CHANGING RICE BOWL

Hong Kong University Press thanks Xu Bing for writing the Press's name in his Square Word Calligraphy for the covers of its books. For further information, see p. iv.

CHANGING RICE BOWL

Economic Development and Diet in China

Elizabeth J. Leppman

香港大學出版社
HONG KONG UNIVERSITY PRESS

Hong Kong University Press
14/F Hing Wai Centre
7 Tin Wan Praya Road
Aberdeen
Hong Kong

© Hong Kong University Press 2005

ISBN 962 209 723 5

Secure On-line Ordering
http://www.hkupress.org

British Library Cataloguing-in-Publication Data
A catalogue record for this book is available
from the British Library.

Printed and bound by Kings Time Printing Press Ltd., in Hong Kong, China

Hong Kong University Press is honoured that Xu Bing, whose
art explores the complex themes of language across cultures,
has written the Press's name in his Square Word Calligraphy.
This signals our commitment to cross-cultural thinking and the
distinctive nature of our English-language books published in
China.

"At first glance, Square Word Calligraphy appears to be nothing
more unusual than Chinese characters, but in fact it is a new
way of rendering English words in the format of a square so
they resemble Chinese characters. Chinese viewers expect to be
able to read Square Word Calligraphy but cannot. Western
viewers, however are surprised to find they can read it. Delight
erupts when meaning is unexpectedly revealed."

— Britta Erickson, *The Art of Xu Bing*

Contents

Appendixes

Acknowledgments

Grace before meals is good manners for readers
and writers as it is for diners.

— Bradford Smith

Inevitably, numerous people have contributed to the evolution and construction of this book. I owe my enthusiasm for China and desire to specialize in that region of the world most directly to Zhao Hongshen, who introduced me to his homeland and infected me with a desire to learn more. He and Qi Hanshen were also my first tutors in the Chinese language.

Li Fuqi, my "adopted Chinese brother," formed the crucial foundation of my network of connections in China — especially the support at Northeastern University in Shenyang — that made possible the fieldwork on which this book is based. In China, Professor Guan Guangye served as my academic host, and his student, Dr Huang Weizu ("Hudson"), solved endless logistical problems. His wife, Zhao Wen ("Diana"), introduced me to the local Nutrition Research Institute, found student volunteers for all sorts of chores, and was a wonderful, supportive friend. Li Jun was a hardworking and able research assistant and delightful travel companion in the spring; Jiang Shaofei took over those duties in the fall. Thermal engineering students of the Liaoning Branch University Class of 1992 and their families enthusiastically formed my pretesting population and extended warm and gracious hospitality to their first foreign guest.

At the Institute of Nutrition and Food Hygiene in Beijing, Dr Chen Xiaoshu, Li Xiaolin, and colleagues provided information about nutritional composition of Chinese foods, Chinese standards for minimum daily requirements, and general guidance and help for the project.

Foreign Affairs Departments are the gateway to any research in China. Gao Yingxue, director of foreign affairs at Northeastern University, was endlessly patient and helpful, and his assistant, Liu Shiwei, helped especially with the complexities of telephoning in China. Both also helped to recruit families from Shenyang city to participate in the study. Interpreters Wu Weidan and Sun Qiang also gave of their time and efforts. Li Jun, assistant director of foreign affairs for the city of Shenyang, helped arrange fieldwork in outlying areas.

In the field, I am especially indebted to the local officials who recruited families and accompanied me on visits. They include: Zou Xueying (now vice-mayor of Ba Yi Zhen) in Sujiatun District; Ou Yang, Li Jie, and Hou Changxian in Dongling District; Duan Yanjuan in Dengta; Li Fuquan in Beizhen County; and Pang Fengqi and Liu Dexue in Kangping County. To the families themselves, I owe an enormous debt for allowing me a glimpse of their lives.

Dr Ding Xueyong and his wife Gou Dan, Wu Weidan, and the medical staff at No. 2 Attached Hospital of China Medical University in Shenyang helped decipher some of the complexities of published data and the food diaries. Yan Fusheng ("William") and his wife Wang Xin, and Wong Kwan Leung obtained data for me; Dr Jay Gao and Weng Qihao helped to prepare the graphics.

At the University of Georgia, Dr Marian Wang and Dr Nancy Connolty of the Food and Nutrition Department served as consultants on various points related to the nutritional aspects of the study. Dr Kam-Ming Wong helped with matters related to the Chinese language and word processing. Dr Thomas Ganschow, Dr C. P. Lo, Dr Kavita Pandit, and Dr James O. Wheeler helped to shape the study. Finally, I am indebted to Dr Clifton W. Pannell for his long hours of discussion, reading, and guidance on this project.

Elizabeth J. Leppman

A Note on Chinese Names
In line with current usage in Mainland China and in Western writing about the affairs of the People's Republic of China, the *pinyin* system of transliteration of Chinese names is used in this book.

1

Diet, Economic Development, and Culture

Everybody eats. Food is necessary for biological survival; all people must somehow obtain it, whether by collecting it, producing it, or purchasing it. It is, therefore, an item in every household budget.

The initial range of potential foods is a matter of various ecological and environmental constraints (Chang, 1977b: 6). From this range, people, although omnivorous, make choices among many available and potentially nutritious possibilities. K. C. Chang (1977b: 3) says, "For survival needs, all men [sic] everywhere could eat the same food, to be measured only in calories, fats, carbohydrates, proteins, and vitamins ... but no, people of different backgrounds eat very differently."

The reasons are only partly biological; cultural, social, and economic factors shape the selection of foods, and, thus, diet and nutrition. "Nowhere is food value-free," says Reid (1986: 51). "The ways in which it is obtained, prepared, presented, and shared are determined as much by cultural prescriptions and emotional association as by the physiological need to eat." Food and "foodways" (customs associated with food) vary as much as any other ways of satisfying human needs (Young, 1986: 111.)

China is an excellent example of the central cultural element of food, including nutrition, and the economic and cultural forces that impinge upon it. In a world where reports of famine, eating disorders, and overeating pepper the pages of newspapers with numbing regularity, the Chinese feed one-fifth of the earth's population on about 7% of its farmland. According to its own reports, China has managed to provide its 1.2 billion people with a diet that is, on average, adequate in energy content (Calories). Thus, the Chinese situation has the potential to be an example to other crowded, hungry people (Anderson, 1988: ix). China's continued ability to feed its population generates growing controversy as farmland is converted to other uses, the population continues to grow, and rising purchasing power encourages the Chinese to demand more luxury foods (Brown, 1995; Brown and Flavin, 1996; Heiling,

1999; Stover, 1996; Yang and Li, 2000). Set against these concerns is the value of reclaimed land, better farming practices, and an import/export regime that exploits China's comparative advantages (*Beijing Review* 2000; Paarlberg, 1997; Rozelle and Rosegrant, 1997; Smil, 2000).

In addition to the fascination of Chinese cuisine for outsiders, food is of central importance to the Chinese themselves; K. C. Chang comments, "few other cultures are as food oriented as the Chinese"(1977b: 3). The details continue to change because the Chinese have borrowed almost all Western foods that will grow in their country (Anderson, 1988: 116). The continuing adoption of new elements produces spatial variation, as different elements penetrate different places at different times and different rates of acceptance. Even in the same culture, not everyone has the same food habits. Within the same general food style, details vary (Chang, 1977b: 3). Because food and economic and cultural forces vary over space, the comparison of their spatial patterns shows how changes in any of them, including economic development, affect food and nutrition as a component of culture.

China also represents a unique history of economic development. As a Communist (in Chinese terms, socialist) country, it has taken a top-down approach to development, directing its economy through central planning. Since the Third Plenum of the 11th Central Committee of the Chinese Communist party under Deng Xiaoping launched a series of economic reforms in 1978, this central direction has opened the country to new economic strategies, including some experiments with free markets. It has also permitted freer movement between city and countryside than had been possible under the rule of Mao Zedong. The mix of continued central planning and free markets also varies spatially. An examination of how these forces are affecting the diets of people in Liaoning Province can illuminate our understanding of development processes and their impact on diet in general. For example, in Western countries, Engel's Law and Bennett's Law have been found to be generally valid. They focus, however, on the economics of dietary choice. Some particular economic conditions and cultural factors could cause exceptions and violations.

We focus here on the Northeastern province of Liaoning. China is a huge and varied country, and no one province is truly representative of the entire country. Even one province contains great differences from place to place. How this spatial variation works, even within one province, is an important element to understanding the entire country.

Influences on Diet

Diet must supply nutrition, but it is more than just biochemical substances. In the Chinese context, culture has shaped diet over several millennia, and economic development, including urbanization, has brought new modifications. Always, the details vary over space.

Diet and Nutrition

Nutrition involves the biological and chemical processes by which the body receives substances (nutrients) from food and then uses these nutrients to promote growth, maintenance, and repair. Essential nutrients are those that the body itself cannot manufacture and, thus, must receive from food. Food must also provide energy, which is measured in kilocalories, more commonly called Calories. Kilocalories are a measure of the heat energy that is available to the body from a particular food.

Nutrition scientists calculate how many Calories and how much of each nutrient are present in different kinds of food, and how much of each is necessary for human life and activity. Because foods offer these nutrients in a wide variety of combinations, the specific assortment of foods one can choose to meet the requirements is almost unlimited. Not surprisingly, it varies a great deal over space. Nutrition scientists evaluate the quality of diets by comparing the nutrients in the diet to a standard recommended requirement. Many such standards have been developed by national governmental agencies and by international organizations. For many reasons and no matter what the standard, the degree to which diets meet its recommendations also will vary from person to person and, more broadly, from region to region.

Economic Development and Urbanization

Economic development, which also shows a wide spatial variation, is defined most simply, for example, by Todaro, as "the capacity of a national economy, whose initial economic condition has been more or less static for a long time, to *generate and sustain* an annual increase in its gross national product of perhaps 5 to 7% or more" (1989: 86; emphasis original). Alternatively, the definition is modified to require that per capita gross national product (GNP) grows faster than the population (1989: 86). "During the 1970s *economic development came to be redefined in terms of reduction or elimination of poverty, inequality, and unemployment within the context of a growing economy*" (1989: 87; emphasis original). In other words, it involves raising the standard of living of the people. Because food is a basic need and closely related to general health, such a rising standard of living should include greater attention to biological survival and the well-being role of food, that is, better nutrition.

Urbanization is a *sine qua non* of economic development (Berry, 1962). Even China, which for a long time tried to avoid much urbanization, has been forced to this conclusion (Pannell, 1981, 1984, 1986, 1992; Pannell and Leppman, 1997).

Terry G. McGee (1989, 1991a) has developed a spatial model of urbanization that is tied to a specific form of Asian development. This model posits an implicit urban hierarchy, by its series of regions exhibiting a continuum of different degrees of urbanization, as a subset of economic development.

Culture

Food selection frequently is based on other considerations in addition to purely nutritional or economic matters. The reasons for such choices must be considered in any evaluation of whether, in fact, economic development and urbanization do lead to changes in nutrition. Why these choices are made and what determines them are among the first questions in any study of food consumption; this research concentrates on those that fall within the general realm of *culture*. Culture is the pattern or style of behavior of a group of people who share it (Chang, 1977a: 3). People who share the same culture tend to share the same food habits. Food preference and preparation are crucial to a people's *genre de vie* or way of life and, thus, a key cultural marker (Sorre, 1962; Vidal de la Blache, 1903).

Food and its associated customs are important parts of culture and comprise a large complex of ideas, behavior, and attitudes. The diet itself has enormous repercussions for our relationships with our environment and with other people near and far. The selection and procurement of food lies at the heart of a group's cultural ecology. We can, in fact, organize studies of human groups and their activities around the theme of their food customs (Zelinsky, 1985), and the study of food habits can be the entry point for examination of a wide range of problems (Bennett, 1946: 554). As with other cultural elements, food customs vary geographically across space (Hilliard, 1972; Kariel, 1966; Shortridge and Shortridge, 1989). Geographical studies of diet and food choices have been based on concepts of cultural ecology (Simoons, 1980, 1994), dietary regions (Bennett, 1946; Kariel, 1966), relocation diffusion (Zelinsky, 1985), hierarchical diffusion (Shortridge and Shortridge, 1989), or economic geography (Hilliard, 1972). *Foodways* (the anthropologists' term) or *food habits* (the nutritionists' term) are the customs of a group that reflect the way a culture standardizes behavior of its members in relation to food, with the result that the group develops a common pattern of eating (Lowenberg et al., 1968: 85).

In traditional China, as in most folk societies, there was a cleavage between the elite culture, or Great Tradition, which was geographically widespread and interconnected over great distances, and the peasantry, or Little Tradition

(Redfield and Singer, 1954), or what Stover (1974) calls the Green Circle, which turned inward and was oriented locally. The Great Tradition/Little Tradition comparison forms a useful baseline to examine the penetration and acceptance or rejection of new food ideas and new sources of information in modern China. While the Communist state apparatus has controlled peasant lives and marshaled peasant labor, the question remains as to whether it has really changed the desires of individual peasants, especially as expressed in something as basic to Chinese culture as food. Furthermore, have these desires and aspirations changed in some places more than others? Specifically, have they changed in some of the regions of the McGee (1989, 1991a) model more than in others? Cities can be expected to be most exposed to new ideas, including new foods. Maoist ideology would even have urban residents "learn from the peasants" (Murphey, 1980), which, if implemented, would result in city dwellers receiving information from rural peasants.

Organization of This Book

The remaining chapters in this book examine diet from the point of view of nutrition, economics, and culture, as well as the survey of Liaoning Province and its results that highlight what Chinese people eat today.

Chapter 2 deals with the concept of culture, especially cultural contrasts between city and countryside. It then discusses nutrition (supplemented by Appendix A) and food, and the mechanisms by which individuals and cultures select what they regard as appropriate foods from the vast array that is available. Applying these concepts to China, it uses a materialist, cultural-ecological approach to review the Chinese diet and the foods that figure prominently in it.

Chapter 3 deals specifically with the foods of China, organized according to the structure of Chinese meals. It then offers an assessment of this dietary regime in terms of its cultural ecology.

Chapter 4 summarizes the vast academic area of economic development. It then explains Terry G. McGee's (1989, 1991a) spatial model of development and urbanization in the Chinese context before focusing on Chinese development, particularly as applied to food.

Chapter 5 provides the geographical and historical background about the study area of Liaoning Province and the application of McGee's (1989, 1991a) spatial model to this region. It also surveys the overall provincial situation of food and diet in the province.

Chapter 6 describes the field survey that was carried out in Liaoning Province in 1994. Its results provide more detailed information at the household level of what people actually eat on a day-to-day basis.

Chapter 7 proposes a modification of McGee's (1989, 1991a) model of spatial development in East Asia to reflect specifically food-consumption patterns. The chapter then reviews what the eating patterns of Liaoning residents indicate in terms of cultural meanings of foods and possible changes in diet, changes that potentially have a great impact on food supplies throughout the world.

2

Culture and Food

China is a developing country, in fact, a rapidly developing country and Liaoning Province is in its more developed east coast region. China's course of economic development has seen many twists and turns, reflecting political shifts and events, but provision of sufficient food and adequate nutrition has remained an important theme throughout. In addition to being a biological necessity, food is also an element of culture and a central focus — perhaps *the* central focus — of Chinese culture. This chapter reviews the roles of food in human lives and the principles governing what individuals and cultural groups select to eat. We begin with the concept of culture, which includes food, and cultural contrasts and comparisons between city and countryside, and then narrow the focus to food itself, both as a biological necessity and as an element of culture.

Culture

Many definitions of culture have been advanced; Kroeber and Kluckholn (1952) identified 160 from which they distilled:

> Culture consists of patterns, explicit and implicit, of and for behavior and transmitted by symbols, constituting the distinctive achievements of human groups, including their embodiments in artifacts; the essential core of culture consists of traditional (that is, historically derived and selected) ideas and especially their attached values; culture systems may, on the one hand, be considered products of action, and on the other as conditioning elements of further action. (181)

They did not end the debate with this pronouncement, and anthropologists (e.g. Bryant et al., 1985; Hiebert, 1976; Hoebel, 1972; Keesing, 1958) continue efforts to define the concept more precisely. Scupin and DeCorse's (1995) definition, "a shared way of life that includes values, beliefs, and norms transmitted within a particular society from generation to generation" (183), aptly states three important commonalities running through the debate: (1) culture includes an entire way of life; (2) culture is a group phenomenon; and (3) culture is learned by each new generation from their elders.

Urban and Rural Culture

Since the founding of the world's first urban places in ancient times, differences in the ways of life between city and countryside have been apparent (e.g. the Biblical story of Sodom and Gomorrah in Genesis 18–9). Sociologists have studied these contrasts, particularly in Western societies undergoing industrialization (e.g. Sorokin and Zimmerman, 1929); anthropologists have inserted the viewpoint of non-Western, non-industrialized societies.

Rural (Folk) Societies

Robert Redfield is credited with initiating the field of anthropological concepts into the study of complex societies. Based on fieldwork in Tepotzlán, Mexico, and drawing on dichotomies of predecessors, such as Ferdinand Tönnies (1887) and Emile Durkheim (1933), Redfield described an "ideal type" of folk society.

> Such a society is small, isolated, nonliterate, and homogeneous, with a strong sense of group solidarity. The ways of living are conventionalized into that coherent system which we call "a culture." Behavior is traditional, spontaneous, uncritical, and personal; there is no legislation or habit of experiment and reflection for intellectual ends. Kinship, its relationships and institutions, are the type categories of experience and the familial group is the unit of action. The sacred prevails over the secular; the economy is one of status rather than of the market. These and related characterizations may be restated in terms of "folk mentality." (1947: 293)

In the Yucatán, Redfield (1941) recognized four kinds of places, each at a different position between the "ideal" folk community and its presumed opposite, an urban place or city. They are the tribal village, the peasant village, the town, and the city, and he concluded that they represent a process whereby all of them eventually become urban (Redfield and Villa, 1934). From the tribal village ideal at one end of the continuum to the city at the other end, each kind of community becomes more culturally disorganized, individualistic, heterogeneous in population and culture, and secular. Occupational structure replaces community and family as means of social organization.

Redfield's peasant community is the embodiment of the folk society or folk culture; he sometimes used the two terms interchangeably. It is semi-autonomous and semi-isolated economically, politically, and culturally. Peasants produce for their families, with a small surplus to sell in the market.

The market is ultimately the city, and, for this reason, peasants need the city. Culturally, the city (Redfield and Singer, 1954) is also the center where the orthogenetic transformation uses the local culture of peasant (and tribal) villages — the Little Tradition — to create the Great Tradition, the overarching, unifying culture that includes moral and religious teaching, the government of a wider area, and an economic system that ties the local communities of the Little Tradition to a larger region. Thus, the Great Tradition contains the Little Tradition. In this primary phase of urbanization, a pre-civilized society develops into a peasant society and its corresponding urban center, which share a common culture, the Little Tradition. The *literati* of the city make this Little Tradition into the Great Tradition, which becomes the core of the indigenous culture. The entire society is fairly isolated and has little contact with outsiders; technology remains low.

Contact with outside cultures stimulates secondary urbanization, which brings a new form that is in conflict with the local culture. New classes, much outside contact, and new forms of urban life bring heterogenetic transformation, which frees intellectual, esthetic, economic, and political life from local control and, thus, fosters change and reform. The spread of Western industrial capitalism has increased heterogenetic transformation in other parts of the world. "Urbanization" as a way of life is primarily secondary urbanization, but Redfield did not really describe the urban end of his continuum in great detail, assuming it to have characteristics opposite to those of folk culture.

Urbanism

Sociologist Louis Wirth (1938) provides the details about the urban end of the continuum. Based on the experience of the United States and the growth of its great cities as part of modern industrialization, he deduced that urban life is based on three characteristics: large numbers of people, high population density, and heterogeneity. In fact, Wirth continues, the urban way of life is not confined to cities themselves; there is no real break between urban and rural areas because rural lifestyles increasingly resemble those of cities. Urbanization is a process rather than a definition, and not all densely populated places are necessarily urban (Davis, 1950).

Many of the interactions in an urban society have to do with economics — making a living and purchasing goods and services — the *pecuniary* or *cash nexus* (Mazlish, 1991). Institutions, geared to making a profit or just maintaining economic viability (the "bottom line"), cater to mass, rather than individual, concerns. Consequently, individuals must form groups to garner enough clout to be effective. For example, workers organize into labor unions because they cannot command higher wages as individuals. Once urban institutions have mastered this kind of organization, they can dominate their hinterland because the sophistication required to serve large numbers of people gives them an advantage over smaller groups and places. The city is also the center of innovation, technological and otherwise, which then spreads to surrounding areas (Reiss, 1955). The city is the center of change, which then spreads out to the surrounding countryside (McGee, 1971: 42).

The Rural-Urban Continuum

Redfield's model generated great controversy, and many modifications have been suggested (Bell, 1992; Dewey, 1960; Foster, 1953; Lewis, 1951; Miner, 1952; Mingione and Pugliese, 1988; Palmer, 1989; Reissman, 1964; Sjoberg, 1952; Stewart, 1958). McGee (1971) argues for a matrix of three urban models — the preindustrial city, the colonial city, and the industrial city (each of which can be either stable or migrant) — and three rural models — folk, peasant, and farmer (that is, commercial farmer). Any combination of these models can exist within a given country.

The particular mix in a country also changes over time, especially under economic development, which involves new occupations for a sizable segment of the labor force. Specifically, they shift from primary industry, mostly farming, to nonfood-producing occupations in manufacturing and services, which are associated with cities. Because all elements of a culture are integrated, the lifestyle of these people also changes (Foster, 1962).

Some people in a developing society make changes in their occupations by migrating to cities, but, as development proceeds, more and more people who stay in the countryside also leave farming or at least develop a more commercialized agriculture geared to the urban market. Johann Heinrich von Thünen's (1966) model of an isolated state on a homogeneous plain describes the spatial arrangement of the types of agriculture that develop around such an urban market. Closest to the city are intensive farms producing such perishable commodities as dairy products, eggs, fruits, and vegetables; extensive grain farming surrounds such regions, and livestock ranching is farthest away. This basic arrangement has been found in both developed and developing countries (e.g. Ewald, 1977; Griffin, 1973; Horvath, 1969).

Swedner (1960), reducing Sorokin and Zimmerman's (1929: 611) description to graphics, shows that, over time, there is a divergence and subsequent convergence of rural and urban lifestyles. Foster (1953) and McGee (1971: 57) agree that this process of divergence followed by convergence has been taking place in such developed countries as the United States.

The rural-urban or folk-urban continuum and its various modifications are useful as a device for measuring the degree of difference, as seen in food habits, between the city and countryside in China. As development proceeds, urban occupations become more widespread as workers leave agriculture for employment in manufacturing and services. Urbanization produces obvious changes in the landscape, as fields and individual houses are replaced by large factories, multi-storied apartment buildings and office towers, and city streets. It also produces a different kind of social environment with high population densities, different class and status structures, and a more heterogeneous, less closely related population. The lifestyle and cultural ecology — the interrelationship of individuals with their physical and cultural environment — are different in urban areas than in rural areas.

Urban and Rural Culture in China

The growth of industry, manufacturing employment, and urban centers under the Dengist reforms has brought about great changes in all aspects of life for millions of Chinese, both city dwellers and rural folk. As Wirth (1938) pointed out, employment in a factory or service firm is different from farming; living in an urban environment is different from living in the countryside. In developed countries, commercialization of agriculture and mass communications and transportation bring many aspects of urban culture to the countryside (Murphey, 1980: 9).

In traditional China, the rural peasantry turned inward and was oriented locally. The rural elite (the gentry) by contrast, had a worldview more like that of the urban elite than that of the peasantry (Fei, 1953). The elite culture depended on the peasantry for subsistence and could not exist without it. The elite decided such matters as national religion, political organization, and arts and philosophy; the elite also was the literate portion of the population. The elite, centered in urban areas, also appropriated to itself the resources of the countryside, especially food. The traffic, however, was not just one-way: the city provided the countryside with manufactured goods and fertilizer in the form of night soil. The economy was interconnected; the meeting point was the market. The relationship was symbiotic; cities were regarded as presiding over the ideal "Great Harmony," serving the country as a whole, and organizing, managing, defending, and nurturing the rural base that supported them (Murphey, 1980: 22).

The terms of trade favored the urban elite, who were educated, concentrated spatially, and united relative to the atomistic Green Circle of the countryside, which remained comparatively powerless. Nevertheless, the Green Circle, after generations in the same environment, had honed its survival skills. Even if the elite suffered disaster, the Green Circle was resilient. Flood or drought or warfare might bring famine, but the Green Circle would survive.

There was no sizable middle class to mediate the two cultures (Murphey, 1980: 21). The rare peasant who left the Green Circle (e.g. by passing the civil service examinations) thereby joined the elite. A peasant who prospered and acquired land and other trappings of wealth was still a peasant.[1] The political counterpart to the economic "hinge" of the market was the *yamen*, the local representative of the government who administered the law.

Under such circumstances, new ideas spread slowly at best. The cities of traditional China, moreover, were not centers for change, but were seats of imperial authority and cosmic centers of China's Great Tradition(Murphey, 1954, 1969, 1980). The treaty ports were supposed to be beachheads of modernization and, indeed, became the seedbeds of ferment that gave birth to nationalism and communism in China. They failed, however, to develop effective linkages with the rest of the country and had very little impact on the vast, largely rural hinterland of China (Murphey, 1970, 1974, 1980). An urban hierarchy, with some very large cities at the top and enormous numbers of small villages at the bottom but a great gap between, was also a hindrance to the flow of information (Murphey, 1980: 98). Communication among villages was impeded by their lack of contact. Of course there were changes in technology, food, and other cultural elements among the peasants over China's long history, but the Green Circle remained isolated, very much within the tradition of China's Neolithic village (Stover, 1974). Tradition remained — and still remains — strong (Zhang, 1993). For most peasants, the only sources of information were local; for the elite and urban dwellers, information sources were more varied.

Food and Diet

Every living being, in order to survive, requires air (specifically oxygen), water, and food. We need food to supply energy and the chemical substances necessary for the maintenance and growth of the body (Zhao, 1988). Food also may play a role in disease prevention.

Nutrition

Nutrition is the total process of the body taking in, absorbing, and using food substances (Whitney, Hamilton, and Rolfes, 1990: 2). Every food item is a complex of materials, which the body handles in various ways and uses for different purposes. Water constitutes a large percentage of most foods. Other substances are used by the body for energy and for growth, repair, and maintenance of tissues. These substances are called *nutrients*. An *essential nutrient* is one that the body cannot manufacture and which, therefore, must be acquired by eating. Recommendations for amounts of most nutrients, based on age, activity level, and other factors, have been established in most countries, many based on the work of United Nations agencies (China Academy of Preventive Medicine, 1991; Lieberman, 1987; National Research Council, 1989). In addition to water, there are five classes of nutrients: carbohydrates, fats, proteins, vitamins, and minerals.

When metabolized, three classes of nutrients — carbohydrates, proteins, and fats — produce energy for the body (Whitney, Hamilton, and Rolfes, 1990: 3). The most common way of measuring this energy is according to the heat energy, in *calories,* that is produced when the substances are metabolized. A calorie is the amount of heat required to raise one gram of pure water from 14°C to 15°C — a small amount of heat. The energy available in foods is many multiples of that amount. For convenience, therefore, the unit used in measuring food energy is 1,000 calories, or one kilocalorie (expressed as 1 Calorie or 1 kcalorie or 1 kcal; "Calorie" with a capital C will be used hereafter). When metabolized, 1 gram of carbohydrate or protein yields 4 Calories, and 1 gram of fat yields 9 Calories. Thus, the amount of energy available from eating any specific food depends on the mix of carbohydrates, proteins, and fats in that food. The Food and Agriculture Organization (FAO) of the United Nations has estimated that the average adult needs 2,360 Calories to maintain health (de Blij, 1993: 149), but the specific amount of energy needed depends on age, body size, growth, physical activity level, and climate (China Academy of Preventive Medicine, 1991; Develin and Horton, 1990: 5; National Research Council, 1989). Consequently, the average number of Calories recommended for different countries also varies, depending on such factors as climate and the age/sex structure of its population (Bergman, 1995: 212). A description of the nutrients and their role in human nutrition is in Appendix A.

Malnutrition

Malnutrition is a condition in which food intake is insufficient to maintain the person in a physical state in which he or she can adequately perform such tasks as physical work, resist or recover from disease, or maintain an adequate level of growth or processes of pregnancy or lactation (Payne, 1985).[2] The physiological effects of inadequate food have been known for centuries, and the media have made us all familiar with images of starving people who suffer from wasting, severe emaciation, and eventual death in famine-stricken lands (Latham, 1990). China has been plagued with famines for centuries (Dando, 1980; Mallory, 1926).

Inadequate food intake leads to deficiency in available energy necessary for work. If the breadwinner of the family is thus affected, vulnerability to poverty increases; if the homemaker suffers, child care may be neglected.

Because the brain matures rapidly during pregnancy and in the first few years after birth, malnutrition during pregnancy and infancy has been blamed for intellectual and physical stunting (Newman, 1995), although the measurement of intelligence in non-Western cultures has proved problematic (Thomson and Pollitt, 1977). Malnutrition spread over a large portion of a population hinders the group's adaptation to its physical and cultural environment and, thus, its viability and survival.

Deficiencies in specific nutrients lead to recognizable disorders, for example, lack of iron to anemia, lack of Vitamin B_1 to beriberi, and lack of Vitamin C to scurvy (Appendix A). Such deficiencies can be treated by increasing the intake of foods rich in the missing nutrient, or, in certain cases, with supplements in pill form.

Taken as a whole, nutritional status also seems to have an impact on disease prevention. Malnourished people suffer from more infections — especially of the respiratory and gastrointestinal tracts — than do well-nourished people (Alexander, 1985). Moreover, by reducing appetite and tolerance for food, infectious diseases aggravate malnutrition. Culturally based restrictions on specific foods during illness further reduce nutritional levels.

As causes of death in developed countries have shifted from infectious (contagious) diseases, such as smallpox, cholera, and diphtheria, to degenerative diseases of old age, such as heart disease and cancer, diet has been a research approach in the quest for causes and treatments of these conditions (e.g. American Cancer Society, 1996). Generating great public attention, much of this research is very preliminary, and some is very controversial.

In summary, people need food to supply energy for bodily functions and for physical activity, as well as for growth and maintenance of body tissues. Carbohydrates, proteins, and fats provide the body with energy; protein also supplies the all-important "building blocks" for body tissues. Vitamins and minerals aid in the metabolism of these substances and protect tissues from deterioration. While the array of necessary substances and their roles may seem bewildering, eating a variety of foods in sufficient quantities meets the body's nutritional needs. The role of food and large quantities of particular nutrients in disease prevention and treatment recently has attracted a great deal of attention among researchers and the general public, but remains controversial.

Nonbiological Bases for Food Choices

Physiologically, our bodies need nutrients, but people do not eat nutrients, they eat food. By trial and error, individuals and groups work out combinations of foods that provide adequate nutrition. Modern scientists can create hypotheses about these choices on nutritional grounds — they are effective because they keep the population healthy — but the thinking that went into those prehistoric choices was based on other kinds of reasoning. Even with all our modern knowledge of nutrition, many of our food choices are made entirely on other grounds (Farb and Armelagos, 1980).

Human beings are omnivorous, that is, we eat both plant and animal foods. Virtually everything that is digestible and nontoxic, at some time and place, has been used for food, even clay and starch (Bryant et al., 1985; Hunter, 1973; Loveland, Furst, and Lauritzen, 1989; Vermeer and Frate, 1975). As early humans developed and migrated to different parts of the earth, they first tried eating anything available. By trial and error, they discovered which foods were dangerous (poisonous) and which seemed to give greatest satisfaction, whether from taste or nutritional benefit.

A resident in a locality for any length of time quickly developed intimate knowledge of the available resources and their seasonal cycles. A move to a new environment meant starting the process again. Geographer Maximillian Sorre (1962) calls the collection of foods that a cultural group accepts, its *dietary regime.*

A dietary regime is based on a staple food, generally a grain or tuber, with other foods added for flavor and nutrition. The staple foods that were domesticated in Neolithic times (Childe, 1983; Sauer, 1969) depended on such physical factors as soils and climate, and these patterns have endured (Kariel, 1966). Wheat dominates from Southwest Asia across Europe and eastward to northern China; rice in southeastern China, Southeast Asia, and Japan; taros, yams, and bananas in the southwestern Pacific; and maize (corn) in the Americas (Spencer and Thomas, 1969: 165).

Plants, however, have been carried to new parts of the earth, especially to regions of similar physical environments. Following the voyages of Christopher Columbus in the late fifteenth century (the Columbian Exchange), contact between Eurasia and the Americas greatly increased such transfers in both directions (Crosby, 1972; 1991; McNeill, 1991). Finally, plants have been introduced into areas of very different environments by breeding them for specific qualities, such as tolerance for cold or drought (Spencer and Thomas, 1969: 366).

All of these factors continue to operate in the realm of food production (agriculture) and, consequently, the foods that people eat. Moreover, increased transportation and industrialization in the nineteenth and twentieth centuries have greatly added to the variety of available foods, both fresh foods brought in from elsewhere and manufactured foods. At the same time, the diversity of the primary raw materials — plant and animal species used for food — has decreased as commercial farming and monoculture replace the huge variety of species that grows naturally in an environment.

Psychological Factors in Food Choice

> The appetite for food and sex is part of our nature.
>
> — Mencius (VI A:4)

Food is necessary to the survival of the individual. Thus (along with sex, which involves relationships with another person), it is vital to the survival of the species (Back, 1977). The same can be said for other animals, but humans also derive enormous psychological pleasure from food, in many cases derived from prehistoric survival needs (Tiger, 1992).

From birth onward, food is strongly connected to personal security (Fieldhouse, 1986: 27). In terms of Maslow's (1954) Hierarchy of Human Needs, food is needed first for basic biological nutrition (equivalent to Maslow's first need for sustenance of life). The immediate need for food is the first priority; when that is satisfied, consideration can be given to future food needs — planning how to get the next meal. Experience and experimentation with people who were starving or chronically underfed — for whom food security was lacking — found that the malnourished become more variable in personality, more irritable, and less able to do not only physical but also mental work. Food becomes the consuming subject of their thoughts and even their dreams (Farnsworth, 1997; Keys et al., 1950). Fear of food shortage and the inability to meet this basic need, shows up when people stockpile bread and milk before a predicted snowstorm, even to the point of purchasing more than they can use.

The second of Maslow's (1954) needs — for status and belonging in the social structure — finds expression in uses of food for social acceptance and status. At the highest level, food serves as a means of self-realization, or creativity. A person who is satisfied by the basic biological needs, and for belonging and status, can use food to express creativity. Exotic foods and new recipes offer such experiences to the venturesome. Uneducated adults and young children, who tend to be insecure in their status and unsure of the stability of their food supplies, are less venturesome, although children who eat a variety of foods at home are more likely to do so at school. Travel and other experiences that expose people to new foods also lead to more venturesome culinary tastes.

Economic Factors

If food is to be eaten, the economic system of the culture group must, in some way, provide the means to obtain it. People must either produce or purchase their food. Those who produce food are farmers; to them the "cost" of their food is opportunity cost. The portion of their production that they eat, they do not sell. The cost of food is a major determinant in the selection process, even among people who know which foods are most nutritious (Basta, 1977; DeWalt, Kelly, and Pelto, 1980). Obviously, people with higher incomes have more money to spend on food, but the relationship is not quite so simple. Ernst Engel, a nineteenth-century German statistician, was the first to examine the relationship between income and food expenditure (Mansfield, 1988: 89–91, 128). Based on expenditure diaries of families in Saxony, he found that, as income increases, so does the total amount spent on food; however, the proportion of each unit of increase that goes for additional food expenditure declines (Figure 2.1a). In other words, the higher the income, the lower the income elasticity of demand for food. As a result, the percentage of total income that goes for food, the so-called Engel's ratio, declines with higher incomes (Figure 2.1b). High-income households spend a smaller percentage of their income on food than do low-income households. The studies that have tested Engel's Law, as this pattern has come to be called, have confirmed the Law's validity in various countries around the world. In low-income countries, food consumes one-half or more of most families' incomes (Sanjur, 1982).

People also modify their dietary regimes — the specific array of foods they eat — as their incomes rise. Cereal grains and potatoes are generally the least expensive foods to produce and to buy. Consumers with more money can pay more for food and can afford to replace such staple foods with more desired but more expensive foods, such as vegetables, meats, oils, and dairy products. Merrill K. Bennett (1941) used this principle to compare national diets worldwide. The ratio of cereal grain and potatoes to other foods becomes a measure of well-being according to Bennett's Law:

> The national ratios of cereal-potato calories to total food calories ... provide a rough indicator of relative per capita levels of national income, or of relative consumption levels, planes of living, or economic productivity so far as these may correspond one with the other.... The national ratios of cereal-potato calories to total food calories may be regarded as an indicator of relative qualitative adequacy of national diets. (374)

In the Western experience, people have shifted from diets heavy in bread and potatoes to those with more meat, sugar, and fat (Grigg, 1995).

The Giffen effect (Williams, 1990) is a seeming contradiction to the basic principle that rising prices bring a decline in demand. If the price of a staple food increases, demand for it actually might rise if, at the same time, the prices of alternative foods also increase (as in general inflation); people cannot afford the alternatives, and the staple food, although more expensive than before, is still the least expensive food available. Everything else costs even more, and, therefore, in order to obtain enough Calories to survive, households must consume more of the least expensive alternative, driving up the demand and, consequently, the price.

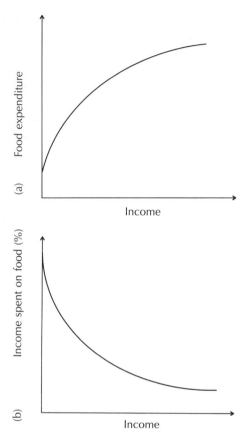

Figure 2.1   Engel's Law: (a) Food expenditure rises with income; (b) Percent of income spent on food declines with rising income.

The purchase of expensive, prestigious foods by low-income people would seem to contradict economic constraints on food selection. Use of such foods, however, plays an important role in breaking the monotony (in both flavor and nutrition) of a diet that is comprised almost totally of staple foods. Even "junk foods," which contain large numbers of Calories but little nutritive value, play a role in providing Calories, especially for the young, whose rapid growth demands extra energy that may not be supplied by a diet of mainly staples (Messer, 1984). Production of sugar, in fact, has been encouraged in order to give workers a cheap source of extra Calories (Mintz, 1979; 1996).

Government pricing interventions, including rationing, may modify the economics of food procurement. Rulers have regulated food distribution since ancient times, and governments in many countries today maintain various kinds of food programs (Scandizzo and Tsakok, 1985).

Cultural Factors

All of these biological and psychological needs can be met economically through an almost infinite variety of edible substances. Acceptance of a substance as food depends on availability and price plus *food appeal*, a combination of taste, fragrance, color, and texture, which intimately is linked with the psychological image and social status of the food (Aebi, 1981: 4). Furthermore, it is a dynamic process that can change with the situation (Booth, 1981).

How a group and its members go about accomplishing this task depends on their culture. Culture includes the evaluation of which foods are preferred and, therefore, attract sufficient demand to raise their cost and make the work of procuring or producing them worthwhile. Because food is necessary for basic survival, its provision has enormous environmental impact. Ultimately, because cultures are integrated, it touches on the group's entire way of life (Zelinsky, 1985).

Cultural groups initially select foods from the local environment; they may then "force nature's hand" into providing the selected foods by raising the requisite plants and animals (farming) and abolishing competing species. Modification of the environment by fertilization, application of pesticides, irrigation, drainage, construction of greenhouses, terracing, and other measures — all applications of technology — increases supplies of chosen favored foods. Transportation technology allows foods to be available that cannot be produced locally, or at least cannot be produced all year-round.

The use of the environment as a source of food necessarily shapes a group's relationship with that environment, its cultural ecology. At the simplest technological level, a group selects from what the environment offers, making no attempt to modify that assortment. Farming and increasingly sophisticated agricultural technology enter the environmental system at ever more basic levels, modifying water availability, soil nutrients, competing species (weeds and pests), terrain, and even temperature. The environment is forced to yield more of the desired crop (at least to a point), but it also may produce unintended consequences in the form of pollution, vulnerability to flooding or landslides, and other problems.

Some foods, once procured or produced, are eaten as is, but many are processed in some way. Human groups have invented a wide assortment of ways of preparing foods, such as boiling, baking, parching, broiling, and frying. This distinctly human trait adds to the enormous variation of human foodways and also is determined by culture. The concept of *cuisine* includes not only the food items but also their preparation for eating, specifically (1) the selection of a set of basic (staple or secondary) foods; (2) the frequent use of a characteristic set of flavorings; (3) the characteristic processing (chopping, cooking) of the foods; and (4) the adoption of rules about acceptable foods and combinations, festival foods, social context of eating, and symbolic uses of foods (Messer, 1984: 228). Roland Barthes (1961) writes,

> When he buys an item of food, consumes it, or serves it, modern man [sic] does not manipulate a simple object in a purely transitive fashion; this item of food sums up and transmits a situation; it constitutes an information; it signifies. (21)

Especially in developed societies, where inputs of mechanical energy have greatly increased the amount and variety of food available, cultural values have a greater impact on food intake, even overriding physiological signals of satiety (Mennell, 1985).

Anthropological Models of Diet

The factors and forces that create and modify a group's dietary regime and cuisine have been primarily the concern of the fields of sociology, and social and nutritional anthropology. Noting what cultural groups eat dates from ancient times (Messer, 1984; Sorre, 1962), but modern nutritional anthropology centers around several theoretical viewpoints.

According to *structuralists*, who dominated social anthropology in the 1960s and 1970s, humans are, by nature, above the humdrum of adapting to their environment because they live according to the meanings they impose on the world through their ability to deal in symbols (Ross, 1980: xix). Food choices involve a statement of the eater's identity: how that person regards him/herself and wishes others to regard him or her (Atkins and Bowler, 2001: 273–4; Caplan; 1997; Lupton, 1996). This statement of identity varies, depending on the location in which it takes place. For example, eating a Big Mac makes a different statement in the United States versus China (Yan, 1997). We mentally organize the concept of "food" into categories, generally designated by pairs of antonyms, such as dark/light or sweet/sour (Fischler, 1988; Lévi-Strauss, 1963a, 1969, 1991). Structuralists stressed the symbolic aspects of food: Thanksgiving to Americans means "turkey," and Valentine's Day means "chocolate." Human ability to deal in symbols makes eating not only biological nourishment, but also symbolic expression (Atkinson, 1978, 1980, 1983; Lévi-Strauss, 1963a, 1963b, 1970; Murcott, 1988; Rozin, 1990).

While animals eat by instinct, humans must learn what to do when eating (Childe, 1983). They learn from elders in their cultural group, and, therefore, they learn the cultural conventions about eating. These conventions include what the culture accepts as food and what foods are appropriate for the socially identified occasion. The structuralist view, therefore, suggests that there is a correspondence between an occasion and food (Douglas, 1966; Murcott, 1988; Schutz, 1988).

Materialists of the 1980s were more concerned with the practical, rather than the symbolic, aspects of eating, arguing that culture is, first and foremost, the way a human group copes with its environment in the daily business of surviving, producing, and reproducing (Harris, 1979a; Ross, 1980). Meaning follows, rather than precedes, activity; symbolism follows practicality. Eating certainly has a material as well as symbolic aspect, and people's social, economic, and political systems for obtaining food have an enormous impact on their physical environment. Thus, materialists focus on economic and political forces involved in a culture's foodways.

Foods that people prefer generally provide better nutrition than non-preferred foods (Harris, 1986: 15). They offer a more favorable balance of benefits over costs in three overlapping spheres: (1) effort and labor required to get the food; (2) comparative costs of effort and labor among types of foods; and (3) relative nutritional value. Ecological constraints, consequently, impact a culture's food choices (Harris, 1986: 16).

The Marxist interpretation of food selection (Mintz, 1979, 1996) stresses power relations, both economic and social, in the development of a human group's foodways (Goody, 1982). In a capitalist system, supply and demand for foods, as anything else, re-adjust until they are in balance. Food habits diffuse hierarchically from city to countryside and from upper classe to lower because the elite hold economic power to organize political interests, colonial aspirations, and mercantilism — the social organization of production. Mass (as contrasted with restricted) literacy, especially among women, is an avenue for the general public to learn about elite customs, which they can then attempt to copy. In most societies, women cook at home, while most men cook professionally. If men, but not women, learn elite cuisine, it is less likely to spread to the home.

Thus, materialists focused on how a food might be selected originally (or not selected) for inclusion in a society's dietary regime. Once included, food certainly takes on symbolic roles in a culture group's way of life.

The *ecological* perspective (Rappaport, 1971) takes a holistic view of human behavior, including foodways. It examines customs and habits with the question of whether "behavior undertaken with respect to social, economic, political or religious conventions contributes to or threatens the survival and well-being of actors and whether this behavior maintains or degrades the ecological system in which it occurs" (Rappaport, 1971: 7). Thus, this perspective sees individual biological requirements for nutrients and psychological needs for nurturance at the center of the system. Such needs, of course, vary with the species (in this case, human being), but also are modified by developmental stage, activity level, reproduction, genetic characteristics, and stressful situations throughout the life cycle (Jerome, Kandel, and Pelto, 1980).

Classification and Dietary Selection

Whatever the overarching theoretical model, people develop food habits from that part of the society with which they have regular contact. Furthermore, individuals express their identity by their choice of foods (Crouch and O'Neill, 2000). Both objective and subjective factors contribute to food habits. Objective factors include physical, biological, and technological influences, while subjective factors are cultural, social, and psychological. The physical and cultural availability of food, in an economic setting, determines both objective considerations and subjective responses. Physical availability includes such factors as the natural environment (soils, climate, and ecology), technological development (cultivation practices; mechanization; and storage, transportation, and processing facilities; industrialization), economy (subsistence versus market, level of purchasing power, and proportion of imports), and social structure (land tenure systems, education level, and health facilities).

Within this general scope, people's food habits come from the subgroup of which they are a part. What is "culturally available" is an edible substance that one's culture has accepted as food. From the first day of life, the influence of the biological need for energy and nutrients declines as a mechanism of food choice that is replaced by external conditions (Maus and Pudel, 1988). Thus, every culture passes along categories of fitness for eating (Fischler, 1988a, 1988b) into which everything in the world can be classified:

> Inedible
> Edible by animals
> Edible by other kinds of humans
> Edible by my kind of people
> Edible by me

At the most basic level, such selection comes from various sensory qualities of food, such as taste and smell, texture, color (and other visual characteristics), and perceived qualities such as "fillingness" (Messer, 1984: 218). In many cultures, taste and smell (which are closely related physiologically and sometimes linguistically) identify and rank foods by their suitability and desirability for eating. They can be classified as sweet, bitter, sour, pungent, disgusting, or bland (Messer, 1984). Classic experiments by Davis (1928) showed that infants prefer sweet foods over bitter, indicating an inborn instinct. Such a predisposition matches the sweet taste of breast milk, nature's designed first infant food. A preference for sweet-tasting foods, no doubt, also protected early humans from consuming unripe fruits, which are bitter or sour, and led to eating ripe ones, which are sweet (Tiger, 1992).

A food's visual appearance is another important criterion for acceptance (Messer, 1984). For many cultural groups all over the world, the lighter the food's color, the more acceptable it is. So pervasive are established colors for foods that we teach young children color words by associating them with fruits and vegetables: a banana is yellow (although some are red); an apple is red (although some are yellow); and an orange is orange (although some are green). Odd colors may be acceptable only under certain social conditions (e.g. green beer on St. Patrick's Day).

Likewise, texture is a further sensory characteristic that classifies food as acceptable, preferred, or appropriate (Messer, 1984). Along with flavor, it plays a large role in the acceptability of newly introduced foods, especially the preparation of grains (as grain, grits, or bulgur versus flour or meal) and their glutinous properties (as in flour or rice). Crispness, crunchiness, or softness are other texture qualities that people come to expect from their foods, as in the food industry's stress on dry cereal that remains "crisp and crunchy" in milk (Lieberman, 1987).

Whether food is served in its natural state or is transformed in some way also affects its acceptability, as a self-described gourmet cook in Pennsylvania rejected sushi with the horrified exclamation, "That's raw fish!" Humans are the only animals that cook their food, and cooking clearly makes more substances edible. Cooking methods are commonly called "cuisine," but that is only the first part of what "cuisine" means. At a deeper level, in the imagination, it "transfers nutritional raw materials from the state of Nature to the state of Culture. It conjures and tames the dangerous forces of nature" (Fischler, 1988b: 284). By extension, it is a system of classifications and rules that give order and meaning to the world, beginning with what is and is not appropriate food, whether for religious or other reasons.

In most cultures, the preferred source of protein is animals, especially large, gregarious animals because they yield the most nutritional benefit for the effort involved in procuring them (Harris, 1979b). "Meat hunger," according to Harris (1986: 22), exists because "while plant foods can sustain life, access to animal foods bestows health and well-being above and beyond mere survival.... Animal foods get their symbolic power from [the] combination of utility and scarcity." The key is the quality of animal protein (Appendix A).

Of course, qualities of foods also can lead to their avoidance, especially in the case of allergies. A whole host of foods that are eaten and enjoyed by many can provoke mild or severe allergic reactions in certain individuals. Chocolate and strawberries are well-known examples, but more basic foods, such as wheat and peanuts (including peanut oil), can also produce violent, even fatal, reactions. A common allergic reaction to milk, especially among Asian and African adults, is caused by a lack of the enzyme lactase that aids in digestion of lactose, the sugar in milk (Harris, 1985; Kretchmer, 1972; McCracken, 1971; Simoons, 1980).

Individuals can — and frequently do — change the classification of a particular substance as life progresses (Allport, 2000). Youth may eat "weird" things as part of a general rebellion against their parents and the "establishment," but a more frequent impetus is the encounters with new groups of people and their foods, especially as a result of travel (Simoons, 1994: 322). Nevertheless, the meanings and classifications remain fairly stable in the group as a whole. People tend to like what is familiar; repeated exposure reassures that the food is safe. Of course, repeated exposure that produces unpleasant side effects reinforces distaste (Rozin, 1987).

Foods may have prestige value that has nothing to do with their nutritional value. For much of human history, adequate food was available only to the elite. To eat a large amount of food was a sign of high social status. As more adequate food became available to increasing portions of society, the rich could no longer "out-eat" the lower classes. Specific foods and ways of preparing them became the mark of social status, and this taste begins to develop in infancy (Bourdieu, 1984; Fernández-Armesto, 2002: 101–30). Prestige depends on a food's availability because something that is available in abundance will become common and inexpensive. When economic conditions improve, changes in diet and other food habits due to improved economic conditions apparently are based on social prestige factors of food (Bryant et al., 1985).

In classifying foods as fit or unfit to eat, allergic reactions explain only a few food avoidances. The explanation of the pork taboo among Muslims and Jews as related to the danger of trichinosis generally has been discredited (Harris, 1986; Simoons, 1994), but an alternative explanation for that and other taboos is still a matter of debate. Materialists, such as Harris (1986), trace it to cultural ecology, while Simoons (1994) maintains a more symbolic explanation.

Eating means taking substances into the body, crossing the barrier that exists between the outside and the inside of ourselves. Doing so involves a certain risk, for the food literally becomes a part of the person who eats it: "Mann ist, was Mann isst" ("You are what you eat") physically and also symbolically (Fischler, 1988: 279; May, 1996). Humans eat both plants and animals and, thus, are subject to the "omnivore's dilemma" (Rozin, 1976). Because everything is potentially a source of food, people expose themselves to the dangers of ingesting harmful substances as they seek new sources of nutrition. If "you are what you eat," you may "become" polluted by contact with something less than desirable.

Disgust seems to be a universal emotional reaction, a "socially constructed biological safeguard" against consuming something dangerous (Fischler, 1988b). Exactly what provokes disgust is determined culturally, but substances associated with animals are regarded more commonly as disgusting than plant material (Rozin, 1990). By the same token, flesh foods are the most common subjects of taboos. Both plant and animal foods may suffer low evaluation as expressions of social status; chitlins and beans in the South were tropes for poverty until they became a symbol of black pride in the late 1960s.

The symbolic aspect of food choices is particularly strong in holiday or celebration foods (Farb and Armelagos, 1980). Nonetheless, most holiday foods have (or at least once had) a practical basis in surviving a season of low supply or redistributing food to poor classes in the society (Messer, 1984: 229). Foods for celebrations tend to be: (1) scarce, which puts a high priority on them; (2) high quality; (3) expensive, which makes them desired; and (4) difficult and time-consuming to prepare. As people move away from local communities and their traditions, particularly in the urbanization process, symbolic uses of food and their accompanying rules may lose force in daily practice, remaining only in the case of major festivals and holidays (Messer, 1984).

What constitutes appropriate food for different meals also varies (Fischler, 1988b; Leppman, 2002). The Japanese regularly eat miso soup for breakfast, but when Campbell Soup Company tried to promote soup for breakfast in the United States, the campaign fell flat. In spite of its high cholesterol and salt content, the traditional American and British breakfast is bacon or sausage and eggs.

The roles of family members, by age and gender, in the production, preparation, serving, and cleaning up of meals vary from culture to culture. When food appears on the table, it is generally eaten; therefore, who has power over the various areas of food provision is also critical to which foods are selected. Kurt Lewin (1943) described various "channels" through which food moves; these vary from one culture to another, but may include farmers, transportation systems, wholesale and retail outlets, processing and packaging companies, and others. Each channel is controlled by a "gatekeeper." Within a family, whoever does the menu planning and the grocery shopping, and whoever decides what crops to plant or what to grow in a vegetable garden, becomes the gatekeeper to that channel and, thus, exercises a degree of power over the family's diet (Bell and Valentine, 1997: Chapter 3; Crouch and O'Neill, 2000: 186).

Dietary Change

Much of the research on food choice and other foodways has been conducted as part of efforts to change a group's diet in order to improve its nutritional level. The nutritionists' goal is to encourage the adoption of a healthier diet; anthropologists contribute an understanding of the cultural imperatives that may be stronger in dietary choices than a desire for nutrients.

Foodways, along with other culture traits, change over time. According to Larry Naylor's (1996) model of culture change, innovation begins when there is an interaction with the environment and the realization that current adaptations are, in some way, deficient. New responses, through innovation or discovery, are devised and then passed along through interpersonal interaction to others. Most cultural change today is directed change, initiated by some person or group external to the proposed acceptors, or *target group*. The authority directing the change must first convince a core of *innovators* in the target group to accept the idea; the innovators will then pass it along to the rest of the population until it has been adopted by a sufficient majority to be considered part of the target group's culture. The efforts of conquerors, revolutionary governments, and advertisers are examples of directed cultural change.

In any group, members vary in their acceptance or resistance to change (Abler, Adams, and Gould, 1971: 405). Innovators, generally high-status individuals who are less fearful of losing status, are more daring and willing to deviate the most from established patterns (May, 1996: 59). In fact, the association of a new food with high status may be an impetus for its adoption, for example, the consumption of Western soft drinks in many developing countries, and the shift to rice as the preferred staple food throughout Indonesia after independence (Soemardjan, 1985: 169). High status may be more cultural than economic; persons with limited funds may find that adopting a new food is a relatively inexpensive way to express cultural distinction (May, 1996: 60). Among those who accept change, timing varies from early changers, to moderates who must see at least preliminary evidence of the benefits of the innovation, to late changers who require proof. Finally, there are always some people in a group who will not or do not adopt the innovation or change. In any case, if the new food eventually becomes widespread and is no longer distinctive, it loses its role as a marker of status (May, 1996: 61).

An individual's or group's acceptance of new foods depends on physiological hunger and thirst, as well as on evaluation of the new food in terms of what is experienced through the senses and the acquired attitudes toward it (Schutz, 1988). Attachments to the social structure surrounding food are stronger at some points than at others, and changes in diet are more successful when they are introduced at the weak points. Fieldhouse (1986: 15–6) lists five factors that contribute to attitudes about new foods: (1) relative advantage of the new food; (2) compatibility with cultural values; (3) complexity of using the new food; (4) trialability (whether it can be sampled first in a limited way); and (5) observability of effects. Modern society changes faster than past societies did, due to more travel and mass communications (including advertising), which make people aware of other cultures, less bothered by minor differences, and more amenable to new ideas (Sanjur, 1982: 286). Modern, developed cultures value newness, variety, change, and convenience. As with other cultural traits, foodways, however, generally remain more stable in traditional cultures, where sameness is valued.

Food habits can, in fact, be very resistant to change, especially if they have been built into children's early experience and are associated with pleasure (Bourdieu, 1984). As we have seen, food habits and customs develop over long cultural experience; they are not a passing fancy. New items, at first, may be ridiculed and strongly resisted before being accepted and taken for granted, perhaps under conditions of famine when "hunger becomes the best cook" (Aebi, 1981: 4). Rozin (1976) ascribes this *neophobia* to the "omnivore's dilemma" (Fischler 1988b). Because humans are omnivorous, they can eat a much wider range of foods than herbivores (e.g. cows) or carnivores (e.g. cats). Consequently, their potential sources of good nutrition are much greater, but they also are more likely to be exposed to poisons. Once they find a safe and satisfying dietary regime, they are loathe to experiment further, lest they ingest something toxic. Preparation of a newly introduced food according to traditional culinary methods and with traditional flavorings reduces the neophobia and makes the food more acceptable by resolving the omnivore's dilemma (Fischler, 1988a: 204).

Food may also take on social, cultural, and even religious roles. The more roles an individual food item has for a people, the more resistant it is to change (Soemardjan, 1985: 168). Most resistant to change is the choice of the staple food (Crosby, 1972: 74, 106–7, 169; Fieldhouse, 1986). The farming system of most cultures is tied intimately to the production of the staple, and this, in turn, affects many other aspects of culture, including major holidays and religious beliefs. Much more amenable to change is the assortment of accompaniments to the staple food. If their flavor is agreeable, these foods are accepted more readily, and add interest, variety, and nutritional value (Sanjur, 1982: 288–9; Soemardjan, 1985: 169).

Because cultures are integrated (all elements and traits are connected to each other), changes in diet usually come with changes in other aspects of life. If these new traits are sufficiently central to the entire cultural system, their effect may be to bring about changes in attitudes, similar to those nutrition educators encourage when they try to improve diets.

Commercialization and new trade relations may lead to the marketing of food that, at one time, had been used only locally, and the resulting income then used to purchase other, previously unknown foods. In industrialized countries, even the basic categorization of foods has changed, as more food preparation shifts from home to factory, and, thus, the origins of the ingredients become increasingly obscure to the consumer (Fischler, 1988b: 289).

The quintessential example is fast food, prepared by a meticulously detailed set of instructions that are exactly the same at all company outlets throughout the world. The enormous growth in popularity of fast food has also led to increasingly mechanized production of potatoes (french fries) and meat in general (Schlosser, 2001). In the United States and Europe, a reaction is beginning to set in. General affluence makes a wide variety of foods available, and changes in belief systems that focus on concerns about ecology and the safety of commercial food supplies, coupled with an aging baby-boomer generation that is concerned about prolonging youthful vigor, has helped to fuel the popularity of health foods and vegetarianism (Kandel and Pelto, 1980).

The migration of people is among the most widely studied changes affecting diet. Food choices are among the last cultural traits that migrants change. They will adopt the language and dress of their new home before they adopt its foodways because language and dress are public, but most eating takes place in the privacy of home. If they eat some meals in a public setting, such as work or school, the family Sunday dinner (or equivalent) retains the traditional menu of their original home (Sanjur, 1982: 286). Nevertheless, migrants' dietary regimes do undergo modification. Some previously used foods, especially fresh produce, may simply be unavailable in the new homeland, and migrants find items that they like among the foods of their new home. Changes in food habits are one measure of acculturation (Jerome, 1980). Migrants to different countries potentially face the most radical changes (Fitzgerald 1986; Grivetti and Paquette, 1978), but domestic migrants, especially those of minority ethnic groups, also meet new foods in their new homes (Jerome, 1980). At the same time, migrants bring new foods and cuisines to their new homes, often by establishing ethnic restaurants (Zelinsky, 1985), and such foods may become so much a part of the new homeland that they cease to be regarded as "foreign" (Pillsbury, 1998).

Changes in diet, no matter what the circumstances, can improve nutritional status and health, or they can have the exact opposite effect (Allport, 2000). Acculturation and accompanying dietary improvement brought better child nutritional levels to the Central Highlands of New Guinea (Dennett and Connell, 1988), but selling green sea turtles in order to purchase commercial foods reduced the nutritional levels of the Miskito Indians of Nicaragua (Weiss, 1980). Similarly, in a highland community in Mexico, using pesticides to increase the yield of food crops had the unfortunate side effect of killing wild plants that poor people used for food (DeWalt, Kelly, and Pelto, 1980). Pollock (1975) found that maintaining supplies of both indigenous and imported foods was the best strategy for Namu Atoll in the Marshall Islands of Oceania. The correlation between consumption of fast food and obesity in the United States, and one that is becoming similar in other countries, is another example of a dietary change that has had adverse effects (Schlosser, 2001).

3

The Chinese Dietary Regime

In keeping with the rest of Chinese culture, the dietary regime of present-day China is the result of thousands of years of development. Some elements are indigenous, while others have been imported. Food is a pivotal part of any culture, but, for various historical reasons, it is especially central to Chinese culture. China has been characterized as having a food-centered culture; even the greeting equivalent to the English "How are you?" is "Have you eaten?" (Simoons, 1991: 14). The Chinese have developed a system of farming and of cooking that, given adequate supplies, can feed 22% of the world's population on 7% of the earth's farmland (Wittwer et al., 1987: 1). That in itself makes the Chinese dietary regime worthy of our attention because China may have lessons for other hungry peoples (Anderson, 1988: ix).

The Chinese not only are concerned about the production of food, but of nutrition and preparation as well, and it vies with the French, in taste and nutrition, as one of the best cuisines in the world. For this reason, it has generated a large literature, including historical/cultural treatment (Anderson, 1988; Chang, 1977b; Simoons, 1991) and numerous cookbooks (e.g. Antolini and Tjo, 1990; Hom, 1990a, 1990b).

The Structure of Chinese Meals

The basic structure of the Chinese diet and of individual meals was laid down in the Zhou period (1122–221 B.C.) and has continued ever since (Chang, 1977a: 40; May, 1961: 17). This structure, rather than individual ingredients, makes Chinese food distinctive, giving it its "Chineseness" that endures, regardless of the introduction of new individual foods (Sokolov, 1990). As Figure 3.1 shows, the Chinese word for the combination of food and drink — *yinshi*, is a compound of *yin* meaning "drink" and *shi* meaning "food." Not surprisingly, *yin* is associated with the element "water." *Shi* ("food") is further

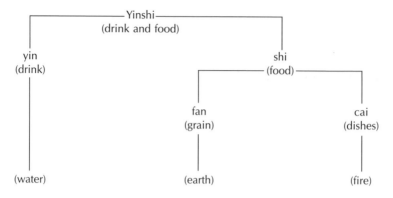

Figure 3.1   The structure of Chinese food and drink. (Source: Chang, 1977a: 40.)

subdivided into *fan*, or "grain" (literally and specifically cooked rice), associated with the element "earth," and *cai*, or "dishes," with the element "fire." Even if the *fan* and *cai* parts of the meal are eaten in the same mouthful, as in *jiaozi* (dumplings), *baozi* (stuffed buns), or *xianbing* (stuffed pancakes), the distinction remains (Chang, 1977b: 7–8).

Fan

Historically, the domestication of cereal grains was the key to the development of a civilization. Mangelsdorf (1953: 50) says, "No civilization worthy of the name has ever been founded on any agricultural basis other than the cereals." The Chinese meal structure has retained this central place for cereal grains; the *fan* or grain is the "main" part (*zhushi*), and *fan* is often used to mean "meal" or "food" in general. Without *fan*, the meal leaves the diner hungry; without *cai*, it is simply less tasty. Although restaurant orders are usually for "dishes" (*cai*), and the *cai* may be the center of a child's attention, *fan* is assumed to be the important part of the meal (Simoons, 1991: 15, 18).

Rice

The Western perception of the Chinese is that they eat a great deal of rice — and they do. Although rice was not the first cereal grain domesticated in China, it has become, by far, the most important, not only in China but in the rest of East Asia as well. Because of this region's dominance in world population, rice is the most important cereal grain in the world (Wittwer et al., 1987: 139). In China, the rice bowl is a metaphor for food and well-being in general.

Rice was first domesticated by the Majiabang and Hemudu peoples at the delta of the Yangtze River in China around 8000 B.C.(Glover and Higham 1996: 435). Both long-grain (*Oryza sativa indica*) and short-grain (*O. sativa japonica*) varieties have been found in the archaeological remains (Andersson, 1934: 336; see also Ho, 1975: 61–73). In the Huang He (Yellow River) valley, it has been found in small amounts, indicating that it was a food for the elite on ceremonial occasions (Ho, 1969). The regionalization of China into rice in the south and other grains in the north was in place by the Han dynasty (207 B.C. to A.D. 200); that same pattern endures today (Buck, 1937; Yü, 1977: 42). Millet (see below), however, was still the favored grain, reflecting the location of China's core area in the north. Rice was second (Yü, 1977).

During the Song dynasty (960–1279), the Liao (Khitan, an Altaic people) established their kingdom in what is now northeastern China, eventually extending it from what is now Beijing to Korea. They, in turn, were conquered by the Jurchen (Manchu, or *Manzu*), a Tungus tribe, in 1125. In 1127, they took the Song capital of Bianjing (now Kaifeng); in southern China, the Song reorganized and were known as the Southern Song, with their capital at Hangzhou. In 1234, the Mongols conquered the Jurchen empire of Jin.

The loss of the northern lands affected the agriculture of the Southern Song, and, during this period, the Chinese diet took on a definitive shape and developed into a remarkable cuisine (Anderson, 1988: 69). Agriculture became more scientific because the peasants were under pressure to produce more food for urban populations and for trade, but much of that development was a continuation and intensification of trends that had begun earlier (irrigation, fertilization, crop rotation etc.). The truly revolutionary innovation was the use of new crop varieties, especially fast-maturing rice from Champa (now Vietnam), which was introduced in the eleventh century (Anderson, 1988: 77).

Its rapid adoption indicates that it filled a perceived need among farmers and others alike. Rice already had become the pre-eminent grain in China. At this time, China was confined to the rice-growing region, and for the first time, the south contained the political, economic, and cultural core. With the loss of the agricultural lands of the north, agriculture in the lands left to the Southern Song became more intensive, and rice was an important factor in this development (Anderson, 1988: 79).

Rice comes in a great many varieties, and different cultural groups favor different qualities. The rice grown in southern China, *O. sativa japonica* or *sinica*, is short-grained and sticky and, thus, easy to eat with chopsticks. "Glutinous" rice is especially sticky, although the term is a misnomer: rice does not contain gluten, and the stickiness is a function of amylose (a derivative of starch), which makes up about 90% of milled rice (Swaminathan, 1984).

The great variability of rice, a result of natural selection and selective breeding, gives it a geographical distribution that is almost unparalleled among plants (Swaminathan, 1984). In the hot climates of southern China, it is grown in fields that can be flooded during part of the growing season — so-called paddies or wet-rice. Rice also can be grown — indeed grows wild — in natural marshlands, as it was in the original Neolithic agricultural area of northern China in times before the Chinese developed irrigation (Ho, 1969). It can also be grown as a dry-land crop, providing that natural rainfall is sufficient (about 80 inches or 2,000 mm per year). Fast-maturing varieties have extended greatly its latitudinal extent, and the northernmost rice paddy in the world is in far northern Heilongjiang Province, at Mohe on the Amur River (Heilong Jiang) at 53°31' north latitude (Zhao, 1994: 182).

Not only is rice versatile, it also responds well to labor inputs (Anderson, 1988; Bray, 1994). Starting seedlings in nursery beds and then transplanting them into flooded paddies, in addition to the work of terracing and building irrigation works, pays off in higher yields. As will be discussed later in this chapter, rice feeds a dense population better than any other cereal grain — it requires many workers, but it also feeds them.

Millet

Millet was the cereal grain on which China's Neolithic Revolution was based (Ho, 1969); however, it later was overtaken by rice as a staple. Its modern Chinese name *xiaomi* literally means "little rice," and the grain today is regarded as food for poor people.

Agriculture in China first developed in the middle valley of the Huang He and its tributaries, especially the Wei and the Fen, a region called the *Zhongyuan* or Middle Plain. Here are found some of the world's great deposits of loess (wind-blown) soils, which are easily worked with primitive tools. Rainfall, however, is sparse, averaging less than 20 inches (500 mm) per year, and such dry conditions also seem to have prevailed at the end of the Pleistocene when agriculture began, as is evident in the preponderance of sagebrush remains (*Artemisia tridentata*) in the strata of that period (Ho, 1969). Thus, grass cover was sparse, and the soil's minerals had not been leached out. Furthermore, the loess-covered uplands were safe from the legendary floods of the Huang He, "China's Sorrow." In this area, the Yangshao culture, named for a village in Henan Province, developed by at least 5000 B.C. and perhaps earlier. The best-known Yangshao site is Banpo, just outside the modern city of Xi'an (Banpo Museum, 1987).

Two kinds of millet formed the base of early Chinese farming culture: *Setaria italica* (foxtail millet) and *Panicum miliaceum* (panic millet). The first has been shown in laboratories to have the highest "efficiency of transpiration," that is, of all the cereals, it is best suited to dry conditions (Wittwer et al., 1987: 203). While *P. miliaceum* has not undergone such testing, its drought resistance is well known (Ho, 1969: 16). Ho Ping-ti (1969) argues effectively that both are indigenous to the Zhongyuan. Millet remained the staple grain through the Shang (1766–1122 B.C.) and the Han dynasties. In the northern lands, it continued as the staple through the time of the Liao-Jin. Although today it is not usually a staple, it continues to be grown as a dry-field crop, especially in the north.

Millet is highly nutritious, with a protein content (especially two essential amino acids) higher than rice or maize and more oil than wheat or rice (Wittwer et al., 1987: 203). Rich in Vitamin B_1 and containing Vitamin A, it is a popular food for women after childbirth. Millet usually is eaten as porridge (*xiaomizhou*). *P. miliaceum* also is used for brewing.

Wheat and Barley

Wheat (Mangelsdorf, 1953) and barley both represent early imports to China from southwestern and central Asia, probably by the middle of the second millennium B.C. (Harris, 1996: 565). In fact, the early word for "wheat" — *lai* — has the same pronunciation as the word for "to come" and was written with the same character (Ho, 1969). Along with another import — corn, or maize — these plants dominate grain farming in northern China today. As standards of living rise in developed countries, wheat products comprise more of the diet; China is following this trend (Gamble, 1933; Wittwer et al., 1987: 157).

Wheat and barley were first domesticated about 8000 B.C. in Southwest Asia, under climatic conditions of summer drought and winter rainfall. The rainfall regime of northern China is just the opposite: most rain falls in summer, and winters are dry. Thus, in prehistoric times, wheat did not fit the agricultural environment of China at all and, though known, was regarded as a curiosity at best (Anderson, 1988; Chang, 1977a; Simoons, 1991). Techniques for raising wheat developed only when population density warranted the effort involved (Anderson, 1988: 20). During the Han dynasty, the introduction of the technology for noodle making gave wheat another major boost in popularity (Yü, 1977).

By the Tang dynasty (A.D. 618–907), the principal wheat-raising area was near the capital of Chang'an (modern Xi'an), a region that still produces winter wheat (Schafer, 1977). The raising of winter wheat, together with summer millet, spread as the availability of flour milling technology greatly increased the uses and popularity of wheat. "Foreign" cakes made from wheat flour, topped with sesame seeds, and baked in barrels became popular; it has been reported that they were sold on street corners in Chang'an, presumably by Iranians (Anderson, 1988; Schafer, 1977). They are still made and sold in the markets of China, in both round and oblong shapes. Archaeological remains also have yielded fried sweet cakes of wheat flour (probably something like doughnuts) and dumplings with wheat-flour wrappers (*jiaozi* and *huntun*). A "Brahman cake" was made of steamed wheat paste (Schafer, 1977).

During the Song dynasty, wheat continued to gain in popularity as the technology introduced during the Tang dynasty became more established (Anderson, 1988). Noodles made from wheat became a common staple for both rich and poor (Raichlen, 1992), although the story that the Chinese invented noodles and Marco Polo took the idea back to Italy is apocryphal.

Although barley is *damai* ("great wheat") and wheat is *xiaomai* ("little wheat"), wheat is actually the more important grain in China today, second only to rice. In addition to noodles, wrappers for *jiaozi* and spring (egg) rolls, and baked and fried cakes, wheat is also made into steamed bread, with or without filling, and pancakes. In the 1980s, the Chinese government actively began promoting increased use of Western-style sliced yeast bread (*Lancaster* [Pennsylvania] *Intelligencer Journal*, August 15, 1985). Cake, including birthday cake, and cookies also are becoming popular.

Sorghum

Sorghum, called *gaoliang* ("tall grain") in Chinese, probably was domesticated first in Africa, south of the Sahara. Its introduction into China is still puzzling, although it probably came from India around A.D. 300; claims that it arrived around 1000 B.C. would require reassessments of contacts between China and Africa (Ho, 1975: 380–4; Bray, 1984). Population pressure in the eighteenth and nineteenth centuries increased its importance (Simoons, 1991). Liaoning is one of the leading producers today (Wittwer et al., 1987: 205).

Sorghum's advantage is its ability to withstand the vagaries of weather; it is resistant to both flood and drought, and it matures quickly. It produces grain that is edible, although not a favorite food, and its stalks have many uses, including fencing material and fuel. Thus, it is widely grown as a kind of insurance, even displacing millet in northern China, especially in the Northeast (Simoons, 1991). It is prepared and eaten like rice, but is less expensive. During the Japanese occupation of the Northeast, the Japanese ate rice, while the Chinese (especially the poor) ate sorghum, which is easily grown in that region without irrigation (Hsu and Hsu, 1977). Sweet sorghum also is used to make sugar (Wittwer et al., 1987: 206).

Corn (Maize)

Corn, or maize (*Zea mays*), was the great cereal grain of pre-Columbian America, domesticated first in the highlands of Mexico, by at least 5000 B.C. It crossed the oceans to Eurasia and Africa, as a result of the great Columbian Exchange (Crosby, 1972), reaching China by the middle of the sixteenth century (Ho, 1955; Simoons, 1991), and knowledge of it spread rapidly. It could be grown on slopes that were too steep for terracing into rice paddies, such as the west and southwest of China, where its introduction allowed the population to spread (McNeill, 1991: 46, 54–55). In Qing times, it enabled migration into the hilly lands of Yunnan, Guizhou, and Sichuan from the overpopulated Yangtze Valley (Spence, 1977). Corn was considered an experiment elsewhere, possibly because areas where it later became important (including the northeast) were not yet developed (Perkins, 1969).

Corn requires less water than rice, but it produces more Calories per unit of land than wheat (Wittwer et al., 1987: 169). It can be grown on hillsides and uplands where rice cannot grow. Today, it occupies a band from the Northeast to Yunnan in the Southwest; in other words, it is less dominant in areas where rice and wheat can be grown easily.

Liaoning roadsides lined with cornfields are reminiscent of Iowa, in the United States, and corn production per hectare there is the highest in China (Wittwer et al., 1987: 172). In the river valleys, where irrigation water is readily available, however, rice takes over. Unlike in the United States, most Chinese corn feeds people directly, although increasing amounts are fed to animals. During the Maoist period, poor people in the northeast ate very little except corn (Ding, 1994; Li Fuqi, 1994). Today, more favored foods have taken the lead; most corn is eaten in the form of cornmeal pancakes, stuffed cornmeal buns, and boiled corn on the cob (a popular street snack).

Potatoes and Sweet Potatoes

Yams and taro, both root crops, have a long history of cultivation in Southeast Asia. In China, however, they gradually were displaced by rice, possibly because Chinese migrants from the north were more accustomed to grains as their staple food (Simoons, 1991). Grains are easier to cultivate and more convenient to use; they store well and can be cooked with less fuel than the tropical tubers. Unlike Africans, Chinese do not regard yams as a prestigious food (Simoons, 1991).

Sweet potatoes (*Ipomoea batatas; digua* or "ground squash" in northeastern China) and white or Irish potatoes (*Solanum tuberosum; tudou* or "soil beans" in northeastern China) came much later, via the Columbian Exchange from America (Crosby, 1972; Ho, 1955). Although Westerners tend to eat them as vegetables, sweet potatoes fill the role of *fan* in the Chinese diet, and they can be made into flour. They came to China through Manila by the end of the sixteenth century; a governor of Fujian province encouraged their cultivation for famine relief in 1594 (Anderson, 1988: 97). They grow in areas not suited to rice, and — important in famine times — they mature quickly. The introduction of sweet potatoes, along with maize, made possible the enormous growth in the Chinese population during Ming and especially Qing times by adding "insurance" foods in case the main staple crops of rice and wheat should fail. Both crops can also be grown on land not suited to rice, such as steep slopes or dry land (Anderson, 1988; Crosby, 1972).

Sweet potatoes, however, have never been a favorite staple food. The ease of growing them has done nothing to increase their prestige, and they are regarded as a food for the poor, for pigs, or, if absolutely necessary, for an emergency food in a famine (Anderson, 1988). To call someone a "sweet potato eater" is an insult (Simoons, 1991).

Today, sweet potatoes baked in barrels — a secondary rather than a staple food — are a popular street snack in northern cities in the autumn. In addition to Calories (more than white potatoes), sweet potatoes are rich in beta-carotene, the precursor of Vitamin A, which generally is low in the Chinese diet. Hence, baked sweet potatoes not only are handwarmers in cold weather but fill an important role in nutrition (Simoons, 1991). However, many adults who are old enough to remember the terrible famine of the early 1960s, when sweet potatoes were the only food available, still shun them because they are a reminder of a time for which they are not at all nostalgic (Li Fuqi, 1994).

White potatoes were first domesticated in highland Peru and reached Taiwan by 1650 and the mainland by 1700. French missionaries helped to spread them in the eighteenth and nineteenth centuries. They never attained the importance in the diet of China that they did in Europe, but they are widely grown and considered a good "insurance" crop in case grain fails. Generally, they are eaten as a vegetable, as part of *cai* in a meal: stir-fried, boiled, or added to soup (Simoons, 1991).

Soybeans

Northeastern China's great gift to the world's diet is the soybean (*Glycine max*). As its Chinese name, *dadou* ("great bean") implies, it is a legume, but it is counted as "grain" in Chinese statistics. It may have been domesticated as early as 3000 B.C., but a more probable time frame is the Shang dynasty, (1766–1122 B.C). (Chang, 1977c) or Zhou dynasty (1100–771 B.C.) (Chang, 1977a). Proto-Tungusic tribes in the Northeast seem to have been the first cultivators (Ho, 1975).[1]

The soybean probably was first grown for its role as a fertilizer. As with other legumes, its roots contain nodules in which nitrogen-fixing bacteria live; they take atmospheric nitrogen and "fix" it in the soil so that it becomes a nutrient for plant growth (Katz, 1987: 47–51). It was regarded as the most important legume by 2000 B.C. and listed by the mythological Shen Nong as one of the five sacred grains essential to Chinese civilization (Wittwer et al., 1987: 184). By Han times, it was a common part of the ordinary Chinese diet (Yü, 1977), and the coming of Buddhism, with its ideal of a vegetarian diet, increased the popularity of soybeans (Anderson and Anderson, 1977).

The beans can be boiled, but most Chinese eat soybeans prepared in other ways. The preparation of bean curd (*doufu,* or in Japanese and English "tofu") may have been developed in Han times (Yü, 1977: 81). *Doufu* has a number of varieties, not only the white blocks of varying degrees of firmness, but also pressed into *choudoufu* (literally, "stinking bean curd") and *gandoufu* ("dry tofu"), which looks a little like sheets of yellow kraft paper. In winter, it is often sold frozen.

Soybeans can be prepared as flour and then used like wheat flour. They also can be made into dried powder, to which hot water is added to make milk (*dounai*). In a country that generally eschews dairy foods, *dounai* provides a source of calcium as well as protein. Unlike most legumes, soybeans also contain oil, which is the major cooking oil in China (and the traditional basic ingredient of margarine in the West). Fermented soybeans are used to make soy sauce. Waste from soybean processing is pressed into cakes, which are used as fertilizer and were an early export from northeastern China.

To the poor of China over hundreds of years, the soybean, especially in combination with grain, economically has provided nutrients — proteins and calcium — that would otherwise be missing in an almost purely vegetarian diet. Soybeans contain the most protein per pound and per acre of any plant food (Anderson and Anderson, 1977; Mote, 1977) and is readily available to the body. In fact, a pound of dry soybeans has more protein than a pound of beef or any other food, although, Calorie for Calorie, beef is richer. Soybean protein is more nearly complete (in terms of essential amino acids) than any other grain protein. Furthermore, preparation of soybeans, as *doufu,* extracts the carbohydrates, leaving the protein (along with oil, precipitates, and coagulates), thus improving the protein-to-calorie ratio (Anderson and Anderson, 1977: 347).

As mentioned, soybeans, especially as *doufu,* also provide calcium (Wittwer et al., 1987: 183). Thus, the early Chinese need for dairy products was not so important, and dairy herds were shunned as a mark of differentiation from the "barbarian" nomads in the north and northwest. Although preparation of *doufu* destroys much of the thiamine, riboflavin, and other B vitamins (which are water-soluble), it concentrates iron and preserves Vitamin A (Anderson and Anderson, 1977). In a diet low in meat, the iron content of soybeans is important.

Cai

The vegetable and/or meat accompaniments of *cai* give Chinese food its richness, variety, and flavor. These non-staple foods come in an almost infinite variety and, of course, add important nutrients to the diet. The following discussion is by no means exhaustive; it serves only as an introduction to the foods commonly found on northeastern Chinese meal tables.

Vegetables

The word *cai* means "vegetables," and most *cai* consists of vegetables. Similar to *fan,* some of today's common vegetables are native to China, while some are imports. Plastic sheeting is a major technological advance that has increased the variety and quantity of vegetable production in northern China. Surrounding both large and small urban areas are suburban districts with rows and rows of greenhouses constructed with tamped-earth walls on the north side, sloping tamped earth walls on the east and west, and sheets of plastic on the top and south sides. In winter, straw mats are attached to the top of the north wall and can be rolled down over the plastic at night and rolled up to admit sunlight during the day. Although hours of daylight are short in winter, cloudy days are few in the dry monsoon. Some greenhouses also have small stoves for additional heating.

Plastic also is used to cover newly planted vegetable seeds, both to warm the ground and to retain moisture. Rice seedlings are started under plastic and then transplanted to flooded paddies. The price of plastic sheeting has become a public concern in connection with food production and frequently is reported in the press. Also of concern is the manufacturing process itself and the pollution it causes. Clearly, however, it is a technological advance that has had a major impact on China's ability to feed a growing population and improve its nutritional status (Wittwer et al., 1987).

The most common vegetable is cabbage, the so-called Peking cabbage (*Brassica pekinensis*) from northern China. Bok choy is more common in the south, although "little bok choy" or *youcai* ("oil vegetable") is grown and eaten in the north. Evidence of cabbages has been found at the Yangshao site of Banpo, just outside Xi'an, in the form of a pot of seeds that evidently were being saved for the following year's planting, indicating that its cultivation in China goes back to at least the fifth millennium B.C. (Simoons, 1991). Chinese varieties of cabbage have more vitamins than Western cabbage (which the Chinese also eat), is very filling, and rich in fiber (Anderson, 1988).

Cabbage is grown in abundance in summer, harvested in early autumn, and laid out to dry. It then can be stored dry or pickled to make *suancai* ("sour vegetable"), similar to sauerkraut. Formerly, it was the only vegetable available in northern China in winter (Jones, 1992), but recent reforms, increases in greenhouse cultivation, and transportation of vegetables from warmer climates (Xiang, 1992) have decreased the demand for cabbages because the variety of available produce has increased markedly (*Christian Science Monitor,* February 18, 1993). Nevertheless, cabbage remains an important component of the Chinese diet and is an ingredient in *jiaozi,* stuffed buns, and filled pancakes.

The largest class of fruits that are eaten as vegetables in China are the cucurbits (*Cucurbitaceae*), collectively called *gua* in Chinese: cucumbers and squash. (Those eaten as fruit will be considered later in this chapter.) Chinese cucumbers (*Cucumis sativus,* or in Chinese, *huanggua,* "yellow squash") are the long, narrow European type and are eaten raw or incorporated into stir-fried dishes. The cucumber's origins are uncertain, but it has been grown in China since ancient times. Various kinds of squash, some of them imports from the Americas, are used in stir-fries or soups.

The onion family (*Allium*) has over 500 members indigenous to the Northern Hemisphere, especially to grasslands (Simoons, 1991). Given China's cultural origins in such a region, it is not surprising that members of this family have been important in the Chinese dietary regime since ancient times, and China is one of the areas where these plants were first domesticated.

The dominant vegetable of this group is the Welsh or bunching onion, *Allium fistulosum,* or *cong* in Chinese. It looks like a giant green or spring onion and has been grown for a considerable period. It may be used as a garnish or flavoring in a dish, but in the north, it may be the principal vegetable. As with Chinese cabbage, it can be dried for storage and, along with cabbage, formerly was the main source of vitamins in winter. It is also an ingredient in *jiaozi,* stuffed buns, and filled pancakes.

Western onions (*A. cepa*) are a more recent addition to Chinese food, as is its Chinese name *yangcong,* "foreign onion." Its flavor is stronger than that of the Chinese onion and is primarily used as an ingredient in stir-fried dishes.

Garlic (*A. sativum*) is also an import, but it came much earlier; it has been cultivated in China for millennia and has its own Chinese name, *suan* (Anderson, 1988). The bulbs, *suantou,* are chopped and added to stir-fried dishes and to the stuffing for *jiaozi;* they also are chewed raw and regarded as a preventative for many diseases (Brody, 1984). The stalks of the plant, *suantai,* are eaten or stir-fried, and have a slightly milder garlic flavor than the bulbs.

Chinese chives (*A. tuberosum*), called *jiucai* in Chinese, are flat-leaved and have a similar taste as garlic. They can be stir-fried and used as an ingredient in *jiaozi.*

Among the root vegetables, besides potatoes and sweet potatoes discussed previously, the most important in northern China are carrots and turnips. Carrots (*Daucus* spp.) reached China from Central Asia during the Yuan dynasty (1279–1368), hence, the Chinese name *huluobo,* or "Iranian radish" (Anderson, 1988). Carrots and turnips are added to soups and stir-fried dishes and frequently are carved into fantastic shapes for banquet dishes. Also widespread, and frequently confused with turnips, are various kinds of radishes. The peanut (*Arachis hypogaea; huasheng* in Chinese, or "born from flowers") also grows underground (despite its name) and first was domesticated in South America, by at least the first millennium B.C. (Simoons, 1991: 280). It seems to have reached China before the early part of the sixteenth century (Ho, 1955:

191–2). It has adapted well to sandy soils that could not be used for rice and has a high protein and fat content. Nevertheless, it spread slowly. Even as late as 1700, it was a luxury banquet dish, rather than an everyday food. Like the soybean, it seems to have been adopted first for its nitrogen-fixing properties (Simoons, 1991). By the twentieth century, in both city and countryside, it was a common food (Buck, 1937; Gamble, 1933: 102). Along with maize and sweet and white potatoes, it made possible the great increase in population in China in Ming times because it supplies amino acids complimentary to grains, thus providing an inexpensive source of protein (Ho, 1955). Peanut oil is favored over soybean oil for cooking. Peanuts also are an ingredient in stir-fried dishes and are often roasted and eaten as a snack.

Eggplants (*Solanum melongena*), both purple and green, seem to have come from India in the distant past (Anderson, 1988). Chinese eggplants are harvested when they are smaller than Western eggplants — and, consequently, are less bitter (Simoons, 1991). They are common in stir-fried dishes, where they add bulk, making the dishes more filling.

Relatives of the eggplant — peppers and tomatoes — were imported from the Americas. Of these, chili peppers (*Capsicum annuum*) are, by far, the most important. While eggplants and tomatoes long remained confined to European-influenced coastal areas, the chili pepper spread rapidly all over China after its introduction through Macau by the Portuguese (Lan, 1996; Simoons, 1991). In addition to increasing immeasurably the flavor of bland grains, the chili pepper provides vitamins A and C, iron, calcium, and other minerals (Anderson, 1988; Simoons, 1991). It is identified most closely with the cuisine of Sichuan and Hunan provinces, but is used to flavor dishes elsewhere. Sweet (bell) peppers are used widely as an ingredient in stir-fried dishes.

Tomatoes (*Lycopersicon esculentum*) were introduced in the 1500s; they go by several names, all indicating their foreign origin: *fanqie* ("foreign eggplant") and *xihongshi* ("Western red persimmon"). At first, their use was confined to Western-influenced coastal areas, but they now have spread widely and are used in various stir-fried dishes or served raw as a cold dish.

The Chinese use a wide variety of shoots in dishes, especially beans and bamboo, mushrooms and other fungus, and seaweed (in coastal areas). Wild plants, some of which entered the dietary regime by necessity during a famine, may become incorporated in the mainstream diet, or they may become luxury items (Maynard and Swen, 1937), like the delicately flavored *qumacai* of Liaoning Province. Southern Chinese are said to eat everything with four legs except tables, everything that flies except airplanes, and everything from water except boats. While northern Chinese diets show somewhat less variety, the *fan-cai* structure of Chinese meals has enabled the introduction of new ingredients, without disrupting the general dietary plan. Thus, the incorporation of new foods has been fairly easy, especially in times when the basic food supply is assured.

Meats

As mentioned, the Chinese traditionally eat comparatively little meat. Their largely vegetarian diet and eating grain directly, rather than feeding it to animals, is part of the explanation for their ability to feed such a dense population on so little farmland. The role of soybean products, especially the various forms of *doufu*, as meat substitutes has already been mentioned. This situation is changing, however, and the Chinese are developing a fondness for meat as their economic situation improves. When asked to list favorite foods, students at Northeastern University in Shenyang invariably mentioned meat, indicating that it was a rather rare treat and, consequently, was valued.

By far, the most common meat is pork. Whether Chinese pigs were first domesticated in China from wild pigs or were imported from elsewhere is uncertain, but they were very much a part of Neolithic China (Simoons, 1991). They have remained important ever since (Tsang, 1996); the character for "family" in Chinese is made up of the character for "pig" with a roof over it, and the word "meat" without any qualifier is understood to mean "pork." The price of pork in China, as beef in the United States, is a matter of public concern (Liang, 1995; Zhang, 1995).

Pork is highly nutritious because it contains iron and B vitamins, as well as protein. Cooking pork with its bones in a vinegary sweet-sour sauce softens the bones and releases the calcium for use by the body, a valuable bonus in diets that contain very little milk (Pyke, 1968).

Apart from their role in human nutrition, pigs play an important part in the agricultural system of China. They, along with chickens, function as living garbage cans in rural China, eating agricultural and kitchen scraps along with prepared feed. Thus, they function as mechanisms for turning potentially useless garbage into food for humans in the form of pork and ham. They also provide fertilizer and, for that reason, were spared at the height of the Cultural Revolution's frenzy to "grow grain everywhere." Mao Zedong characterized the pig as "a small fertilizer plant" (Wittwer et al., 1987: 111).

Chickens are also scavengers. Like pigs, their history goes back so far into antiquity that the origins of their domestication have been lost, but they may have been used first for cockfighting, a sophisticated form of divination (Simoons, 1991). Ducks, also domesticated early, contribute to the agricultural system by eating weeds and bugs in rice paddies. Along with geese, they provide feathers and down for quilts and clothing, as well as food. Chicken and duck eggs, both fresh and salted, are eaten, although "thousand-year-old eggs" are really not that old (*China Daily*, June 23, 1994).

Domestic sheep, goats, and cattle apparently came to China in Yangshao times from southwestern Asia. Gradually, these animals were concentrated in the drier lands to the north and northwest; settled agriculture became dominant in the wetter south and southeast. To the settled farmers, the nomadic animal herders, lacking cities and written language, were considered "barbarians," and, by extension, so was their dependence on animal foods. Throughout history, the frontier zone between settled agriculture and pastoral nomadism has been a zone of contention; the Great Wall was built to mark and defend the boundary of Chinese farmers.

In southern China, water buffalo have long been used as work animals, while oxen were used in the colder north. Today, mules, donkeys, and horses more commonly fill this role. The role of cattle as work animals, together with Buddhist teachings, led to a decline in the demand for beef by the time of the Tang dynasty (Simoons, 1991).

The major market for mutton is China's Muslim population, which shares with other Muslims a prohibition against pork because it is considered "unclean." One of the great insults that Maoist China perpetrated against the Muslims was insistence that they raise pigs and eat pork. More recently, Muslims have developed a somewhat distinctive cuisine based on mutton and have opened numerous restaurants featuring such dishes.

Dogs may have been the first animals to be domesticated, possibly as early as 12,000 B.C. in southwestern Asia (Simoons, 1991). While Westerners generally (but not totally) have eschewed eating dog meat, it has been a small part of the Chinese diet for centuries. During the Maoist years, especially after the famine that followed the Great Leap Forward, there was a campaign to eliminate dogs because they competed with people for food; keeping dogs was prohibited in cities. More recently, dogs have become pets, especially in the countryside, and dog meat can be found in restaurants in all areas, although more commonly in the south.

Where it is available, seafood is valued highly among the Chinese. Banquet fare frequently includes shrimp and sea slugs and is incomplete without a large, whole fish (including head and tail) that has been steamed, deliciously seasoned, and beautifully decorated. It is placed on the banquet table with the head pointing toward the guest of honor, who is supposed to eat the eye. An enormous variety of fresh- and saltwater fish are eaten, although Western favorites, such as tuna and salmon, are considered appropriate only as fertilizer (Simoons, 1991). Aquaculture in artificial fish ponds, long a practice in the south, is becoming more widespread in the north. Along with better transportation from coastal to inland regions, this development has made seafood more readily available farther from the coasts.

Fruits

Fruit seems to have been a more important part of the Chinese diet in earlier times than in recent history (Freeman, 1977). By the late nineteenth century, fruit was not central to the thinking of either farmers or eaters (Anderson, 1988), and fruit growing occupied a very small percentage of farmland. Today, fruit is grown in orchards, including some in Liaoning, but it is still regarded as something of a luxury — for example, a popular gift when one visits a home or to take to a visitor's hotel room. Fruit is often eaten as a snack, before a meal, and, less frequently, as a dessert.

Citrus fruits apparently have been cultivated in southern China since ancient times. Today, they are grown mostly in the Southeast and are sent to many parts of the country. Grown in Guangdong Province, the litchi or leechee is another tropical fruit that is linked to China. A wild form grows on Hainan Island; it was domesticated in antiquity and already grew around the Gulf of Tonkin when the Han reached that region.

Of the *Prunus* species (plums, peaches, apricots, and cherries), the peach (*P. persica*) is native to China. Its domestication dates from antiquity; remains have been found in Zhejiang dating from the fourth or fifth millennium B.C. It is prized, not only for its fruit, but also for its flowers, and symbolizes long life and immortality, a mysticism that survives in the New Year's custom of placing a spray of peach branches over the door.

The Chinese greatly love melons, and the country has its own distinctive varieties, especially the very sweet Hami melon from Xinjiang. Watermelon is a particular favorite; the best watermelons are said to come from Lanzhou, but they are grown in many other areas of the country as well. Watermelon seeds are also eaten as a snack. The fruit was introduced from Central Asia in the twelfth century, hence, the Chinese name *xigua*, Western gourd.

Berries are a minor element in the Chinese diet. An exception is the recent addition of strawberries. Formerly available from local sources in season, they are now being sent from southern China to colder regions in winter, at the same time of year that California strawberries appear in markets in northeastern United States.

Beverages

The expression "all the tea in China" shows the importance of that beverage in the national culture. The location of its first domestication is uncertain (Dekker, 1995; Evans, 1992), but Chinese tea (*Camellia sinensis*, var. *sinensis*) appears to be native to warm areas, from Assam in India through Myanmar (Burma) and the Indochina Peninsula to southern China.

The plant is an evergreen shrub, and the variations among different kinds of tea reflect the processing of the leaves. They include: black tea (called *hongcha* or "red tea" in Chinese), which is fermented and produced for export; oolong, which is semi-fermented; green, which is unfermented; and scented, such as jasmine or chrysanthemum (Anderson and Anderson, 1977; Simoons, 1991). There are infinite varieties of each, as well as a wide assortment of medicinal teas (*China Daily*, June 6, 1994). People who cannot afford tea usually drink plain boiled water, either hot or cooled.

Tea is prepared by placing dried leaves directly into cups or pots and pouring boiling water over them. Teabags may be found in hotel rooms and restaurants, but the Chinese keep loose leaves in a tea caddy. To be sure that boiling water is always available, they keep it in thermos bottles; this water is also safe to drink. Tea is associated with hospitality and is the first thing served to guests in a home or at a restaurant. Hence, it is drunk before, rather than during, a meal. Rarely is anything added to the tea, although in former times, milk, salt, and other flavorings were used. Tea also can be used as a flavoring, for example, when hard-cooked eggs are steeped in tea and sold as a street snack.

Beer is a popular drink with meals, and many kinds of beer are produced in China, some of them (e.g. Tsingtao) for export. Most cities have a local brewery, and the industry, some of it in the form of joint ventures with foreign firms, has been growing rapidly (*China Daily Business Weekly,* December 26, 1993-January 4, 1994). In 1979, the total output was 700,000 metric tons; in 1991, it had reached 8.13 million tons. Although per capita consumption is only about eight liters (two gallons) per year, it is growing by 10% to 15% annually, especially among young adults, who find it less expensive and believe it to be healthier than distilled liquor (Snyder, 1992).

Grape wines have been produced in China since at least the Han dynasty, and Marco Polo reported that grape wine was available, although rice wine, flavored with various spices, was preferred (Freeman, 1977). Today, China produces various kinds, including sweet dessert-type red wines and the widely known Great Wall white wine.

The technology for distilling liquors was developed during the Song dynasty, with the first technical manual dating from 1117, but these liquors apparently were not widely known (Freeman, 1977). They include the famous *maotai* and more common *baijiu* (literally "white wine"). In any case, they are virtually obligatory for toasting at banquets, where they are served in tiny cups.

One of the most widely recognized symbols of China's Opening to the World since 1978 is the rapid growth of Western soft drinks, especially Coca-Cola and Pepsi-Cola (*China Daily Business Weekly,* June 19–25, 1994), although native soda has been available for some time. Instant coffee is now available in China, and there are coffee houses in towns and cities. Starbucks operates a restaurant within the Forbidden City in Beijing.

As mentioned previously, dairy products are not favored in China. Many Chinese adults suffer from lactose intolerance, caused by an insufficiency of the enzyme lactase for digestion of milk sugar, or lactose. There have been periods in Chinese history, however, when more dairy products were used. This occurred when Chinese upper classes had more contact with leaders of nomadic herding peoples and there was more intermarriage. In Tang China, fermented milks, including kumiss (fermented mare's milk), were in greater demand than fresh milk (Simoons, 1991). Conquest by the Mongols, who were a milk-using people, highlighted for the Chinese a connection between milk and the enemies of China, making milk less desirable. The Manchu, who became the rulers of the Qing dynasty, are also a non-Han people, but use of dairy products seems to have been confined to scattered pockets during their rule.

Today, there is a dairying industry in China, and pasteurized milk is available. Children, who do not suffer from lactose intolerance, drink it, and some non-Han enjoy it. Yogurt (where the processing pre-digests some of the lactose) and ice cream are two dairy products that all Chinese can eat and are becoming increasingly important.

Snacks

The veritable explosion of petty street vending in China's informal labor sector has made snacks widely available. The equivalent of potato chips and pretzels are found everywhere, along with all kinds of candy (including chocolate, a newcomer), prepared foods, sodas, ice cream, and popsicles. Peanuts (originally an American food), sunflower seeds, and watermelon seeds are traditional snacks.

The Cultural Ecology of the Chinese Diet

As mentioned at the beginning of this chapter, Chinese culture is food-centered. Not only do people think about food almost constantly, their great poets have written about it (Kwok, 1991; Lin, 1935). As the common saying goes, the Chinese don't just eat to live, they live to eat. A long history of a precarious food supply and repeated famines (Dando, 1980; Mallory, 1926) undoubtedly has contributed to food's status as pivotal in Chinese life.

The traditional regional dividing line in Chinese agriculture and diet is between the rice-growing south and the wheat-growing north with the dividing line at the Qingling mountain range and the Huai River (Buck, 1937; Zhao, 1993). The south is warmer and wetter; precipitation is also more dependable. The division, however, is by no means pure, as each region grows some of the other grain, as well as varying amounts of other staples (Buck, 1937).

Nutrition and Health of the Chinese Diet

In an environment of high cholesterol and obesity, high rates of heart disease and cancer, Western scientists are looking to the diet for clues to control these problems. Not only is the dominantly vegetarian diet of the Chinese a more efficient use of land than the consumption of animal products, it may also be healthier (Brody, 1990; Henderson, 1994; Roberts, 1988). It is lower in fat and higher in fiber.

Most agricultural systems are based on a carbohydrate-rich staple crop, with a backup crop in case of failure. Carbohydrates are the direct product of photosynthesis and the main nutrient of plant foods; most people get the majority of their Calories from carbohydrates. Thus, the most successful and most efficient staple crop is one that provides not only carbohydrates but also other nutrients. The best such crop is rice, which provides both a high Calorie content per unit of land and also protein and B vitamins. Wheat is less productive per acre, although it provides more protein and B vitamins. The backup crops in China — corn, buckwheat, millets, sorghum, and barley — are in a lesser position precisely because they yield less per unit of land and are less nutritious. A rice-based diet, therefore, provides plenty of carbohydrates from the staples and also, in all likelihood, most of the protein (Anderson and Anderson, 1977: 346). Much of the rest of the protein is made up from the soybean, which also provides iron, B vitamins, Vitamin A, calcium, and a host of other nutrients. The many vegetables in the Chinese diet, especially peppers, are rich in vitamins, and the Chinese enhance their diet by eating very little sugar.

Chinese cooking techniques also add to nutrition. Rapid cooking, use of broth for soups, and the searing heat of stir-frying not only save fuel, but also help to conserve vitamins. Use of iron woks adds iron to the food.

As incomes rise in China, however, the same thing is happening to the diet that happened in the West: a nutrition transition (Chapter 4) that encouraged the increase of degenerative diseases (Grigg, 1995; Popkin, 1993). The Chinese are consuming less grain and more meat, eggs, and sugar; meat consumption increased by 200% in the 1980s. Western fast-food chains appear in more and more cities, where they enjoy considerable prestige (Chee, 2000; Lozada, 2000; Yan, 1997). "Diseases of affluence" (cancer, heart disease, hypertension, and stroke) are increasing (*China News Digest*, June 30, 1992).

Historical Perspectives

The Chinese dietary regime was laid down in the Zhou dynasty. It underwent the most modification during three periods of disunity, when rivalries stimulated innovation. During the Warring States period and concluding in the Qin and Han dynasties, such new technologies as iron tools and irrigation impacted agriculture. New crops were introduced from the West, and, finally, the newly created central government developed an overall agricultural policy, including standard measurements and the ever-normal granaries (Swann, 1950; Zhao, 1991).

In the second major period of innovation, centered in the Wei dynasty following the Han dynasty, when Buddhism had a major impact, great agricultural encyclopedias were written, and more crops were introduced from western Asia. Southern China developed into a region of economic and cultural prominence.

Finally, during the Song Dynasty when there was the rapid development of agriculture, land use, and cooking, the Chinese dietary regime assumed the form that exists even today, with the addition of individual ingredients (Anderson, 1988: 131). Agriculture, which heretofore had been developing extensively, changed fundamentally to become more intensive. In the twelfth century a major turning point came, with multiple cropping, land reclamation, and fertilization with higher-yielding varieties (Chao, 1986: 194, 198). The Columbian Exchange, beginning in the sixteenth century, brought new ingredients to the Chinese diet (Crosby, 1972, 1991; Ho, 1955; McNeill, 1991; Stover and Stover, 1976: 115–6) and made possible the spread of settlements to new areas and a growth in the population. The basic structure of Chinese meals, however, did not change.

The longevity of the Chinese diet alone should give an indication that it works; it provides nutrition that is adequate for the survival of the people and the system. It was so enduring that, by the Qing dynasty, China worked itself into a "high-level equilibrium trap" (Elvin, 1973) in which greater and greater demands were placed on the system without introducing any notable technological innovations. The population grew faster than agriculture could expand, and famine and threat of famine were an ever-present specter (Dando, 1980; Mallory, 1926; Spence, 1977: 261; 1999). Sons were needed in the highly labor-intensive agriculture, but the system could no longer feed the additional people.

The poor nutritional status of the Chinese in 1949 was not a result of their traditional cuisine, but in the disparities in distribution of wealth that had been increasing for at least a century and a half. Elite appropriations of income went on: by 1800 people were starving, while the court ate well. "Surplus" in the sense of expropriated wealth had become greater than "surplus" in the sense of wealth beyond what people needed for subsistence (Anderson, 1988: 115). Such a pattern has been called "involution" — growth without development, where a traditional agricultural system is driven harder to feed more people without any real changes. Eventually, it can no longer keep up with population growth, and more and more people sink into misery. Because land is expensive relative to labor, labor-saving technology is not applied. In previous periods of Chinese history, slow population growth and frequent technological advances kept available food and the number of people in balance. By the end of the Qing dynasty, the reverse was true (Anderson, 1988: 123).

The imbalance helped lead to the century of disruptive revolutions that ended the long imperial age in China and, eventually, brought the Communist party to power. The Taiping Rebellion, the Hakka-Cantonese wars, the Yunnan Muslim rebellion, and the almost constant warfare after 1911 also periodically reduced the labor supply in the fields, especially in the south.

Urban and Rural Diets in the Early Twentieth Century

In the early twentieth century, John Lossing Buck (1937) led a team of investigators who surveyed agriculture and food in China. While Liaoning Province and the rest of the Northeast (Manchuria) were not part of the survey, one location in Liaoning was included, and the results give an indication of the situation in China, as a whole, and specifically that in northern China. Food production and Calorie consumption were barely adequate, and sales to urban markets and other kinds of maldistribution deprived a significant number of rural residents of good nutrition. While the proportion of the food that farm families produced for themselves varied widely, most families purchased at least some of their needs, such as animal products and vegetables (Maynard and Swen, 1937).

The northern staple grain of wheat can be used as an example. Farmers would sell their highest-quality wheat and then purchase less expensive and less nutritious millet, sorghum, oats, or corn for use at home. Gamble (1954), in his study of Ting Hsien in Hebei Province, also found that millet was the most commonly consumed grain (109). Maynard and Swen (1937: 416) concluded, "It must be assumed, therefore, that the substitution is not a matter of taste but one of economic necessity."

For the country as a whole, Calories were provided proportionately by the following foods: grains, 83%; legumes and vegetable oils, 9%; potatoes and other vegetables, 5%; animal products, slightly more than 2%; and fruits and sugar, slightly less than 1% (Maynard and Swen, 1937: 410–1). Most of the animal food was pork; farm families ate few eggs because most were sold.

In the wheat-growing region (northern China), millet, sorghum, and corn were reported in addition to wheat. Because wheat is an excellent source of protein as well as carbohydrate (Maynard and Swen, 1937: 416), protein consumption in the wheat region was above the minimum. In fact, in no place with adequate food supplies did the survey find deficiencies in protein consumption. This protein, however, was almost all of vegetable origin because the diets contained so little food from animal sources. Gamble (1954) also found that meat was used only at festival times, and 75% of that was pork (113). Maynard and Swen (1937) came to

> a clear conclusion: considering the farm population of the country as a
> whole, the average intake of protein may be considered adequate in both

quantity and quality ... however, ... an average may conceal — and in this case certainly does — enormous inequalities between regions and between families. (420)

Calcium consumption was deficient everywhere, but it was closer to minimum requirements in the wheat-growing north where soybeans, wheat, and leafy vegetables were grown. Phosphorus and iron were adequate unless total food intake (Calories) was too low. Vitamins A and D were found to be inadequate; Vitamin B was adequate, providing that grain was not highly milled; and Vitamin C foods were abundant, but information about the preservation of this easily destroyed vitamin was not available (Maynard and Swen, 1937).

Another 1926 survey in Peiping (Beijing) gives us information about urban families in northern China. These families also used more wheat than any other grain (Gamble, 1933), as well as rice, which was rather expensive compared to wheat because it had to be transported from southern China. Only the wealthiest families could afford to make it their most frequently used grain, although even low-income families would eat it on special occasions. For the latter group, maize flour was the principal grain, followed by millet. Unlike rural families, urban families did not eat sorghum in large amounts.

Pork was the most commonly used meat, except, of course, by Muslim families, who favored mutton. Among families that ate pork, the average consumption was about 1.5 pounds per month, but the actual consumption varied widely because more was eaten at the time of Spring Festival (Chinese New Year) and Mid-Autumn Festival (at the time of the September full moon). Mutton also was eaten by non-Muslim families; beef and chicken were less common. Egg consumption averaged less than one per week, and seafood consumption was small. Milk was available but expensive; only the higher-income families drank it. Although almost all families in the survey ate bean products, the consumption was low.

The most common vegetable was cabbage, and other vegetables were used in season. Fruits, even in season, were uncommon, and the amount varied little by income. Melons, pears, peaches, apricots, persimmons, and apples were used the most (Gamble, 1933: 108).

These two important surveys show that the traditional rural diet of northern China provided sufficient energy, but was nutritionally marginal. Urban families, in general, were better off; most of them could eat higher quality (and more desired) grains, more animal foods, and more fruit. Urban families spent 13 times as much for fruit and miscellaneous foods (including meals eaten out) as rural families (Gamble, 1954: 110). Rural families spent 50% or more of their food budget on vegetables, including 21% of their food expenditure on sweet potatoes, which the city residents disdained as a country food.

The Rural-Urban Continuum in the People's Republic

Years of civil war and the Japanese invasion, beginning in the 1930s, disrupted agriculture and economic life in China. The result was widespread hunger, with many, especially poor people, going to bed hungry (Hsu and Hsu, 1977: 315). In 1949, the Chinese Communist Party took control of a nation of more than 500 million malnourished, sick, and weary people (Piazza, 1986: 1).

The Chinese Communist party was born in Shanghai in 1921. Shanghai was a treaty port, and the founding of the party there was a result of the intellectual ferment engendered from the presence of foreign ideas and the stark contrast with China's comparative backwardness.

Communism, however, did not fare well in the cities of China. Not only was the urban proletariat small, but it was not attracted to communism. Fleeing from near extinction, the Communists took refuge in the countryside, where, under Mao Zedong, they found support among the rural peasants — the "real" Chinese, untainted by "bourgeois spiritual pollution" (Murphey, 1980).

When the Communists seized the treaty ports and established the People's Republic of China in 1949, they sought to turn the "consumer" cities, principally treaty ports, into "producer" cities that would serve the entire country. Coastal cities were geographically too marginal and too well situated for foreign influence (as their history as treaty ports attested); they also were vulnerable to attack (as the Korean War of 1950–3 threatened to demonstrate). Hence, investment would be directed inland (Chapter 4).

At the same time, ideologically, the Maoists sought to eliminate the distinction between manual and mental work, between countryside and city. Manual work was typical of the countryside; the urban elite did mental work and were now to "learn from the peasants" and emulate their "pure" attitudes and hard physical labor. At the same time, rural areas would be transformed by new technology, so that they would be more like the cities. The cities, in turn, would curtail their luxurious living to aid the countryside, and, eventually, the two areas would converge (Murphey, 1980: 35).

To win the support of urban dwellers for this program, the new government treated them differently. In the mid-1950s, all Chinese households were classified as either "agricultural" (*nongye*) or "non-agricultural" (*feinongye*). Just as before 1949, food supplies in the cities were considerably better than those in the countryside because rural produce was siphoned off to support industrialization (May, 1961). While the famine that resulted from the Great Leap Forward hit cities as well as the countryside, favored treatment of the cities continued. The Dengist reforms, in fact, have returned the focus to the coastal cities with the establishment of special economic zones and open ports. Coastal locations also are poised best to receive foreign investment and to manufacture goods for export. The importation of modern technology also increases the dualism between urban-based manufacturing and rural-based agriculture, which is still largely non-mechanized (Kueh, 1989: 431).

In spite of Mao's praises for the peasants and stated objective of making the city and countryside equal, the differences remain marked (Hsu, 1985; Johnson, 1997; Shen et al., 1996). The income gap alone has widened (Zweig, 1987). In 1994, the average per capita income among urban residents was 2.9 times that of rural residents (SSB, 1995).

Chinese urban residents in the 1980s were consuming even larger quantities of more valuable foods (meat, eggs, vegetables, and fruits) than their average income would predict. The low cost and restricted availability of rationed foods (especially grain and cooking oil), as well as housing and fuel, were causing a "spillover effect" on un-rationed non-staple foods (Wang and Chern, 1992). Because rural residents did not have access to subsidized, rationed food (or other goods), this effect led to further differences in lifestyle and diet between city and countryside. Since China's Opening to the World policy began in the late 1970s, Western-style supermarkets and fast-food chains have moved into the country's largest cities, increasing the differences in diet between city and countryside.

When it was pointed out to a student how he had moved up the urban hierarchy during his lifetime, he remarked that he had no desire whatsoever to move down the urban hierarchy. Traditional Chinese poets and scholars may have written rhapsodically about the countryside, retiring there, but millions of Chinese peasants today "vote with their feet" and move to the cities, with or without official permission.

While the Communist state apparatus has controlled citizens' lives and marshaled their labor, the question remains as to whether it really has changed the desires of individuals, especially as expressed in something as basic to Chinese culture as food. If cities are the hearth of the Great Tradition and recipient of ideas from a wide region, they can expect to be exposed to the newest ideas, including ideas about food. Maoist ideology would have urban residents "learn from the peasants" (Murphey, 1980), an idea consonant with Redfield's development in cities of the Great Tradition out of the Little Tradition from surrounding rural areas. In such a case, urban dwellers would receive food information, as well as food itself, from the peasants in the countryside.

The McGee (1989, 1991a) *zhenxianghua* model (Chapter 4) posits a continuum of regions with differing degrees of urbanization. The degree of cultural change could expect to vary accordingly (Chu and Hsu, 1979; Chu and Ju, 1993). With more sources of information, more foreign investment, and a longer history of food security, the city should show the greatest innovation in diet and food choice as part of culture, while the sparsely populated frontier shows the least, and intervening areas falling in between.

4

Food Production to Food Purchase:
Economic Development and Urbanization

Major changes in lifestyle, including the way households provide food for themselves, accompany the multifaceted societal transformation, collectively called economic development. Economic development, by Todaro's definition, involves economic growth, that is, rising gross national product (GNP), "the capacity of a national economy, whose initial economic condition has been more or less static for a long time, to *generate and sustain* an annual increase in its gross national product of perhaps 5 to 7% or more (1989: 86; emphasis original). Many examples of economic growth, in which the main beneficiaries have been the elite of the society and little benefit has reached the masses, led an increasing number of critics during the 1970s, including Todaro, to redefine the GNP "*in terms of reduction or elimination of poverty, inequality, and unemployment within the context of a growing economy*" (1989: 87; emphasis original). This aspect is especially important to socialist economic development (Lippitt, 1987).

Industrialization and Labor Force Shift

Evidence shows that, as per capita income (well-being) rises, the share that industry or manufacturing contributes to the society's GNP also rises; the share of agriculture and other primary (resource-gathering) activities declines (Kuznets, 1966). This parallels Engel's Law that predicts the declining expenditure of the individual household on the products of primary industry, especially food. This pattern of a declining contribution by agriculture and a rising contribution by industry is common, but the rate at which it takes place varies among countries (Chenery and Syrquin, 1975).

Paralleling the change in the share of GNP contributed by manufacturing is a shift in the composition of the labor force from predominantly agricultural to industrial. Industrial workers' lifestyles are fundamentally different from farmers': instead of growing their own food, they are paid cash wages and use this money to buy food (and other necessities) from farmers who remain on the land.

Those farmers, in turn, now are producing, not just to feed their families, but to sell in the marketplace — in other words, they increasingly become commercialized (Harriss, 1989). Ultimately, they may produce one or two specialty crops (wheat, corn, soybeans, or milk) for which they receive a cash income. They may continue to grow food for their own use, as was the case in the American pre-Civil War South (Hilliard, 1972), or they may purchase their food in a market, along with the urban industrial workers. They also may have vegetable gardens for home use and consume some of their cash crop (e.g. drinking milk from their dairy herd), but, in most cases, if they eat any of their production, it is only after it has been combined with output from other farmers and manufactured into finished goods.

Western Experience

Theories about this transformation date back to David Ricardo's (1817) *Principles of Political Economy and Taxation* and have been expanded and elaborated ever since (Buttrick, 1960; Gillis, et al. 1983; Lewis, 1955; Ranis and Fei, 1964). Over time, agriculture suffers from diminishing returns because more effort is required to grow a declining amount of produce to meet the demands of a rising population. Eventually, adding workers produces less and less additional crops, and they become surplus labor. Industry can draw on these workers without diminishing the food supply because the workers really are not producing anything.

The introduction of capital allows both the founding of industry and the equipping of subsistence farmers to become more commercial by replacing some of the human (and animal) power with machines. Of course, capital costs money, too, but the cost of hiring former subsistence farmers is initially low enough so that the higher value of industrial products can cover both capital and labor costs.

This classical model shows a rural labor surplus that allows drawing agricultural workers into industry, with no effect on wages until the surplus is exhausted. In the neoclassical model, development of agriculture and industry must be balanced from the beginning. Drawing off too many agricultural workers eventually begins to decrease the food supply that industrial workers, who do not produce food, must have available for purchase. As we will see, this happened in China in the Great Leap Forward.

These models have concentrated on two sectors of the economy: agriculture (primary) and manufacturing (secondary). In the history of today's developed countries, employment in primary industry drops during development, while the share of the labor force in secondary industry first rises rapidly and then declines (Clark, 1957; Fisher, 1939). Meanwhile, the service sector also grows. In today's less-developed countries, however, agricultural employment drops rapidly, and manufacturing employment growth is small (Chenery and Syrquin, 1975; Pandit, 1990). The service sector is left to take up the slack. Today's developing countries can adopt all of the labor-saving technology that has been introduced over the past two centuries; consequently, their manufacturing sector requires far fewer workers than did the first factories of the Industrial Revolution. Furthermore, today's less-developed countries have faster-growing populations, producing a larger labor force, and high rates of rural-to-urban migration, even in advance of widespread industrial job opportunities. Given the imbalance between a more highly automated manufacturing sector (requiring fewer laborers) and a burgeoning population (providing more laborers), the surplus is left to the low end of the service sector, much of it in informal occupations , such as day labor, petty vending, small-scale repairs (e.g. bicycles, umbrellas, or shoes), fortune telling, and even begging, prostitution, and crime. Similar to manufacturing workers, these people are not producing food and must purchase food for cash.

Oshima's Model for East Asia

The starting point in the labor situation in rice-growing East Asia, as Harry Oshima (1987, 1993) explains, has been different. Rice feeds large numbers of people, because it produces many Calories and good-quality protein per unit of land, but it also requires enormous amounts of labor at planting and harvest times. Consequently, East Asia's rice-growing regions, at least before the rapid population growth that began in the late 1960s, had labor shortages during those seasons. At other times of year, there was little farm work, producing a seasonal labor surplus. In such a situation, the solution to the problem of surplus labor is not to draw workers from agriculture to full-time, year-round factory work, but rather to keep them in farming and provide work for the slack seasons. Multiple cropping; diversification into fruits, vegetables, and animal husbandry; fishing; and off-farm seasonal employment in labor-intensive industries allow the continued production of the staple crop of rice, while providing new sources of additional income. Eventually, the agricultural labor force becomes employed fully all year-round, and rural wage rates begin to rise. Mechanization spreads to farms and factories, raising productivity and, thus, GNP per capita.

Urbanization

Implicit in all of these models is the movement of workers from farms to factories, which are primarily located in urban areas. In the Western experience, urbanization was part and parcel of industrialization and, thus, of economic development.

Urban-Rural Relationships

Cities have been in the world since ancient times (Childe, 1983; Sjoberg, 1960), but the process of their development took on a much greater scale with industrialization (McGee, 1991b). The larger amount of capital necessary for industry also drew investment into transportation, giving the cities better accessibility to sources of raw materials and markets. The gathering of the industrial workforce in the cities provided both a concentrated labor force and a market for factory products. The first countries to become highly urbanized tended to be technologically advanced and developed (Berry, 1962; see also Unwin, 1989).

If the most highly developed countries are also the most urbanized, what roles do cities play in the process of development? According to Marxist theory, the world is arranged as a series of centers, each surrounded by a periphery, in a nested structure. Each center draws to itself the resources of the surrounding periphery as far as its power allows it to reach (Frank, 1967). On a world scale, the developed countries, with their sources of capital and demand for goods, are the center and the less-developed countries the periphery (Wallerstein, 1974).

Applied at a national (or smaller) scale, once industry and related high income-producing activities (banking, shipping, and commerce) have been established in a given location, then labor, capital, raw materials, and skills flow in to support it (Friedmann, 1966; Hirshman, 1988). The result for the peripheral countryside is a *backwash effect*, the reduction of these resources for use in rural areas. There is some movement from city to countryside in the form of spread effects (e.g. higher prices paid for food), but, overall, the center has appropriated to itself the resources of the periphery, as Marxist theory predicts, and the disparity between the city (which gets all the resources) and countryside (which loses them) increases through circular and cumulative causation (Myrdal, 1957). Even governments, which could influence the process, usually do not act effectively in the interest of lagging regions. Furthermore, the surplus that the economy generates benefits the dominant class: capitalists in capitalism, people who work for a living in socialism, or government bureaucrats in statism (Lippitt, 1987).

These models were based on the historical experience of developed countries, and Reissman (1964) saw them being repeated in less-developed countries. McGee (1991b), however, questioned the role of the city as a center of change in developing countries, and Berry (1969a, 1969b) noted that growth does not always "trickle down" or spread out from cities to the periphery because the process is confounded by high rates of population growth and rural-to-urban migration that outstrip metropolitan growth. Marxist André Gunder Frank (1967) and Lin Piao (1965) saw the cities of less-developed countries as centers of continued colonialism.

Systems of Cities

No city exists in total isolation from other cities or from the countryside surrounding it. Transportation and communications systems link cities with each other, and, as the individual cities grow, the direction of their growth mirrors those links.

Megalopolis

Growing, industrialized American cities have spread out over former rural land, as the technology of intra-urban transportation has developed and various cultural forces have enticed urban workers to live in more rural settings. Manufacturing and services followed this market and expanded farther into the suburbs. Because access to the cities and newly emerging suburban centers, with their attraction for employment, shopping, and other opportunities, has continued to be important, much of this spread has taken place along transportation routes that link the cities: railroads and highways, reinforced later by airline service. Jean Gottmann (1961) termed the series of coalesced cities along the Eastern Seaboard of the United States "Megalopolis." Similar converging urbanized regions have been identified in other countries (e.g. Canada by Yeates, 1975; England by Herbert, 1982; the Netherlands by Hall, 1982).

The McGee Model

Terry McGee (1989, 1991a) applied the concept of Megalopolis to Asia as it has undergone rising rates of urbanization (proportions of the population living in cities). He found that Gottmann's prediction of the spread to other parts of the world of cities with larger commuting fields and the mix of urban and rural land uses was correct, but, in East Asia, it is apparent that some unique characteristics in these areas are taking on urban characteristics (1991b). He gave the name *kotadesasi*, coined from the Bahasa Indonesia term *kota,* meaning "town," and *desa,* meaning "village," to his model to highlight the mixture of urban and rural activities taking place in the same area. The Chinese equivalent would be *zhenxiang* (*zhen* means "town," and *xiang* means "village"); the process involved is *zhenxianghua* (*hua* refers to a process of becoming). The Chinese terms will be used hereafter.

As with Megalopolis, *zhenxiang* regions have developed in areas surrounding major cities and along the transportation links between them. Six main features can be identified. First, they start with a large population, primarily growing wet rice on small farms. Second is the great mixture of non-agricultural activities, sometimes within the same household. While one member of the household continues to farm, another may commute to a nearby job in town; someone else may work in local industry or in retailing.

Third, like Megalopolis, *zhenxiang* regions display great mobility of people and goods, especially with the introduction of trucks, buses, and inexpensive motorcycles. The availability of cheap transportation, both public and private, enables commuting, as well as transporting products from farm and factory. Some of the residents of the *zhenxiang* region go into business that provides this transportation.

Fourth is the increasing mixture of land uses; agriculture, industry, markets, services, and other land use exist side by side. While non-agricultural activity provides a ready market for farm produce, it also can cause air and water pollution. In East Asia, most land has been under cultivation for centuries, so the new activities prevent the land from producing food. In contrast, Megalopolis spreads over vast areas that were virtually wilderness.

Fifth, women increasingly are involved in non-agricultural labor in *zhenxiang* regions. They are in demand for factory and service labor, but their shift away from agriculture also reflects a shift from the monoculture of rice to a more diversified agriculture, including fruits, vegetables, and livestock. As Oshima (1987, 1993) found, diversification evens out the seasonal demand for labor.

Finally, these *zhenxiang* regions are somewhat nebulous from the viewpoint of state authorities. By definition, they are becoming more urbanized, in terms of economic activities and ways of life, but may still be regarded as rural by the government. Informal sector activities may find less interference and regulation in such an environment.

The greater mix of activities and the increased mobility of people and goods lead to increased fusion and interaction between what were formerly distinct urban and rural areas. Nevertheless, set in context, the *zhenxiang* areas form one of five types of regions in the overall model (Figure 4.1) (McGee, 1991a).

The first region of the spatial economy in McGee's model is the major cities of the urban hierarchy. In East Asia, these cities are often very old and have large populations.

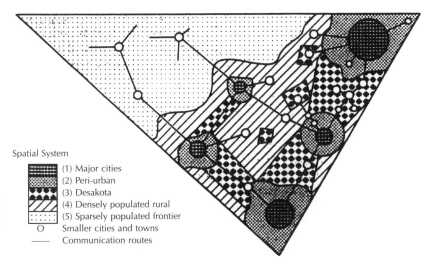

Spatial System

	(1) Major cities
	(2) Peri-urban
	(3) Desakota
	(4) Densely populated rural
	(5) Sparsely populated frontier
O	Smaller cities and towns
——	Communication routes

Figure 4.1 Spatial configuration of a hypothetical Asian country. (Source: McGee, 1991a: 6.)

The second region is the peri-urban zone that surrounds the cities. As with suburbs in the West, they are within commuting range of the cities, sometimes extending as far as 30 km from the cities' cores.

The third region is the *zhenxiang* region of very mixed economic activity as previously described. These regions tend to follow transportation corridors between the cities and have a high-density agricultural population, usually (but not always) engaged in wet-rice cultivation.

The fourth region is located farther from major transportation routes, but still has a dense population, primarily engaged in agriculture. In many, but not all, parts of East Asia, the dominant crop is still wet rice.

Finally, in many parts of East Asia, a sparsely populated frontier has yet to feel the effects of the dynamism of areas near either cities or major transportation corridors. It may represent potential for land reclamation and agricultural development.

Applying his model to East Asia, McGee (1989) found three types of regions, based on the growth of population within urban cores. In the first group (Japan and South Korea), most population is urban, although agricultural land use persists, even within cities.

In the second group, a great deal of change is taking place, especially industrialization and a decline in the production of staple crops (specifically, rice). Among the regions in this group are Taiwan and those based on coastal cities of Mainland China. Regions in the third group show some resemblance to the second group, but have high population growth and slower economic development. Sichuan Province in China falls into this category.

Ginsburg (1991) also notes increasing rural-urban interaction in various parts of Asia, notably in the southern part of Jiangsu Province (Sunan) west of Shanghai. Especially important is the growth of transport for both people and goods, primarily road transport in the form of buses and trucks.

The Nutrition Transition

Because they form part of a group's total way of life, learned by each generation from their elders, both food and the economic system are part of culture. Culture is integrated, that is, each component is related to every other component (Hoyt, 1961). Furthermore, the various aspects of culture are dependent on each other, so that a change in one leads to accommodating change in others. Economic development encompasses fundamental changes in the economic structure of the society, including urbanization, that is, the movement of increasing numbers of people from rural to urban settlement patterns.

Over the long course of human history, major changes in economic and social structures, such as the Neolithic Revolution and the Industrial Revolution, have led to changes in diet (Bryant et al., 1985). Following and intricately intertwined with the Demographic Transition, has been what Barry Popkin (1993) calls the Nutrition Transition. Actually, in human history there have been several nutrition transitions, each marked by great changes in foodways and other aspects of life, and taking place at different times and different rates of speed in various parts of the world. Popkin's model consists of five patterns of diet, related to the economic and population structure. Different subpopulations in the same region may follow different patterns in the model.

Pattern 1 is Collecting Food. Hunting and gathering comprise the economy; plants and wild animals make up the diet, which exhibits great variety. Food processing is rudimentary at best, although fire was controlled very early, allowing people to cook food and, thus, eat even more different things. This variety generally leads to good nutrition, despite a subsistence existence and primitive technology. Birth rates are low, death rates are high, and life expectancy is short. Population growth is, of course, very low, and most of the people are young.

Pattern 2, Famine, follows the Neolithic Revolution. Permanent settlements, based on cultivation of a single staple crop or nomadic herding of a few species of animals, cut down on the variety in the diet and, thus, the nutritional status. Crop farmers (especially women and children) may suffer from low fat intake, and nutritional deficiency diseases emerge. Poor nutritional balance reduces the average stature and resistance to epidemic disease (Allport, 2000). The system is labor-intensive, with few tools and a subsistence-level existence. Although systematic crop storage begins, total dependence on local food sources means that local crop failure brings famine and many deaths, offsetting high birth rates; life expectancy remains low. The population is young. Most people live in rural areas; there are only a few small, crowded, and unsanitary cities.

Pattern 3, Receding Famine, accompanies the Industrial Revolution. Improved agricultural and transportation technology (the second agricultural revolution) once again bring increased quantity and variety of food, and rising cash incomes enable people to consume more animal protein, fruits, and vegetables. New food processing technology also enhances the variety of available foods. Variety, however, is still circumscribed, and women and children are still subject to nutritional problems. Infectious diseases grow with increased urbanization and crowding, but these diseases decline with better control techniques. Specific nutritional deficiency diseases begin to disappear, and the average stature increases. Cooking technology advances, along with agricultural and industrial technology (which manufactures both), but acquiring this technology requires higher incomes, which are available only to certain segments of the population. Nonetheless, the general living standard improves, as seen in a decline in death rates, which, with continued high birth rates, leads to rapid population growth. The population gradually begins to age, as birth rates begin to decline and life expectancy increases.

Pattern 4, Degenerative Diseases, marks the gradual aging of the population as birth rates fall. People eat more fat (especially animal products), more sugar, and more processed foods, leading to less fiber consumption. Food technology proceeds at a high rate, even producing artificial sweeteners and fats. At the same time, fewer jobs require heavy physical work because machines replace human (and animal) muscle power, and the service sector grows. Household appliances replace muscle power at home. Income disparities continue, and even increase, as mechanization and the service sector require higher levels of education. Obesity (currently a major concern in America; Critser, 2003), problems for the elderly (a growing component of the population), and various disabilities follow the changes in diet and lack of physical activity. Infectious diseases decline to the point of disappearing. Urbanization continues; cities spread out into the suburbs.

Pattern 5, Behavioral Change, shows the public response to problems brought on by Pattern 4. Automation continues in manufacturing, and the service sector continues to grow — including providing exercise opportunities for those holding sedentary occupations. Health education programs, both public and private, promote better diets to control degenerative diseases, and rates of heart disease and some cancers decline. Food preparation technology changes in response to public demands for less fat and processed foods, and more fruits, vegetables, and whole grains. For example, fresh produce consumption is increasing in the United States, especially in the Los Angeles,

San Francisco-Oakland, and Boston metropolitan areas (Shortridge and Shortridge, 1989), resulting in decreased obesity and increased bone strength, and leading to longer disability-free life expectancy. The proportion of elderly in the population increases, as does the urbanization of rural areas within the range of cities.

As with the Demographic Transition, the Nutrition Transition is based on the experience of Western societies. David Grigg (1995) found that western Europe, except for the Mediterranean region, has gone through the transition to Pattern 4, and tastes are beginning to change in line with Pattern 5. Abdel Omran (1971) traced a related "epidemiologic transition," citing the role of food in resistance to contagious disease. The model forms a useful way of encapsulating dietary change under the impact of economic development in China.

Economic Development in China

Since the establishment of the People's Republic in 1949, development in China has been directed toward two major objectives. First has been industrialization, especially the development of a heavy industrial base. Second has been the alleviation of the worst aspects of poverty, including hunger and malnutrition. In these pursuits, two major constraints have been: the severe limitations on the amount of farmland and international isolation. These two constraints have sharpened the tension between the two major objectives. Land scarcity in a farming system that already was highly intensive and limited opportunities for international trade across the Bamboo Curtain curtailed progress in agriculture, the principal income source for the poor. Competition for resources between the two major objectives also was aggravated by international isolation, which forced the country to rely only on domestic resources.

Nevertheless, China has made progress toward meeting both objectives of economic development (Kantha, 1990). Industrialization has grown significantly, not only in heavy industry but also in consumer goods, because large amounts of state capital have been poured into manufacturing, mining, and energy production.

The average Chinese standard of living has risen, and, for the most part, the worst effects of poverty have been alleviated, primarily through local initiatives (Schell, 1986; 1989). Poverty persists, however, especially in rural areas (Lo, 1990; WuDunn, 1993). Despite the rhetoric about the equality of city and countryside, urban residents continue to enjoy higher cash incomes, larger subsidies, and more amenities than rural residents (Morgan, 2000). More public investment still goes into urban pursuits, such as manufacturing, than into rural pursuits, such as agriculture. The divide between urban and rural persists.

Agriculture and Food in the People's Republic

When the Communists came to power in 1949, a century of intermittent warfare and maldistribution of food had left the country with a weary and hungry populace. The history of agricultural development within people's memory colors their attitudes toward food, especially in relation to Maslow's (1954) Hierarchy of Human Needs (Chapter 2).

Maoist Policies

The first few years after the establishment of the People's Republic of China marked a recovery from warfare, and the economic situation generally improved, including availability of food supplies (Wen, 1990; Zhao, 1993). Under Mao Zedong's leadership, ideology drove an ambitious program of land reform, followed by the establishment of cooperatives and communes (Leeming, 1989; Taimni, 1994), all dedicated to meeting the two major objectives of economic development. In 1958, a campaign began that was to reorganize rural China into agricultural communes and, simultaneously, to speed up economic development of industry, designed to overtake Great Britain within ten years. The campaign disrupted rural production, especially as it drew too many peasants from farming into manufacturing, both in the cities and in rural industry. Because Mao was committed to the campaign, economic reports continued to be rosy, while food production actually plummeted. The result was the worst famine in Chinese history, in which an estimated 30 million people died of starvation, malnutrition, and related disorders (Ashton, Hill, Piazza, and Zeitz, 1984; Becker, 1997; Lardy, 1983; Lin, 1990). Relaxation of the campaign, the return of peasants to farming, and imports of grain brought recovery after 1962.

During the Great Proletarian Cultural Revolution (1966–76), emphasis in agriculture was on grain production and regional self-sufficiency (Ho, 2003). Production was in the hands of tens of thousands of communes, each containing several thousand households (Lin, 1990; Piazza, 1986: 21). All commune members earned "work points" on which wages were paid for showing up at work, regardless of how much they produced. In addition to grain, a few pigs were permitted because they provided fertilizer for the grain (Leeming, 1985). For a while, even private plots were eliminated, so households could not produce vegetables for their own use. Piazza puts it bluntly: "The people's commune system, and centrally-administered agricultural planning system, have been important *impediments* to increasing agricultural production" (1986: 16; emphasis original). Although acute starvation was rare after the disaster of the Great Leap Forward in 1960 to 1962, diets, especially in rural areas, were bland, monotonous, and unbalanced

(Piazza, 1986: 17). In spite of the consumption of *doufu*, they also lacked adequate protein (Whyte, 1972).

Incomes rose, but surpluses were siphoned off for support of the state's primary concern, the growth of heavy industry (Lippitt, 1987; Nolan and White, 1984; Oi, 1989). Agriculture was neglected; agricultural production increases barely kept pace with growth in population (Lardy, 1983: 154; Lippitt, 1987; Pannell, 1985: 173). Contrary to the concept that economic development should mean better quality of life for the masses of people, diets did not improve.[1] Economist Nicholas Lardy says, "China is probably the only country in modern times to combine, over twenty years, a doubling of real per capita national income and constant or even declining average food consumption" (Lardy, 1983: 159). Furthermore, in spite of the Marxist-Maoist ideological imperative of equality, the production and consumption of cereal grains and other foods became more, rather than less, uneven with increasing disparities between urban and rural areas, as well as from one region of the country to another (Lardy, 1983: 147).

Dengist Reforms

In 1976, Mao Zedong died, and two years later Deng Xiaoping consolidated his power as premier. China's economy was a shambles, wracked by ten years of chaos during the Cultural Revolution. At the Third Plenum of the 11th Central Committee of the Chinese Communist Party, held in December 1978, a major reform program of China's economy under the slogan of the Four Modernizations was launched.[2]

Beginning in Sichuan province in 1979, communes began allocating plots of land to individual households and contracting with them to produce a certain quantity of grain. Anything the household produced over and above the contract could be kept or sold on the free market. In 1983, communes began to disband, and the state contracted directly with individual households to produce grain. Again, production over and above the contracted amount was the peasant family's to dispose of as it wished (Croll, 1988; Lin, 1988; Taimni, 1994). Agriculture had diversified from the Maoist monoculture, especially as specialized households engaged, either full- or part-time, in non-agricultural pursuits, from which the family kept the profits (Bray, 1994; Fei, 1989; Travers, 1986; Wittwer et al., 1987). The reforms also encouraged the re-establishment of farmers' markets in towns and cities, giving the peasants an outlet for their products. In short, China adopted some aspects of a market economy (Leeming, 1989; Zhao, 1991).

Now that the peasants' efforts had resulted in higher incomes, production soared (Bray, 1994; Garnault and Ma, 1993; McColl and Kou, 1990; McMillan, Whalley, and Zhu, 1989; Smith, 1991; Walker, 1984, 1988; Yan, 1990). The gross value of agricultural output increased as much in the eight years between 1978 and 1986 as it had in the 21 years from 1957 to 1978 (Field, 1988); between 1978 and 1984, it rose by 8% per year. Grain output was 446 million tons in 1990, almost three times the production in 1952 (Figure 4.2). The per capita availability of staple grain (also enhanced by declining population growth; Hussain and Feuchtwang, 1988) rose by 30%, of vegetable oils by 300%, and of sugar and meat by 200% (Smil, 1985: 116). Farmers were producing other commodities in addition to grain, and other foods were replacing some of the grain in people's diets. By 1993, the average per capita consumption of grain, including imports, was 390 kg annually (*China Daily*, October 29, 1993). With more food available and higher incomes (Lardy, 1984), the overall trend in the Engel's ratios for 1978 to 1986 was downward, both for the country as a whole and for a selection of rural provinces, as Engel's Law would predict (Kueh, 1988: 648).

Figure 4.2 Grain production, total and per capita, China, 1949–2000. (Source: China Statistical Yearbooks.)

These figures are national averages, including food available to both urban and rural people. The consumption amounts and patterns, and the amount spent on food, however, vary geographically (Morgan, 2000; Pannell, 1985; Walker, 1989). The Chinese government increases this discrepancy by its 1955 policy of treating differently the rural (agricultural) and the urban (non-agricultural) citizens. Only officially registered urban residents were entitled to purchase subsidized food. In the Maoist years, virtually all such persons were employees of state enterprises. Today, "temporary" rural workers are permitted to come to cities to work, and their incomes and consumption patterns are included in the "urban" statistics.

Rural people received their food supply from the communes until those rural institutions were disbanded. Today, on average, they produce about half of their food themselves and buy the rest in markets (SSB, 1995). Rural-registered "temporary" residents in cities always have had to provide their own food; the presence of free markets made doing so possible, if somewhat more expensive than buying state-subsidized food. The diets of rural people began a marked improvement almost immediately after the Dengist reforms were launched (Aubert, 1988; Croll, 1983; Piazza, 1986).

Nevertheless, there is still concern that the typical pattern of less-developed countries prevails (Soemardjan, 1985). Rural people, especially poorer ones, spend a high proportion of their income on food (upwards of 60%), and their diets are still unbalanced (Carter, 1997; Kueh, 1988; Leppman, 1999; Morgan, 2000; Shen, Habicht, and Chang, 1996; Walker, 1989; Webb, 1991). They rely on grain for a large proportion of their calorie intake and consume very little protein, especially animal protein (Zheng, 1990). In addition to improving the people's health, replacing some of the grain with animal products could also relieve the pressure on grain production because fodder crops can be raised on land that is ill-suited to food grain production (XINHUA, 1989). Replacing a portion of China's main meat — pork — with poultry and fish also would allow greater protein-production efficiency because these animals consume less grain than do pigs (Smil, 2000: 311). China also will continue to import grain in amounts that it deems appropriate, and these imports will decrease the variability of supplies (Shen, 2000).

Meanwhile, most urban residents have achieved higher levels of nutrition (Cai, 1991); consumption of pork and beer has reached levels that provoke concern about the amounts of grain that go into producing these commodities (Walker, 1989: 472; Zhang and Ma, 1988). On average, urban youth are taller and heavier than were youth in the 1950s (Morgan, 2000; Shen, Habicht, and Chang, 1996). From 1989 to 1991, "Project Food Basket" aimed to improve urban nutrition even more by increasing supplies of non-staple foods (meat, fish, fruits, and vegetables) (Wen, 1989). Convenience foods, including American fast foods, snacks, and frozen foods, also have seen an increasing demand.

Rising incomes and wide availability of a variety of foods led the Chinese authorities to dismantle the 40-year-old food rationing system (Cai, 1993; Jiang, 1988; Li, 1992; WuDunn, 1992). The last ration coupons disappeared in the spring of 1993.

Later in 1993, China announced a new program to improve the nutritional status of the entire population by the year 2000 (XINHUA, June 11 and 12, 1993). Noting the progress of the 1980s and 1990s (Table 4.1), the plan called for increases in protein (especially quality protein) by producing more animal foods, especially seafood; improving food processing; increasing nutrition education; and improving food sanitation, management, and development. In line with experience in other countries, the plan proposed reductions in grain consumption and increases in such higher-value foods as fruit, meat, fish, and eggs.

Table 4.1 Food structure reform program of 1993

Item	1990 (actual)	2000 (planned)	
		Urban	Rural
Calories	2,680.0	2,520	2,630
Grain (kg)	239.0	150	230
Meat (kg)	20.0	34	23
Dairy (kg)	4.2	*	*
Eggs (kg)	6.3	12	9
Fish (kg)	6.5	12	8
Vegetables (kg)	*	140	115
Fruit (kg)	*	33	14

* Not available.

Source: XINHUA, "Food Structure Reform, Development Outlined," FBIS-CHI–93–126, 2 July 1993, pp. 52–58.

Food Supply Prospects

A deeper problem is surfacing: the increase in food production that can be obtained by rewarding the farmers, generated by the reforms, may be reaching its limits (Brown, 1995; Heiling, 1999; Rozelle, Huang, and Zhang, 1997; Stavis, 1991; Tyler, 1996). China's population is still growing despite the one-child-per-family policy. Furthermore, as incomes rise, so does the demand for food — and for better quality food (*China Daily*, October 29, 1993). Especially in a culture as food-centered as the Chinese, people want to eat better as economic prosperity makes it possible. Concern has been raised about meeting these expectations, although other authorities (e.g. Smil, 2000) believe that China's food-supply future is bright.

Rice has been double-cropped (two crops per year) in the Yangtze Valley since ancient times. Today, farmland effectively is increased by more than one-half (index 155) by multiple cropping on the same piece of ground (Zhao, 1994: 70). Irrigation has increased since 1949 (Terjung, Hays, Ji, Todhunter, and O'Rourke, 1985), and land reclamation continues, especially in the Northeast and Northwest.

The net increase in farmland, however, is negative: more land is being lost than gained. At the end of 1991, the total area of farmland stood at 95.7 million hectares (240.9 million acres), a net drop of 19,333 hectares (47,770 acres) from the year before. The amount of farmland per person declined as well, to a little more than 0.07 hectare (0.16 acre). Soil erosion, hydroelectric projects, and industry and urban growth account for most of the loss (*China Daily,* June 13, 1992; Xiao, 1993); construction of tombs also takes up land (FBIS-CHI–92–134, July 13, 1992). Overfishing also is becoming a threat (Wang, 1993).

Chinese researchers are cautiously optimistic about the country's ability to be basically self-sufficient in grain, based on a maximum population of 1.6 billion and 113 million hectares (279 million acres) of farmland (*Renmin Ribao [People's Daily]* Overseas Edition, June 23, 1995; XINHUA, April 2, 1995). China, however, has been importing food (wheat) since the 1960s, when emergency imports helped to relieve the famine that followed the Great Leap Forward, and now regularly imports quality rice, wheat, and barley (*China Daily,* October 29, 1993). Western commentators (Brown, 1995; Brown and Flavin, 1996; *The Economist,* August 12, 1995; Heiling, 1999; Leeming, 1993, 1994) point to China's rising population and rising living standards, poised against the declining amount of farmland, which will result in out-stripping not only China's, but the entire world's productive capacity.

Nevertheless, geographer Vaclav Smil (2000) still regards China as an example to the world of a country that can feed its huge population on very little farmland. He points to slowing population growth and rising commercialization and productivity, despite the very real challenges of water supply, conversion of farmland to other uses, and increasing demand. By using and pricing inputs (water, fertilizer, seed, and pest control) more rationally, reducing post-harvest waste from rot and pests, redirecting dietary aspirations, and investing in research, China's agricultural future is bright (Smil, 2000: 291–315).

Industrialization and Urbanization

The story of China's efforts to industrialize has been studied, described, and analyzed exhaustively (Chiu, 1980; Hodder, 1994; Howard, 1990; Kueh, 1989; Pannell and Ma, 1983). This section briefly will summarize the story, concentrating on the aspects most closely related to the shift from agricultural to industrial employment, which brings about changes in lifestyle because it involves movement from rural to urban occupations and environments.

Industrialization and Labor Force Shift

As indicated in the previous section, Maoist China's chief goal was industrialization, especially the development of heavy industry (producer goods). The base that the People's Republic inherited in 1949 was small. There were industries with strategic importance, such as the iron works at modern Wuhan, and agricultural processing (textiles and flour milling) had been established in the treaty ports along the coast (Howard, 1990). The other major industrial center was in the Northeast (Chapter 5).

During the 1950s, the Communist government restored order and, following the Soviet model, undertook the building of industry. Growth (from a very low base) was rapid, especially in the favored heavy industry. Investment also was directed toward the interior, for reasons of both defense and equity, leading to new growth in such centers as Baotou, Xi'an, Wuhan, Lanzhou, and Taiyuan. The portion of industrial output from the coastal areas consequently declined.

The Great Leap Forward was launched in 1958 to make China equal to Britain within a few years. Millions of Chinese were attracted to work in cities, but rural industries on the newly organized communes were also an important part of the effort. Production by the much-maligned "back-yard furnaces" was substandard and wasteful, but the legacy of rural industry survived and has remained, in modified form, an important part of rural Chinese development (Perkins, 1977).

Recovery after the disaster of the Great Leap Forward depended on more reasonable expectations, especially after the withdrawal of Soviet aid and personnel. Industry was directed to support agriculture as the country recovered from famine. In the late 1960s, progress again was retarded by the Cultural Revolution. At the same time, fearing Soviet attack and the threat of the war in Vietnam, China diverted resources to the construction of the "Third Line" industrial complexes in the interior (Naughton, 1988).

Mao's death and the arrest of the Gang of Four in 1976 paved the way for the series of reforms announced in 1978. For industry, these reforms meant greater independence from micro-management by government planners and the Opening to the World policy, which made available Western expertise in the form of technology, capital, and education and training. Special Economic Zones, particularly in the south, and open ports attracted foreign capital with especially favorable regulatory and financial incentives, once again, turning the focus of Chinese investment and development from the interior toward the coastal areas (Luo and Pannell, 1991; Pannell, 1988). Such locations were the most advantageous for export-oriented manufacturing of consumer goods, and these activities flourished. As incomes have risen and managers have greater freedom to respond to market forces, production for the domestic market also has increased dramatically.

Agriculture, as a share of GNP, generally has decreased since the reforms were instituted, and the share of light industry, as opposed to heavy, industry has risen (Table 4.2).

Table 4.2 China: Shares of gross national product (GNP), 1978–1994

Year	Primary	Industry			Tertiary
		Total	Heavy	Light	
1978	28.1	44.3	56.9	43.1	23.7
1980	30.1	44.2	52.8	47.1	21.4
1985	28.4	38.5	52.9	47.1	28.5
1990	27.1	37.0	50.6	49.4	31.3
1992	21.8	38.6	51.1	48.9	34.3
1993	19.9	41.0	56.0	44.0	32.5
1994	21.0	40.8	52.9	47.1	31.8

Source: State Statistical Bureau, *China Statistical Yearbook, 1995* (Beijing: China Statistical Publishing House, 1995).

A decline in the share of employment (Figure 4.3) has paralleled the decline in the share of GNP contributed by the primary sector. The trend, however, has been uneven, influenced by the same events and policy shifts that have impacted industrialization, agriculture, and urbanization. It has, however, always revolved around the basic administrative division of China's population into two categories: agricultural and non-agricultural. This dichotomy depends on residence and on occupation; most facets of Chinese daily life hang on it . Originally, almost all of the non-agricultural citizens were "staff and workers" in China's state-owned industries and other "work units." They had secondary- or tertiary-sector occupations and were entitled to state-subsidized (and rationed) food, clothing, and other goods, which they obtained at designated state-run outlets in their neighborhoods or places of employment. The state allocated them housing and gave them educational, health, and recreational services through their work unit.

Agricultural (rural) households received no such benefits. When communes were established, supplies of food, as well as education and health services, came from those institutions. Rural citizens provided their own housing. Because only officially registered urban residents could obtain food in cities, persons with rural registration who had left farming to go to cities for non-agricultural jobs would not be able to eat — or to obtain other necessities of life — because the state controlled the entire distribution apparatus (Kirkby, 1985). For a rural resident, obtaining urban household registration was extremely difficult, and, at times, when the household registration regulations were enforced, labor-force shift and concomitant rural-to-urban migration virtually were cut off.

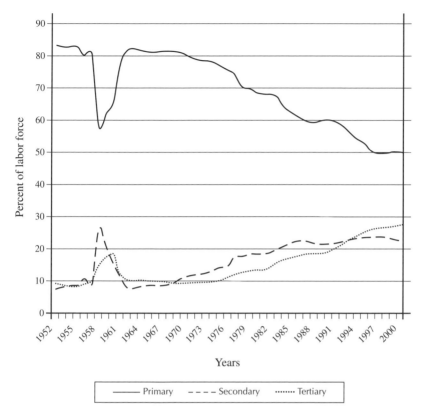

Figure 4.3. Employment by economic sector in China, 1952–94. (Source: China Statistical Yearbooks.)

The Great Leap Forward was one period in which migration to cities was permitted, even encouraged, and the shift was massive, as workers answered the call to jobs in heavy industry for rapid development of the country. However, as the previously discussed neoclassical economic model would predict, the withdrawal of so many workers from agriculture (combined with other problems) led to diaster (Ashton et al., 1984; Becker, 1997; Lardy, 1983; Lin, 1990; Piazza, 1986). Faced with too many people in the cities, for whom subsidized grain had to be supplied, and too few farmers to grow the grain, the state reduced urban employment and sent back to the countryside millions of peasants who had migrated to cities. Never again would the floodgates of migration be quite so open.

During the Cultural Revolution, there was a great deal of movement to and from cities, as young school graduates were "sent down" to the countryside to "learn from the peasants." Hordes of young people traveled all over China, with or without permission, and a general breakdown of order weakened the power of any authority to stop the chaos.

With the reforms of the 1980s and the resulting changes in agriculture and industry, as well as greater pragmatism in the administration of many regulations, migration to cities has increased again. Youths who had been sent to the countryside returned home, with or without permission, and new graduates refused to go. Universities reopened, and students came to cities to study. Furthermore, new industries and construction projects needed workers, and ways were found to move people into such jobs. Rural-registered persons were permitted to take such work on a temporary basis, provided they supplied their own food and other necessities.

At the same time, the household responsibility system uncovered large numbers of surplus rural labor (Zweig, 1987), reminiscent of the theoretical writings of Ricardo (1817), Lewis (1955), and Ranis and Fei (1964). Under the commune system, these workers had been fed and supported, although they produced nothing additional, but households who were responsible for their own profits wanted to rationalize their labor inputs. It is estimated that that about 220 million rural workers in China are surplus (Jan Wang, 1990; Lingjun Wang, 1990; Wang, Liu, and Wang, 1989: 96; Xin, 1991: 43).

The service component of the economy also began to grow (Table 4.2, Figure 4.3). Under Maoism, service activities were neglected in favor of industry, although the provision of services through work units meant that many "industrial" employees were, more accurately, service workers (teachers, health workers, recreation leaders, etc.).

Repair services, restaurants, small shops, and the like, however, virtually were absent in Chinese cities. The Dengist reforms allowed such businesses to be established under collective or individual ownership, and they have burgeoned. A striking feature of the cityscape today is the profusion of petty vendors, service workers, small shops, and restaurants — surely enough of the latter so that every Chinese person could eat out at the same time with room to spare!

The Chinese government, wanting to control the growth of large cities and avoid the shanty towns that have plagued other Third World cities, has encouraged the growth of rural industry and specialized households to absorb surplus rural workers. These policies draw on traditional Chinese home-based handicrafts, as well as the efforts in the Great Leap Forward. As Oshima (1987, 1993) posited, they use surplus rural labor, some of it on a seasonal basis. Farm workers can change occupations without changing residence — or household registration — in what the Chinese call *li tu, bu li xiang* ("leave the land but not the village"). These solutions, however, have been insufficient, and workers have flocked to eastern coastal areas, especially to Guangdong with its booming export-oriented manufacturing sector (Goldstein and Goldstein, 1984; Pannell, 1989; Taylor and Banister, 1991). The size of this "floating population" is not precisely known; official estimates suggest 50 to 60 million persons (*China Daily*, Oct. 24, 1991; Zhang, 1990). Such migrants provide much-needed unskilled labor, petty vending, and services (Zweig, 1987), but complaints of crime, begging, prostitution, and other illegal activities among the "floating population" are increasing. In any case, it is a response to the changing economic and employment realities under the reforms in China, and represents an occupational and lifestyle change for the migrants. In 1994, the percentage of the labor force engaged in services surpassed that engaged in manufacturing (Figure 4.3).

Urbanization

The recent increase in rural-to-urban migration, both legal and illegal, is but the latest chapter in the course of urbanization in China (Figure 4.4). Examination of Chinese urbanization confronts the long, complex history of the country, as well as changing definitions of what constitutes "urban," both before and after the founding of the Communist government in 1949 (Ma and Cui, 1987). Statistics even have been adjusted "after the fact" (Kirkby, 1985; Leeming, 1993; Luo and Pannell, 1991; Pannell, 1984; 1987–88; 1990; Quan, 1991; Ye, 1989).

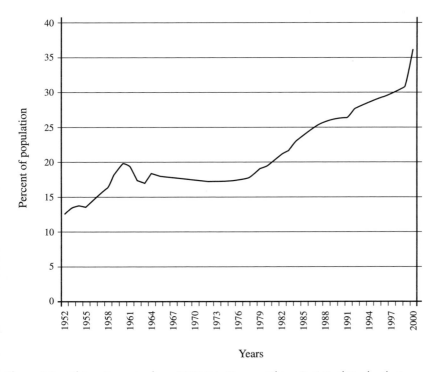

Figure 4.4 China: Percent urban, 1952–94. (Source: China Statistical Yearbooks.)

China's long history of towns reaches back as far as 2500 B.C. (Chang, 1963; Quan, 1991; Trewartha, 1952). From the Tang dynasty to the Ming dynasty (A.D. 618–1644), the proportion of the population living in cities stayed at about 10%, followed by a slight decline during the Qing dynasty (1645–1911) (Quan, 1991: 42). In traditional China, the distinction between urban and rural was fairly clear-cut: towns had walls around them, were seats of authority, and usually were located on roads (in the north) or rivers (in the south) (Orleans, 1982: 271).

Modernization began in the nineteenth century, near the end of the Qing dynasty (Buck, 1978). The Opium War (1839–42) imposed Western will on China and brought about the opening of the first treaty ports and the beginning of the modern period of Chinese cities (Skinner, 1977: 229). The next half century saw commercialization with the building of railroads and port facilities, but China was still composed of several regional urban systems, rather than one unified one (Skinner, 1977). Despite disruptions of civil war, Chinese cities did continue to grow in the early twentieth century (Chen, 1973; Orleans, 1959; Pannell, 1981: 97). Since 1949, the urban proportion of the population has increased, but the process has been sporadic, reflecting ideological shifts and domestic upheavals that impacted agriculture, industry, and the balance between them (Lo, 1990; Pannell, 1981; 1986: 291). In the period immediately after 1949, city populations grew. Land reform drove people from rural areas, the end of civil strife made cities safer again, and the establishment of heavy industry, described in the previous section, attracted workers to jobs and better lives (Chen, 1973). Government policies favored growth of smaller cities and the interior of the country (Buck, 1981; Fei, 1989; Tan, 1986: 140).

During the Great Leap Forward and the contemporaneous establishment of the massive rural people's communes beginning in 1958, the flow to the cities increased still more, outpacing the development of the country (Quan, 1991: 43). Specifically and most critically, it went beyond the nation's capacity to feed the city dwellers (May, 1961: 26). Frightened by this disaster, the Chinese government determined to control migration stringently and keep urban populations low (Ran and Berry, 1989). In an effort to reduce the number of city dwellers for whom the government had to supply food grain, it reduced urban employment and removed about 20 to 30 million persons from cities to the countryside (Orleans, 1982: 279; Quan, 1991: 43). During the Cultural Revolution (1966–76) development of any sort was disrupted badly, and reliable statistics are hard to come by. It is apparent that large numbers of young people were sent into the countryside (Banister, 1987: 177; Orleans, 1982: 280), and large numbers of migrants moved *into* the cities during those years (Orleans, 1982: 280). Self-sufficiency and grain production were stressed, and all forms of trade and commerce were suspect as "capitalistic." Administrative, service, and industrial activities in commune centers gave them town characteristics of population and function (Schinz, 1989: 35), but they were not officially urban.

Reforms beginning in the late 1970s have had far-reaching affects on urbanization (Figure 4.4) (Chen, 1991; Perkins, 1990; Xie and Costa, 1991). Youths were no longer sent to the countryside, and, in general, the government relaxed its rigid opposition to urbanization (Banister, 1987: 177). New economic activities began to revitalize smaller centers (Banister, 1987; Buck, 1981; Ma, 1992; Quan, 1991; Tan, 1986). The 1982 census also counted as "urban" any person who had lived for at least a year within the boundaries of a city or town, even those who continued to engage in full- or part-time farming (Chen, 1991: 363; Pannell, 1990: 218).

At the same time, policy changes favored the formation of small enterprises owned by townships, villages, or individuals. As agriculture became more efficient, such firms would absorb surplus rural labor. Engaging in small-scale industry, construction, transportation, and commercial activities, they resembled the informal sector of other developing countries. They attracted workers to large cities, but also to many small centers (Pannell, 1990: 219). The government also moved to meet the need for urban labor, without adding to the number of officially urban residents for whom it must supply food and other subsidies, by allowing rural people to become "temporary" or "farmer-worker" residents of cities.

Diet in China

Of the complex collection of transformations that constitutes economic development, two have the greatest relevance for a household's foodways: changes in occupation (labor force shift) and changes in the living environment (urbanization). Both aspects of development have been proceeding apace in China, especially under the Dengist reforms. People have been leaving farming. Some have moved to cities in classic rural-to-urban migration. In other cases, the urban environment invades the countryside — rural urbanization — in the form of small factories, especially in the peri-urban zones and in the *zhenxiang* areas. In both scenarios, the people shift from producing their own food to purchasing food in markets, a fundamental change in their way of life. Because all of culture is integrated, we would expect to find that foodways as a cultural element also change; the modern understanding of economic development, furthermore, predicts that nutritional levels will rise.

If urban residents in China enjoy a higher standard of living than rural people, Engel's Law predicts that they would spend a smaller percentage of their income on food. Bennett's Law predicts that they would eat less grain and more vegetables, fruits, and animal foods. Among urban residents, the same pattern should be expected: the higher the income, the smaller the percentage that is spent on food and the lower the proportion that is made up of grain, while the proportion that is comprised of animal foods increases.

Overall Consumption

We begin with the broad picture of consumption in general, including such tangible goods as food and clothing, as well as such intangibles as rent and electricity. On average, urban per capita incomes in China always have been higher than rural incomes. Per capita consumption is a measure of disposable income, because it does not include taxes or savings. It is relevant here because it includes food. Incomes and consumption have been rising in China, but the rise has been uneven; even Deng Xiaoping said that "some must get rich first." In urban areas, average consumption rose from 405 yuan in 1978 to 3,956 yuan in 1994, while rural consumption rose from 138 to 1,087 yuan. In other words, if 1978 is used as a base of 100, the index for urban consumption in 1994 was 289.1, while that for rural consumption was 285.2 (SSB, 1995). Thus, the overall percentage increase was similar, but urban residents still had higher levels of living. Because rural consumption started out lower, it would have had to rise much faster for the two figures to become equal. Because it did not, urban consumption is still higher.

Another measure of the degree of equality of living standards in the two regions is the ratio of urban to rural consumption levels (Figure 4.5). This ratio declined in the late 1970s and early 1980s, as rural incomes rose in response to the Dengist reforms, which first impacted the countryside. Since 1985, however, as reforms took hold in urban areas and the first (and easiest) increases in agricultural output and value had been accomplished, the ratio has climbed steadily. Urban living standards remain higher than rural standards, and the disparity is growing.

Urban Food Consumption Patterns

Turning to the specific issue of food, Engel's ratio is one measure of comparative economic well-being. According to Engel's Law, higher-income families spend a smaller percentage of their incomes on food. Engel's ratio can be calculated as a percentage of total income or a percentage of total expenditures. The first is preferable because it includes savings and taxes as a part of a household budget. The percentage of household expenditure, however, is a valid measure of the place of food because food is a biological necessity, and the elasticity of demand is small. Therefore, the variation in the available data has little impact on the overall patterns obtained.

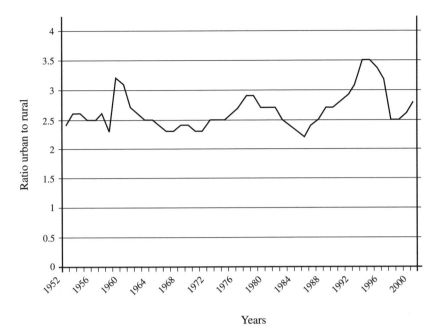

Years

Figure 4.5 Ratio of urban to rural consumption levels in China, 1952–84. (Source: China Statistical Yearbooks.)

The general trend in the Engel's ratio (Figure 4.6) for urban areas, measured as the food portion of expenditures, is downward over time, as is to be expected with rising incomes, but the progress has been uneven. From 1981 to 1983, it rose and then dropped steeply to 52.43% of living expenses in 1986. After a slight uptick to 53.47% of living expenses in 1987, it dropped again to 51.36% in 1988. In 1989, it then turned sharply upward to 54.50%. Moreover, the ratio for rural people traditionally had been higher than that for urban residents, but the rise in the Engel's ratio for urbanites in 1989 changed the relative position. The Engel's ratio for rural areas also rose slightly in 1989, but that for urban areas rose more. The government, alarmed by the urban discontent manifest in the demonstrations in Tiananmen Square in Beijing and other cities in that year, took measures to cool inflation, especially in food prices. Food prices then stabilized, incomes continued to increase, and, since 1990, the Engel's ratio has declined to stand at 39.1 in 2000. The drop between 1993 and 1994 was less than that in the preceding few years, reflecting the effect of the end of food rationing and food subsidies in Chinese cities and the renewed high inflation.

The Engel's ratios (the food portion of expenditures) across income groups in cities for 1994 (Figure 4.7) show a steady decline as income rises. The poorest 10% of households spend more than 60% of their incomes on

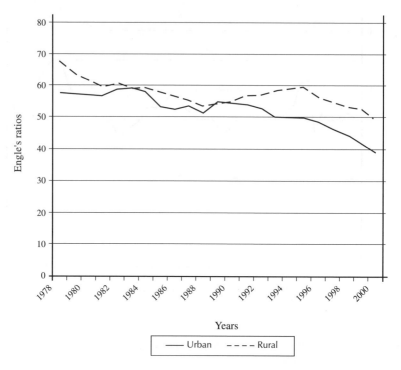

Figure 4.6.   Urban and rural Engel's ratios in China, 1982–94. (Source: China Statistical Yearbooks.)

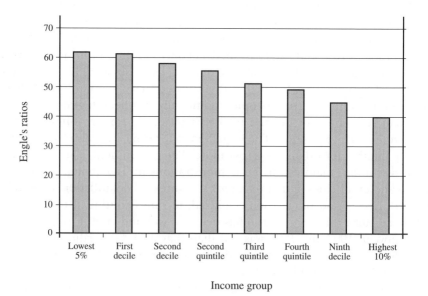

Figure 4.7.   Engel's ratios by income group, Chinese urban areas, 1994. (Source: SSB, 1995: 260–1.)

food, and the ratio declines to 40% for households in the highest 10%. With all households facing basically the same food price structure, this pattern follows Engel's Law more closely than changes over time when simultaneously prices are rising.

According to Bennett's Law, the portion of grain (and staple foods in general) in the diet declines with rising incomes. In urban areas, this pattern clearly stands out (Figure 4.8a), with per capita consumption of grain showing a general decline since 1957 (note that the famine years of 1958–61 are not shown on the graph). At the same time, the consumption of meats and poultry, oil, eggs, sugar, and alcoholic beverages generally has increased (Figure 4.8b).

The tradeoff between vegetables (Figure 4.8a) and meats (Figure 4.8b) in the *cai* portion of meals also appears. In general, consumption of meat has risen, while consumption of vegetables has declined. While pork continues to be the favored meat, by far, it has declined slightly in recent years in favor of poultry, eggs, seafood, beef, and mutton, which fluctuate within a fairly small range from year to year. In other words, the variety of menus is increasing.

Bennett's Law also operates across income groups in cities (Figure 4.9). While grain consumption rises slightly with income, the real increase is in the consumption of meat (here including pork, beef, mutton, and poultry) and seafood. The differential in consumption of eggs and dairy products is much less. Consumption of dairy products can be expected to remain low because they are not a favored food in China; as mentioned in Chapter 3, many Chinese are lactose-intolerant and cannot drink fresh milk. While ice cream and yogurt are gaining popularity in cities, cheese (except on pizza) generally is disliked. Thus, China will probably not follow the Western pattern of greatly increased consumption of dairy products as incomes rise.

Rural Food Consumption Patterns

Rural residents produce more of their own food than do urban residents; In 1994, the country average for rural resident production was 56% of their needs (SSB, 1995). Because they also grow food to sell, what they eat represents "opportunity cost," that is, food for which they do not get cash income. At the same time, they purchase what they do not produce, paying market prices.

As for urban residents, Engel's ratios provide a measure of comparative economic well-being and changes in well-being over time. From 1965 until 1988, the Engel's ratio (Figure 4.6) for rural residents declined. As mentioned earlier, it then rose slightly in 1989, but by less than that for urban residents. In 1990 and the years following, the ratio for urban residents declined, while that for rural people did not; the ratio rose to 59.6 in 1995 before dropping to 49.1 (10 percentage points higher than the urban ratio) in 2000.

In rural areas, unlike cities, grain consumption is considerably higher and

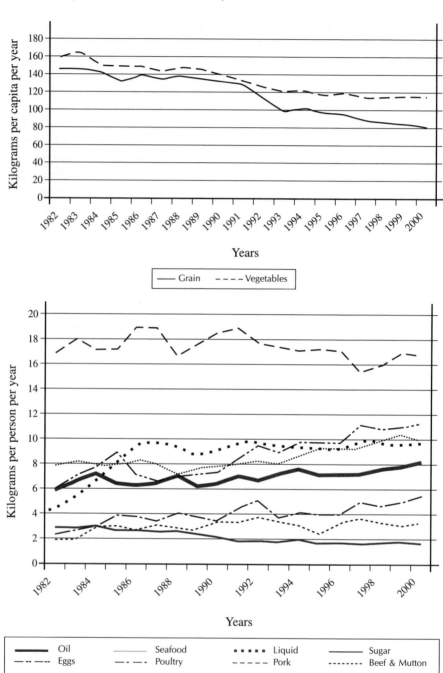

Figure 4.8 Per capita consumption of foods by category in Chinese urban areas, 1982–94: (a) Grain and vegetables, and (b) Other categories of food. (Data source: China Statistical Yearbooks.)

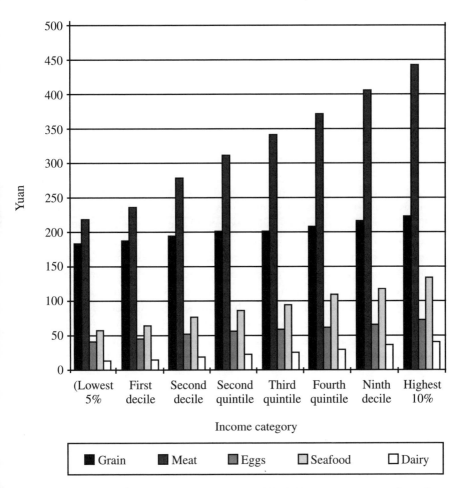

Figure 4.9 Per capita expenditure on categories of foods by income group, urban China, 1994. (Source: SSB, 1995: 264.)

has not declined, despite rising incomes (Figure 4.10a). Vegetable consumption has been fairly consistent, with a slight decline, especially in 1993. Consumption of meats, poultry, eggs, seafood, sugar, and liquor (Figure 4.10b) rose in the late 1970s and 1980s, as the reforms under Deng Xiaoping took hold and the Maoist "grow grain everywhere" strictures were relaxed. Since the mid-1980s, the curve has flattened out. Following Bennett's Law, while the *amount* of grain (staple food) has not declined in the Chinese countryside, the *percentage* of food that it comprises has. The grain consumed also has improved in quality and desirability since 1978 (Figure 4.11), as the percentage represented by wheat flour and rice (fine grain) increased, especially in the early years of the Dengist reforms, although more recently, the curve has flattened out. At the end of the Cultural Revolution, rural diets were even more inadequate than were urban diets, and people needed to continue to eat the same amount of grain *plus* other foods to reach even a minimum nutritional standard. An informant in the field said that authorities are still trying to get peasants to eat enough nutrients, never mind food choices.

A comparison of the consumption of various categories of food between city and countryside (Figure 4.12) shows that rural people still consume more than twice as much grain per capita as urban people. Of non-staple foods — vegetables, oil, meat, poultry, eggs, seafood, sugar, and liquor — urban residents consume more.

The rural diet's dependence on grain drove up the Engel's ratios in the face of rising incomes because grain prices rose faster than incomes from 1992 to 1994. The rise in grain prices also exceeded the income increases in cities, but urban diets are less dependent on grain, so the impact on the family budget was less. In the countryside, by contrast, a 50% rise in the price of grain (Table 4.3) makes a significant difference in food expenditure. Replacing grain with other foods is impractical because those foods are even more expensive, especially on a per Calorie basis. Thus, we see the Giffen effect at work, especially in 1993, when consumption of grain (a less desired food) actually rose despite rising income because of the effect of price increases. Likewise, the proportion of fine grain — wheat and rice — in the diet declined in those years.

Thus, Engel's ratios in urban areas rose in the early 1980s, as more food and a greater variety of items became available under the Dengist reforms. Expenditure on food had been kept artificially low during the Maoist years, not only by rationing, but by the lack of much of anything to buy. It is not surprising that people in such a food-centered culture as the Chinese would spend more of their rising incomes on improving their diets. Table 4.4 provides more details about consumption of various individual foods in urban China as a whole, thus indicating some of the items for which people aspire as their incomes increases. Because high-income people can be expected to spend more on everything than low-income people, foods for which higher-income people spend *less* than lower-income people are those that are less favored. Soybeans are an example; the highest-income group spends less on soybeans than the group immediately below it. Similarly, the lowest 5% of households spends more on soybeans than the lowest 10% overall. Soybeans are an inexpensive protein and, therefore, have no prestige. On the other hand, as we have seen, consumption of meats rises across income groups, more than doubling for some kinds of meat. Sugar increases slightly, but candy triples. Fruit wine, which is closer to a Western than a Chinese beverage, more than doubles, as does beer. Melons and fruits more than double, showing their status as a luxury food. Cake, fresh milk, milk powder, and yogurt are all more

Table 4.3 Changes in consumer prices and per capita incomes in China, 1980–1994 (previous year = 100)

a. Urban areas

Year	Income	Prices		
		Overall	Food	Grain
1980	na	108.1	108.1	100.2
1981	na	102.7	102.7	100.7
1982	107.0	102.1	102.1	99.2
1983	107.0	101.9	103.7	102.1
1984	115.2	102.5	104.0	100.0
1985	124.4	112.2	116.5	103.3
1986	110.8	107.0	107.2	104.1
1987	111.2	109.1	112.0	106.2
1988	117.8	121.8	125.2	114.1
1989	116.2	116.0	114.4	116.9
1990	109.7	100.2	98.8	93.5
1991	112.5	104.5	105.4	120.7
1992	118.6	107.7	105.4	139.2
1993	127.2	114.2	116.5	131.1
1994	135.6	125.0	131.8	150.7

b. Rural areas

Year	Income	Prices		
1980	na	104.4	107.1	107.1
1981	116.8	102.1	103.0	101.1
1982	120.9	101.7	104.4	103.5
1983	114.7	101.2	100.6	100.2
1984	114.7	103.0	101.4	99.6
1985	111.9	107.0	112.5	117.6
1986	106.6	105.0	107.5	113.0
1987	109.2	106.3	108.4	106.1
1988	117.8	117.1	120.9	114.0
1989	110.4	118.8	118.0	125.0
1990	114.1	103.2	101.7	96.7
1991	103.2	102.0	101.3	99.9
1992	110.6	103.9	104.7	112.7
1993	117.6	112.6	112.0	124.6
1994	132.5	123.4	131.9	150.7

Note: na = data not available.

Source: State Statistical Bureau, *China Statistical Yearbook 1994 and 1995* (Beijing: Statistical Publishing House, 1994 and 1995), and calculations by the author.

traditional in the West than in China and are more common among high-income people. The rise in the consumption of yogurt in the high- and highest-income group is striking. This table, then, indicates which foods have greatest prestige in China and the direction toward which we can expect the Chinese diet to move, as development proceeds and the level of well-being rises.

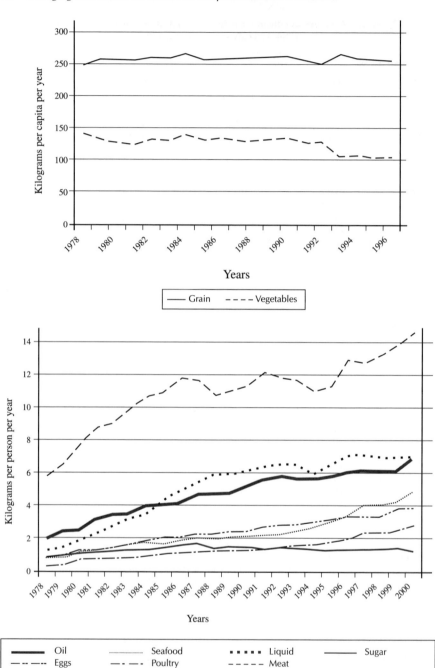

Figure 4.10 Per capita consumption of foods by category, rural China, 1978–94: (a) Grain and vegetables, and (b) Other categories of foods. (Source: China Statistical Yearbooks.)

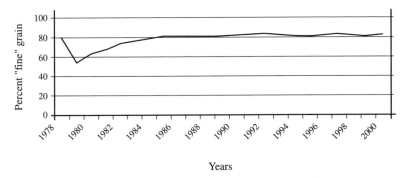

Years

Figure 4.11 Consumption of fine grain in rural areas in China, 1979–94. (Source: China Statistical Yearbooks, and calculations by the author.)

Table 4.4. China: Urban household annual per capita purchases of major commodities, by level of income, 1994 (in kilograms)

Item	Lowest 5%	Lowest 10%	Second decile	Second quintile	Third quintile	Fourth quintile	Ninth decile	Tenth decile
Starches & tubers	13.27	13.20	12.89	13.94	14.44	14.51	14.75	15.66
Soybeans	.24	.23	.26	.24	.29	.31	.36	.34
Bean curd	5.72	5.75	5.98	6.30	6.66	6.86	7.74	8.24
Vegetable oil	6.05	6.58	7.16	7.50	7.44	7.81	8.07	8.36
Animal	.61	.67	.70	.70	.67	.67	.66	.76
Pork	12.76	13.40	15.15	16.03	17.32	18.67	19.50	20.94
Beef	1.27	1.37	1.59	1.92	1.88	2.01	2.20	2.78
Mutton	.74	.80	.86	1.08	1.19	1.24	1.68	1.61
Poultry	2.51	2.67	3.33	3.84	4.19	4.53	5.19	5.72
Fresh eggs	6.88	7.38	8.43	9.34	9.78	10.23	10.91	12.50
Fish	2.46	2.76	3.25	3.62	3.91	4.20	4.43	5.19
Shrimp	.38	.43	.47	.54	.66	.67	.75	.87
Vegetables	100.46	103.14	110.48	116.93	118.91	125.45	136.03	144.59
Sugar	1.35	1.43	1.64	1.72	2.37	1.87	2.01	2.22
Candy	.36	.40	.52	.57	.67	.76	.89	1.03
Liquor	2.52	2.64	2.52	3.00	3.00	3.17	3.06	3.48
Fruit wine	.08	.09	.09	.12	.14	.13	.16	.21
Beer	3.22	3.73	4.95	5.59	6.12	6.81	7.31	8.67
Other liquor	.66	.70	.74	.81	.77	.87	.96	.92
Melons & fruits	22.11	24.23	31.20	36.61	41.43	45.63	49.55	55.00
Cake	1.89	2.05	2.59	2.95	3.41	3.69	4.27	4.58
Fresh milk	2.59	2.94	3.27	4.64	5.13	5.78	7.66	8.80
Milk powder	.25	.26	.30	.37	.42	.49	.54	.62
Yogurt	.13	.14	.17	.25	.29	.33	.53	.53

Source: State Statistical Bureau, *China Statistical Yearbook 1995* (Beijing: Statistical Publishing House, 1995), p. 264.

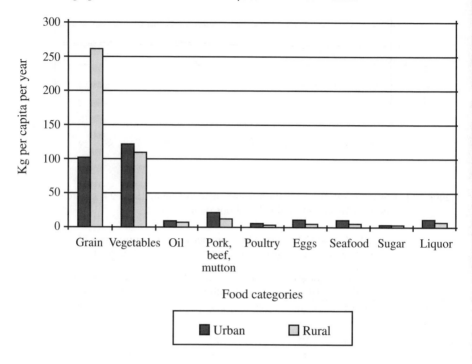

Figure 4.12 Urban and rural Chinese consumption of food by category, 1994.

In the late 1980s, however, the rise in food expenditure and in the Engel's ratio was the result not of new abundance or more prestige foods but of higher prices. In 1988, people cut back on meat and poultry, but, as inflation raged on, such luxuries had been squeezed out of the budget and people had no choice but to increase their spending on food. Everything just cost more. Unaccustomed to such insults after several years of improved living (and eating) standards, they joined the students who were protesting other grievances in the streets of China's cities.

As has been noted, beginning in the 1990s, Engel's ratios once again have declined in the cities. Furthermore, more processed and Western foods have become increasingly available (Jussaume, 2001; Veeck, 2000). They tend to be high in fat and sugar and to be advertised heavily, just as in the West (Guldan, 2000; Guo, Popkin, and Zhai, 1999; Yan, 1997). Similar to the Western experience, urban China is reaching Pattern 4 of the Nutrition Transition (Popkin, 1993), with a shift from communicable to chronic diseases as the main cause of death, and obesity as a major health problem (Campbell, et al., 1992; Guldan, 1999; Ma and Popkin, 1995). As in the Western experience, greater concern for healthy diets is also appearing in China; however, more information on which areas to take appropriate action is needed (Ma, 1998; Smith, 1993).

Since 1989, there have been reports of protests in the countryside, and the press frequently reports measures to insure that peasants get paid and that illegal financial assessments cease (e.g. *China Daily Business Weekly*, November 14–20, 1993; *Atlanta Journal Constitution*, November 12, 1996). While Chinese press reports must be read cautiously, the very fact that such matters are mentioned at all indicates a perceived problem. In the meantime, despite repeated reports of the problems it produces, migration of the "floating population" to towns and cities offers a "safety valve" and some release of the pressure (*China Daily*, December 4, 1994). Real famine, in the historical sense of starvation from lack of food, does not stalk the Chinese countryside today; inflation is a comparatively mild problem. Nevertheless, if food prices continue to rise for rural residents and incomes do not keep pace, a potential source of instability in the Chinese countryside could be in the offing. Chinese authorities are clearly concerned about such a scenario. At the same time, rural Chinese also are changing their preferences, even reducing their desire for meat, perhaps from health concerns, and increasing their desire for rice as opposed to wheat (Wan, 1998).

Plate 1   On a cold winter day, a donkey keeps guard over a greenhouse near Shenyang. The use of greenhouses with plastic sheeting and, in some cases, supplementary heat has increased greatly the variety of vegetables available in Chinese cities in winter.

Plate 2   The re-establishment of traditional farmer's markets in Chinese cities was one of the reforms of Deng Xiaoping . This market is in Dalian.

Plate 3 To lengthen the growing season in Liaoning, rice seedlings are started in "nurseries" under plastic. When the weather warms up and the seedlings are of sufficient size, they are transplanted into paddies.

Plate 4 Old and new technology mingle in a Shenyang street, as cabbages dry for winter storage outside of a store selling electronic goods.

Plate 5   Rural industry was a feature of the Great Leap Forward, and the tradition continues with independent factories, as well as branches of city industries. This machine-parts factory, in the midst of rice paddies, is in Hunhepu, near Shenyang.

Plate 6   A feature of the streetscape of modern cities in China is a nearly endless variety of small restaurants. Ownership varies among large entities, townships and villages, and individual families. Muslim-owned restaurants feature dishes of lamb, rather than pork that Muslims do not eat.

Plate 7 American fast-food restaurants have spread to many cities in China. McDonald's enjoys high status among middle-class Chinese. Under the umbrellas, traditional snack foods are being sold. This McDonald's was in Beijing, but recently has been replaced by an office building. Because fast-food restaurants are in cities, they increase the differences between urban and rural diets.

Plate 8 Rice farming is not highly mechanized in China, and planting seedlings by hand in flooded paddies is still back-breaking, hard work.

Plate 9   Shenyang, typical of McGee's urban center, is a large industrial city of ancient foundation. Office towers and apartment blocks line a major north-south thoroughfare.

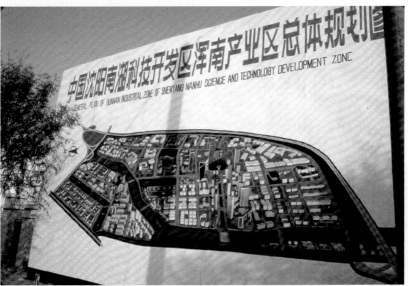

中国沈阳南湖科技开发区浑南产业区总体规划总 GENERAL PLAN OF HUNAN INDUSTRIAL ZONE OF SHENYANG NANHU SCIENCE AND TECHNOLOGY DEVELOPMENT ZONE

Plate 10   A major factor in the loss of farmland around Chinese cities is the spread of urban functions. Here, a new complex, including a factory, as well as housing and other facilities for the workers in the work unit, is planned for land that once was fields to the south of Shenyang.

Plate 11 A beautifully decorated and deliciously seasoned fish forms the final dish of a sumptuous banquet at a city restaurant in Shenyang.

Plate 12 In Kangping County, which borders Inner Mongolia, level land and low population density allow for larger fields. Mechanization, as well as pasture for grazing animals, is easy to introduce.

Plate 13   Shenyang, capital of Liaoning Province, is the ancient capital of the Manchu people before they conquered China in 1644 and became the Qing dynasty. Their imperial palace, like the one in Beijing, is a museum today.

Plate 14   Once harvested, rice must be threshed, a dusty operation that uses a simple electric machine. The work is primarily done by women.

Plate 15 Grazing land is scarce in eastern China because cropland must be devoted to crops that people will eat directly. These animals take advantage of the weeds that grow under a highway overpass.

5

Liaoning Province

To see more clearly what Chinese people eat on a day-to-day basis, we now focus on one province: Liaoning in Northeastern China. This chapter surveys the geography of Liaoning Province, describes the food and diet situation for the province as a whole, and lays out the application of McGee's *zhenxianghua* model. While no one province truly can represent a country as large and diverse as China in all details of food habits, Liaoning possesses characteristics that are repeated elsewhere and are important to understanding China's issues of food supply, nutrition, and well-being.

The timing of this study fell just after the end of food rationing in Chinese cities. Thus, the power of rations and subsidies to skew food choices no longer applied, and people had much more choice in what they would purchase and eat. Of course, as we shall see, old food habits die hard, and the impact of food rations and subsidies remained in people's minds and, thus, influenced their choices. Nevertheless, it is instructive to look at what they were eating at this momentous period in the food history of China.

Geographical Background

Liaoning (Figure 5.1) is the southernmost of the three northeastern provinces of China, formerly known as Manchuria. In latitude, it stretches from 38°43' to 43°26' north, or about the latitude of St. Louis, Missouri, to Milwaukee, Wisconsin. It is the only northeastern Chinese province that has a seacoast. Its total area is 145,900 km² (56,332 square miles), or about the size of Iowa. At the end of 1994, the total population was about 40 million.

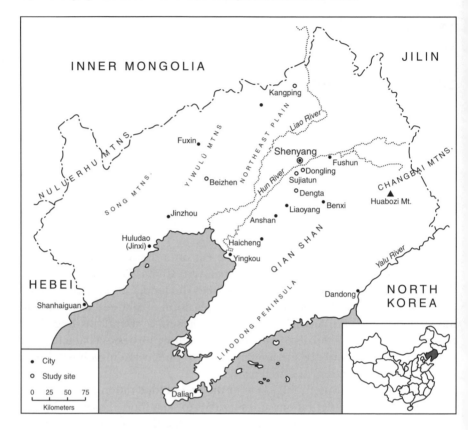

Figure 5.1 Map of Liaoning Province.

Physical Geography

Liaoning has three physiographical regions: mountains on the east and west with a river plain in between. Its climate varies with latitude and topography.

Topography

In eastern China, topographical features trend northeast–southwest; the topographical features of Liaoning follow this pattern. The entire region is geologically part of the Sino-Korean platform or plate, which moved northward from south of the equator in Ordovician to Carboniferous times (between 3 and 5 million years ago) and docked with the Siberian plate in its present location. In this period, Liaoning's coal measures were laid down (Webb, 1994).

Folding and faulting continued, and two parallel normal faults, the result of extension of the crust, uplifted the mountain ranges in eastern and western Liaoning and down-thrust the valley between them (Webb, 1994). The eastern mountains, a part of the Changbai range, are the highest, with Huabozi Shan at 1,326 meters (4,350 feet) the highest point in the province. The Liaodong Peninsula and offshore islands, with the Qian Shan ("Thousand Mountains") as their backbone, are part of this structure.

The western mountains, which continue into Hebei Province, are lower, with the highest peaks in far western Jianping County reaching just over 1,100 meters. Their southern face is very close to the seacoast, leaving only a narrow corridor, which has been of great strategic importance throughout history. Marking and guarding this passage is the seaward end of the Great Wall of China, just across the provincial boundary at Shanhaiguan, Hebei.

The valley between the mountain ranges is part of the Northeast Plain; it is a structural depression, rather than a river-eroded valley. The same structure continues southward, as the Bohai Gulf and the North China Plain, and northward into Jilin and Heilongjiang provinces. In Liaoning, it is drained by the Liao and Hun rivers and their tributaries and has been built up with wind-blown loess and riverine deposits. The silt deposits have hampered the development of harbors at the mouths of the rivers. Thus, although Yinkou (Newchuang) at the mouth of the Hun River, with its access to the hinterland of the plain, was the historic port in the days of junks and became a treaty port, it was too shallow for steamers, and dredging it would have been prohibitively expensive (Cressey, 1934). Dalian, at the southern end of the Liaodong Peninsula, is the province's chief port today.

Climate

Liaoning has a temperature regime like Minnesota, in the United States. Weather varies by altitude and latitude, but the entire province is under the effect of the East Asian monsoon. The result is cold, dry winters and hot, rainy summers (Figure 5.2, Table 5.1).

In winter, the chilling of the huge Eurasian landmass cools the air above it and forms a mass of cold, sinking air over Siberia. Airflow spirals clockwise outward from this high pressure center, bringing northwest wind to Liaoning Province. This air is cold and dry, but, thanks to the stability of the cold air mass, there is little surface wind in winter. An occasional cyclonic depression brings snow. While the total accumulation is small, what does fall, stays on the ground until spring because the temperatures are too low for it to melt.

In summer, the heating of the landmass of Eurasia forms a low pressure cell in which air is rising. Because "nature abhors a vacuum," air rushes in to fill the space left by the rising air. Thus, the counterclockwise circulation around the low pressure cell draws air from the Pacific Ocean over adjacent

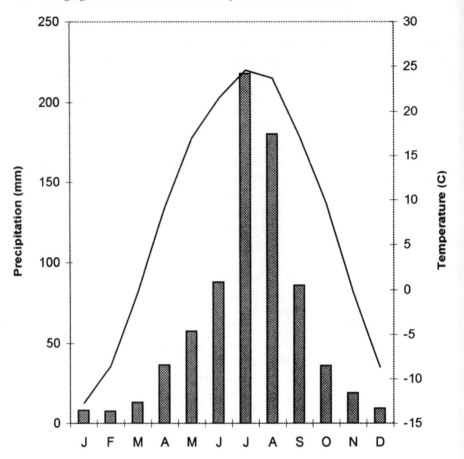

Figure 5.2   Climate graph for Shenyang, Liaoning. Data source: Zhao, 1986: 206.

Table 5.1 Temperature and precipitation by month, Shenyang, Liaoning, 1994

Month	Temperature (°C)	Precipitation (mm)
January	−11.5	3.4
February	−6.6	0.2
March	−0.2	9.2
April	13.0	3.0
May	16.8	88.5
June	23.7	83.2
July	26.7	225.2
August	25.0	338.8
September	17.4	98.9
October	9.6	28.2
November	2.8	10.2
December	−8.4	4.5

Source: Liaoning Statistical Bureau, 1995: 4–5

land areas, including Liaoning Province; this air is warm and moist. Rising over the land, especially the hills, it releases precipitation, and summer is the rainy season. Heat and rain come together (Liaoning Education College, 1983).

In springs, the monsoon systems shift. The winter high pressure breaks down, and the summer low forms over Siberia. Weather is warm and windy. Because Liaoning is close to the drylands of the northern interior of China, spring also tends to produce dust storms. Autumn, when the heat, humidity, and haze of summer begin to clear, is a pleasant time of year.

Human Geography

Chinese development of Liaoning has come rather recently compared to the portion of China within the Great Wall (so-called China Proper); early industrial development was the work of foreigners. Liaoning, along with Jilin and Heilongjiang to its north, is today regarded as an integral part of China, and the regional name "Northeast" (*Dongbei*) is much preferred over "Manchuria" (Zhao, 1994: 184).

History

Little is known of the ancient history of the Northeast. For centuries, it remained primarily the homeland of nomadic herders, such as the Xianbei, Khitan (from whose name the word "Cathay" derives), and a Tungusic people called the Nuzhen, or in Western usage, the Juchen (Jurchen). They lived by a combination of nomadic herding and farming, including pig raising. By various defensive works, including a "Great Wall" of willow trees, the Chinese tried to separate these tribes from their lands. From these tribes arose the Manchu people, who conquered China in 1644 and established the Qing dynasty.

For two hundred years, the Manchu rulers of China virtually prohibited migration by Han Chinese into their homeland, keeping it as a private preserve, although there were some Chinese farmers in the southern part, south of Shenyang. Increasing population and civil unrest south of the Great Wall, and resulting famines, made this policy increasingly untenable, and in the mid-nineteenth century, the Northeast was opened to migration.

At the end of the nineteenth century, the Northeast fell under the sphere of influence of Russia, followed by Japan. The Russians built the China Eastern Railway through the northern part of the region (modern Heilongjiang) to connect the Trans-Siberian Railway with Vladivostok. In the early twentieth century, after the Russo-Japanese War (1904–5), the Japanese, attracted to the Northeast by the abundance of raw materials for their growing industries, replaced the Russians as foreign overlords. They built the South Manchurian Railway in order to link their mines and factories with the port of Dalian. Meanwhile, the Chinese built a railway linking Shenyang with Beijing, giving each of the three rival powers in the region a railway line.

In 1931, the Japanese invaded the Northeast with a military force and set up a puppet state called Manchukuo (Manchu Kingdom), with the deposed last Qing emperor Henry Puyi at its head. The region became a source of industrial resources for Japan, as well as a beachhead from which to conquer additional Chinese territory. What the Chinese call the War of Resistance against the Japanese became part of World War II, which ended with Japan's defeat in 1945.

In almost a half century of occupation, the Japanese had developed a dense railway network; Liaoning still has the densest rail system of any Chinese province (Liaoning Education College, 1983). They also built mines and factories; despite loss of equipment to the Soviets at the end of World War II, this development formed a base on which the People's Republic could build after 1949. Japanese cities were centered near the railway stations, sometimes at a distance from pre-existing Chinese cities, as at Shenyang. Japanese-style houses and commercial buildings are still evident in cities, such as Shenyang, Anshan, Fuxin, and Dalian.

The Northeast was an early base of the Communist People's Liberation Army, and Shenyang was "liberated" on November 2, 1948. Soviet aid helped to re-establish the region's industries, and it remains a base of heavy industry to this day.

Population

Once the Northeast was opened to migration, Han Chinese, mostly from Shandong and Hebei, responded (Cressey, 1934). Initially they were needed to supply labor for railway construction, industry, and farming, and movement was seasonal. Workers would start out for the Northeast in the late winter, just after Chinese New Year, and continue arriving throughout the spring. After harvest in the autumn, they would return to their homes. By the 1920s, more migrants were establishing permanent homes in the Northeast.

About two-thirds came by by boat from Yantai or Qingdao in Shandong, or from Tianjin to Dalian or Yingkou; others came by train from Beijing. Train and boat tickets were inexpensive, and those who could not afford even those low fares came on foot. The South Manchurian Railway estimated that between 1923 and 1929 over 5 million migrants came; about 55% stayed permanently (Cressey, 1934: 223). Cressey describes the migration:

> It is a common sight along the overland road through Shanhaikwan [Shanhaiguan] to see family after family trudging along with all their worldly

possessions loaded high on a creaking wheelbarrow. ... Many immigrants have not even a wheelbarrow and carry their scanty belongings in a little bundle swung from a stick over their shoulders. The misfortunes of many of these people are pitiful, for they have waited until they were destitute before starting and know little of where they are going. (Cressey, 1934: 223)

By the 1930s, southern Liaoning was filling up with people; the frontier had shifted northward. Like the settlers in the American West a century earlier, the migrants were driven by a combination of poverty and warfare in their old homelands and the promise of free or inexpensive land in the new.

The ruling Japanese sent few settlers to the rural Northeast; most Japanese who came to China settled in cities, and they left after 1945. Koreans, who also lived under Japanese rule, did settle in Northeastern China, which they had been doing for about two centuries. Since 1949, more Han Chinese have moved to the Northeast, both to the cities and to the countryside, as have Mongolians and Hui (Chinese Muslims) from the Northwest. As of the 1990 census, the Han comprise 84.4% of the population of Liaoning (*Liaoning Statistical Yearbook*, 1991), and the largest concentration of Manchu people in the country is in the province (SSB, 1995) (Table 5.2). The Manchu have been assimilated into Chinese culture; acceptance of the Qing dynasty by the Chinese people depended on their sinification.

Table 5.2. Ethnic composition of Liaoning, 1990

Ethnic Group	Number	Percent
Han	33,295,000	84.4
Manchu	4,952,859	12.6
Mongolian	587,495	1.5
Hui	263,422	0.7
Korean	230,378	0.6
Yibe	120,101	0.3
Zhuang	2,775	–
Miao	1,240	–
Tujia	1,077	–
Dong	859	–
Tibetan	652	–
Daur	526	–
Yi	438	–
Others	2,839	–
Total	39,459,661	100.0

Note: – = < 0.01 percent
Source: *Liaoning Statistical Yearbook, 1991* (Beijing: China Statistical Publishing House, 1991), p. 439, and calculations by the author.

Despite the migration, the population density of Liaoning (274.6 per km²) is lower than that of other provinces in eastern China. The physiological density (per unit of agricultural land) is 994.3 per km², or 11.7 hectares per person.

Economy and Urbanization

Once settlement from China began in the nineteenth century, Liaoning became a farming region, especially in its section of the Northeast China Plain, and an early center of industry.

Agriculture. The relatively low population density of Liaoning reflects the province's agriculture. Except in the far south, the climate limits farmers to one outdoor crop per year; however, although the growing season is short, it is hot, and the northern latitude lengthens the hours of summer daylight. Furthermore, maximum precipitation comes in summer — "rain with heat" — when crops need it most.

The in-migrating Han Chinese were accustomed to diets based on wheat or rice. Corn, a relative latecomer (Chapter 3), produces more Calories per unit of land than wheat, provided sufficient moisture is available. As the Northeast had no established, traditional grain crop when the Han Chinese began to immigrate, and the soil and climate were suitable for corn growing, it became the dominant grain crop, supplemented by drought-resistant millet and sorghum. Rainfall was insufficient for rice, and irrigation works were lacking. Under Mao Zedong's policy of regional self-sufficiency, the grain ration before the Dengist reforms reflected the local agriculture. With a per capita ration of 35 *jin*[1] per month, 20 *jin* was cornmeal, 6 *jin* was wheat flour, 6 *jin* was sorghum, and 3 *jin* was rice (Ding, 1994).

Koreans and Japanese had introduced the growing of rice, but, as the composition of the grain ration shows, very little actually was grown. During the Japanese occupation, the Chinese ate sorghum, while the Japanese ate rice.

Grain still occupies most of Liaoning's farmland (Table 5.3), but the proportions devoted to each type of grain have changed in recent years. Beginning in 1949, the construction of irrigation works allowed rice paddies to replace sorghum and millet fields in the floodplains of the Liao and Hun rivers (Hsu and Hsu, 1977: 300). Many Koreans are engaged in this kind of farming. Since the reforms under Deng Xiaoping were initiated, farmers have been able to respond to the cultural demand for rice, the traditional favored grain of the dominant Han Chinese majority. One informant said that the shift to rice eating was not a matter of changing tastes, but the farmers "doing their job" and providing what people want to eat. Nevertheless, availability of irrigation water concentrates rice growing in the river valley, resulting in higher population densities (Figure 5.3).

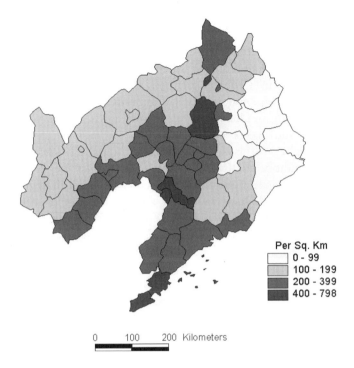

Per Sq. Km
☐ 0 - 99
▨ 100 - 199
■ 200 - 399
■ 400 - 798

0   100   200 Kilometers

Figure 5.3   Population density, Liaoning, 1994. Data source: Liaoning Statistical Bureau, 1995, and calculations by the author.

Table 5.3. Field crops, Liaoning, 1994

Crop	Land		Production (tons)
	Area (1000 ha)	Percent	
Total cropland	3,623.5	100.0	
Grain	3,026.4	83.5	13,371,000
Paddy rice	458.7	12.7	2,977,000
Wheat	162.4	4.5	485,000
Corn (maize)	1,464.6	40.4	6,139,000
Sorghum	321.7	8.9	1,815,000
Millet	109.0	3.0	255,000
Potatoes	95.9	2.6	283,000
Soybeans	318.6	8.8	483,000
Other grain	95.4	2.6	144,000
Oil crops	144.4	4.0	244,305
Peanuts	102.9	2.8	200,079
Sesame	18.1	0.5	14,022
Vegetables	318.3	8.8	11,306,000

Note: Percentages do not add up to 100 because non-food crops are omitted from the table.
Source: *Liaoning Statistical Yearbook, 1995* (Beijing: China Statistical Publishing House, 1995), and calculations by the author.

In the late winter, rice is started as seedlings in special nursery beds placed under plastic. In April and May, the paddies are flooded, and the seedlings are transplanted by hand. Late in the summer, the paddies are drained so that the rice can ripen. It is harvested in October and shocked in the fields to dry. Threshing takes place in a central location; the rice is bagged, the straw bundled for use as basketry material, fuel, and many other purposes, and the waste is burned. Planting and harvest are the busy seasons, and harvest is always a race with the first snowflakes of winter.

Under the Dengist reforms, farmers also have responded to urban markets by increasing the quantity, quality, and variety of vegetables they grow. Winter vegetables are grown in greenhouses, which use plastic rather than glass. From a selection of Chinese cabbage in winter and American-type cabbage in summer (prevalent in 1978) (Ding, 1994; Jones, 1992), markets today offer an enormous variety of vegetables. Farmers close to cities also raise animals for milk (which is pasteurized and packaged at urban dairies), eggs, and meat.

On land that is too rugged for high-value rice, fruit is a crop that commands a higher price than millet, corn, or sorghum. In the hills to the far west, is an area that specializes in pears. Apple-growing areas are along the western shore of the Bohai Gulf and on the Liaodong Peninsula. Also, there are small areas that specialize in growing grapes, often in front courtyards of homes, with other crops occupying the land under the arbors.

The rivers and seacoasts of Liaoning support a fishing industry; better transportation has increased the available market for seafood. Shrimp, many kinds of carp, crab, mackerel, and a host of other fish are landed. Seaweed also is harvested. Inland, artificial fishponds are being constructed for aquaculture.

Industry. The Northeast was the only heavy industrial center in China when the Communists came to power in 1949 (Howard, 1990: 170), the result of Japanese investment and development beginning in 1915. Based on the mineral wealth of the province, the Japanese had developed coal mining in Fushun and Fuxin, the steel center of Anshan, and steel and machine works in Shenyang (Greene, 1961). After 1949, these facilities fell to the Chinese Communists, who organized the industries in a highly centralized, Stalinist pattern to create a "producer" city (Lo, Pannell, and Welch, 1977). Anshan is still China's "Iron and Steel Capital" (Liaoning Education College, 1983), producing more than 7 million tons of steel per year (Zhao, 1994: 99). Some of that iron and steel is used for machinery, automobiles, transportation equipment, and other products made in Liaoning, especially in Shenyang. The areas of Dalian, Shenyang, Fushun, Jinzhou, and Huludao (formerly Jinxi) also support a strong chemical industry, based on petroleum and natural gas deposits, coal, and sea salt. Light industry is concentrated around textiles, with Haicheng a major center. The province grows some cotton, and flocks of sheep are nearby. Silkworms also are grown in the eastern mountains of the province.

Paper making from marsh reeds is found in coastal cities. Small manufacturing plants produce all kinds of daily needs, from tablecloths to washing machines. With the Opening to the World policy beginning in the 1980s, Liaoning has attracted foreign investment, most from Japan because of its former ties with that country (Thomas, 1990; Torbert, 1984). Gillette, Goodyear (*Goodyear Vantage*, Summer 1995), and General Motors are among those who have joint ventures in the province. Dalian is one of China's fourteen official "open ports" (Torbert, 1984), and Shenyang has a high-technology district, which is expanding into suburban Dongling District, south of the Hun River.

Urbanization

Given the long history of industrialization, it is not surprising that Liaoning is more highly urbanized than China as a whole. In a population of just over 40 million, 83.8% live in towns and cities, although only 44.2% have non-agricultural household registration. With a birthrate of 10.7 per thousand and a death rate of 5.8, the natural increase for the whole province was 4.9 per thousand (.49%) in 1994.

Liaoning has four cities with city-district populations of more than 1 million: Shenyang (4,690,000), Dalian (2,520,000), Anshan (1,430,000), and Fushun (1,390,000).

Zhenxianghua in Liaoning

McGee (1989; 1991a) listed south-central Liaoning as an example of *kotadesasai* development, and Zhou Yixing (1991) described it as one of China's "interlocking metropolitan regions." Both placed the region between Dalian in the south and Shenyang in the north, connected by the Japanese-built South Manchurian Railway and, more recently, by a new, limited-access, toll superhighway (*Shen-Da Gaosu Gonglu*).

Region 1 in the *zhenxianghua* model is exemplified by Shenyang and Dalian, as well as by intermediary cities, including Anshan, Liaoyang, Benxi, Fushun, Yingkou, and Haicheng. Shenyang is an ancient city, formerly the capital of the Manchu, and now capital and largest city of Liaoning Province. Dalian, the province's major port, is the second-largest city. It is an "open port" and has a high-technology development zone.

Region 2, the "peri-urban" zone, is composed of the suburban districts of the cities. These districts are under the administrative governance of the cities, but land use is more rural, with intensive vegetable and rice cultivation mixed with urban sprawl, new industrial districts, and rural industry (some are branch plants of city companies). Such suburban zones surround every city, whether officially delimited as suburban administrative districts or not. The greenhouses are distinctive in the landscape.

Region 3 comprises the densely settled, rice-growing, but dominantly rural areas, along the transportation corridor between Shenyang and Dalian. The rural population is dense (Figure 5.3), and a high proportion of people have a rural household registration (Figure 5.4). In addition to farming, land is used for small factories, to which members of farm families commute, often by bicycle. One example is the Liaoning Zhenxiang Clothing Manufacture Company in the county town of Dengta, which is a joint venture with South Korea that draws its entire labor force from the surrounding farm families. The high proportion of GDP from secondary activity also is reflected in relatively high per capita income compared to rural counties located farther from the cities (Figure 5.5).

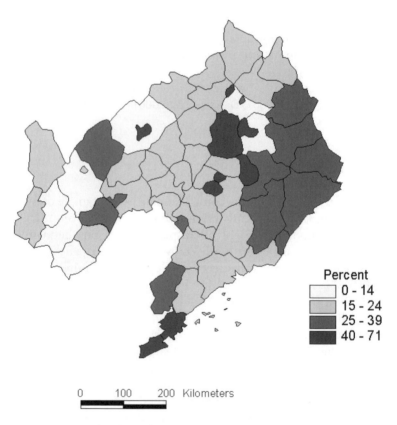

Figure 5.4   Non-agricultural population, Liaoning, 1994. Data source: Liaoning Statistical Bureau, 1995, and calculations by the author.

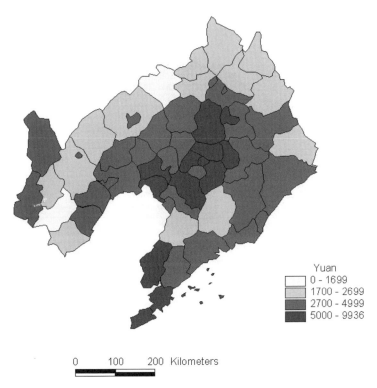

Yuan
- [ ] 0 - 1699
- 1700 - 2699
- 2700 - 4999
- 5000 - 9936

0   100   200 Kilometers

Figure 5.5   Per capita gross domestic product (GDP), Liaoning, 1994. Data source: Liaoning
Statistical Bureau, 1995, and calculations by the author.

Region 4 forms a giant horseshoe around the valley of the Liao and Hun
rivers. Here water for paddy rice is unavailable, and dry-field crops take over.
Population density is lower, and a larger proportion of the gross domestic
product (GDP) comes from primary economic activity (Figure 5.6), with the
proportion from secondary activity correspondingly lower (Figure 5.7).
Beizhen County, for example, has only two small joint-venture companies. It
would like to attract more investment, but location away from a railroad
hinders its efforts.

Region 5 is the sparsely populated frontier. Ignoring the mountain regions
to the east and west because of their lower suitability for agriculture, this
region in Liaoning is best represented by the far northwest along the border
of Inner Mongolia. Population density is low, especially by Chinese standards,
fields are large, and more extensive farming is apparent by the use of large-
scale machinery.

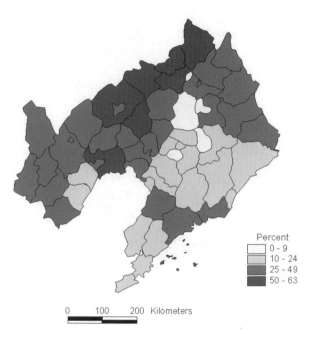

Percent
☐ 0 - 9
☐ 10 - 24
■ 25 - 49
■ 50 - 63

0   100   200 Kilometers

Figure 5.6 Primary production as proportion of GDP, Liaoning, 1994. Data source: Liaoning Statistical Bureau, 1995, and calculations by the author.

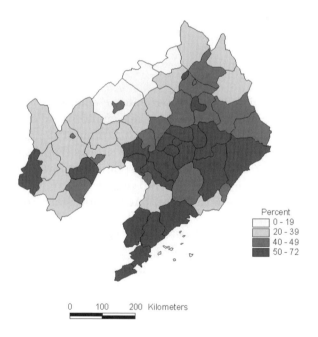

Percent
☐ 0 - 19
☐ 20 - 39
■ 40 - 49
■ 50 - 72

0   100   200 Kilometers

Figure 5.7 Secondary production as proportion of GDP, Liaoning, 1994. Data source: Liaoning Statistical Bureau, 1995, and calculations by the author.

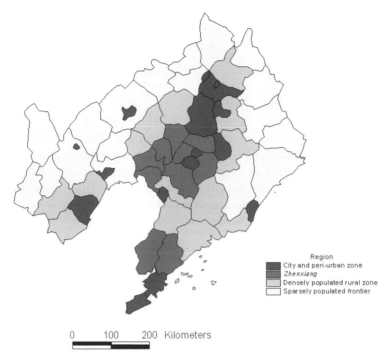

Region
- City and peri-urban zone
- *Zhenxiang*
- Densely populated rural zone
- Sparsely populated frontier

0   100   200 Kilometers

Figure 5.8   Application of McGee's Spatial Model to Liaoning.

In summary, south-central Liaoning Province fits McGee's (1989, 1991a) spatial *zhenxianghua* model of East Asian development and urbanization in a rice-growing region, despite a "gap" in the intensive development at the northern end of Liaodong Peninsula (Figure 5.8). The major cities and connecting transportation lines lie in the valley of the Liao and Hun rivers, surrounded by lands that are less developed, but still densely populated. Along the boundaries of the province are more sparsely populated lands, where agriculture is less intensive and very little industry has been established.

Liaoning, then, is a region with intensive agriculture, raising both rice and dry-field crops in the river-bottom lands of the region's center, and more extensive agriculture to the east and west, where rugged topography and lack of moisture pose limitations. Liaoning has a dominantly Han Chinese population. It was first industrialized by foreign powers and remains a base of heavy industry, concentrated in the agriculturally rich middle of the province. With a relatively dense population and excellent transportation, this part of the province has seen urban-type development in the countryside, as well as the cities, resulting in a rural-urban economic continuum.

Agricultural technology, especially irrigation and greenhouses, as well as transportation, have expanded greatly the variety of foods available under the Dengist reforms. The intensity of agricultural also has increased.

Food and Diet in Liaoning

As one of China's provinces, we can expect Liaoning to display similarities in food and diet to the national picture, but there are some differences. Liaoning is one of China's wealthier provinces: a long-standing base of heavy industry that today is attracting foreign investment and high-tech enterprises. Multiple cropping is limited, but agriculture is productive, especially because of irrigation and greenhouses.

Overall Consumption

As in all of China, urban consumption (a measure of living standards) is higher than rural consumption, today by a factor of nearly three (Figure 5.9). In the early 1950s, as socialism became established in China, the ratio of urban consumption to rural consumption fell (the two areas became more nearly

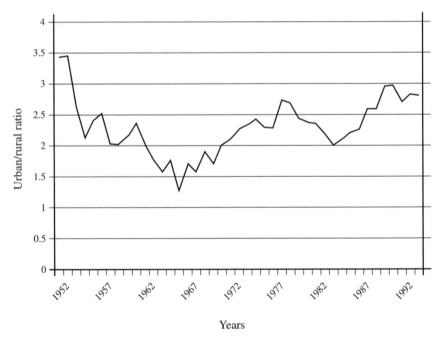

Figure 5.9   Ratio of urban consumption to rural consumption, Liaoning, 1952-94. Source: Liaoning Statistical Bureau, 1995: 116.

equal), then varied through the years of communization of the countryside, the Great Leap Forward, and the famine of the early 1960s. The ratio dropped again after the recovery following the famine, only to begin an irregular climb during the Cultural Revolution (1966–76), and then peak, just as the Dengist reforms were being announced in 1978.

The early years of reforms, under Deng Xiaoping, saw a steady drop in the urban-to-rural consumption ratio (the two areas became more equal again), at least until the earliest and easiest improvements in rural life were complete and reforms had begun in the cities. The low point came in 1984 with a rural-to-urban ratio of 2.03:1; then it started to climb again. Beginning in the early 1990s, there has been a slight decline; the ratio is not as high as it was when the Communists came to power, but, by this measure, urban living standards are clearly higher than rural life in Liaoning Province. Using 1952 as a base of 100, rural consumption in 1994 stood at 393.6, while urban consumption was 403.6 (*Liaoning Statistical Yearbook*, 1995). Rural consumption started from a much lower point (76 yuan compared with 262 yuan), so rural consumption would have to rise by more than urban consumption for the two levels to become equal.

Food Consumption Patterns

Since 1985, Engel's ratios (Figure 5.10), however, have shown a somewhat different pattern than the national one. First of all, there is no consistent downward trend, as would be expected with rising incomes, but, most strikingly until 1993, the urban Engel's ratio was higher than that for rural residents. The Engel's ratio in urban areas fluctuated around 50% of per capita income; a steady decline began in 1990 that reached 43% in 1993 and rose again to 46% in 1994.

Meanwhile, in the countryside, the middle to late 1980s saw a steady decline in the Engel's ratio, from 42.7% of per capita net income in 1985 to 38.9% in 1988. In 1989, following the national trend, it rose markedly to almost 44%, and then, except for 1992, has continued to climb, surpassing the urban ratio in 1993. In 1994 it reached 50.6% before declining.

Across income groups in urban areas, the general pattern is what Engel's Law predicts: the higher the income, the lower the percentage that goes for food (Figure 5.11). The highest ratio, however, is not the poorest 5% of the population, but the next higher 5%. The very poorest group is not receiving enough income to feed itself adequately, so any additional income must be used to purchase food in order to obtain any semblance of an adequate diet. This, of course, assumes that the added expenditure is not contributing just to overeating, but that would be unlikely in the poorest segment of the population. Each higher-earning group, then, displays a lower Engel's ratio, especially the highest tenth.

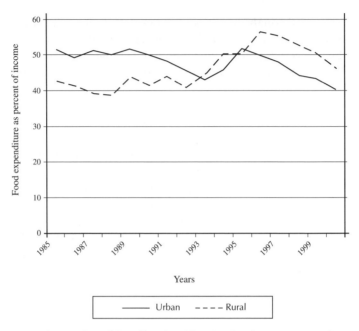

Figure 5.10 Urban and rural Engel's ratios, Liaoning Province, 1985-94. Source: Liaoning Statistical Yearbooks, and calculations by the author.

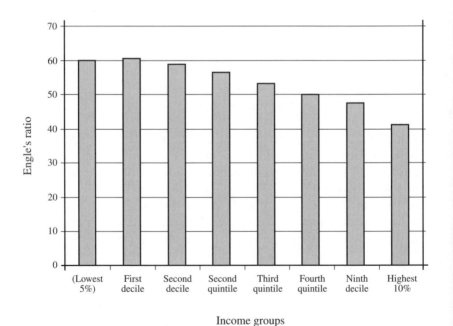

Figure 5.11 Engel's ratios by income group, urban areas, Liaoning, 1994. Source: Liaoning Statistical Bureau, 1995: 121, and calculations by the author.

Dietary Composition

One reason why the Engel's ratio for urban residents resisted falling in the early 1980s, as happened in the country as a whole, has to do with the kinds of foods people were eating (Figure 5.12). The Dengist reforms of those years, by freeing farmers to grow what they perceived would bring the greatest rewards, and by re-establishing markets in which to sell their produce to the public, greatly increased the quantity and variety of food available. The consumption of grain (Figure 5.12a), however, contrary to Bennett's Law, remained almost steady through those years. People were continuing to eat the same amount of grain but were adding other foods to their diet, indicating that the amount available before the reforms had been inadequate. Through the early 1980s, people ate fewer vegetables, but consumption of most other foods (Figure 5.12b) climbed rapidly. People's diets became more varied — and more nutritious. For example, at the end of the Cultural Revolution, diets were seriously short of fat (the ration was only 1.5 kg per person per month), and consumption of oil rose fairly steadily until 1988. Consumption of pork was already substantial in cities, and it even dropped off a bit, to be replaced by poultry, beef, mutton, and eggs. The rise in egg consumption is especially notable; the end of the Maoist restrictions on what farmers could produce led to a rapid rise in the raising of chickens.

All of these meat items, as Figure 5.12a shows, were replacing vegetables in the *cai* portion of meals. In the early 1990s consumption of fresh vegetables dropped, as other foods became available. The statistics do not specify, but probably one vegetable to lose popularity was cabbage, as has been documented in more recent years. Consumption of liquor, a luxury item, climbed significantly. Sugar consumption, however, actually declined slightly because Calories could be obtained from other foods; it has remained flat ever since, reflecting the general Chinese indifference to sugar.

In the late 1980s, some adjustments took place in the *cai* portion of meals, and consumption of grain moved slightly upward. As in the simultaneous rise in the Engel's ratio, this is not supposed to happen with rising incomes! The answer, again, seems to lie in the rapid increase in the prices of food during the late 1980s (Table 5.4). For that period, only the provincial average price indexes are available; from 1990, they are available for urban and rural residents separately. In any case, in 1988, the rise in the cost of food was greater than the rise in per capita incomes, reducing the purchasing power. Families initially economized by consuming less pork, beef, and mutton, and more eggs and vegetables, which are less expensive. Poultry held steady, but very little of that had been eaten prior to that. Then, in 1989, such economies already had been squeezed out of the budget, and more money was allocated to food; the Engel's ratio rose, despite reductions in such expensive items as beef and mutton, as well as oil. (Use of more meat decreases the need for oil because

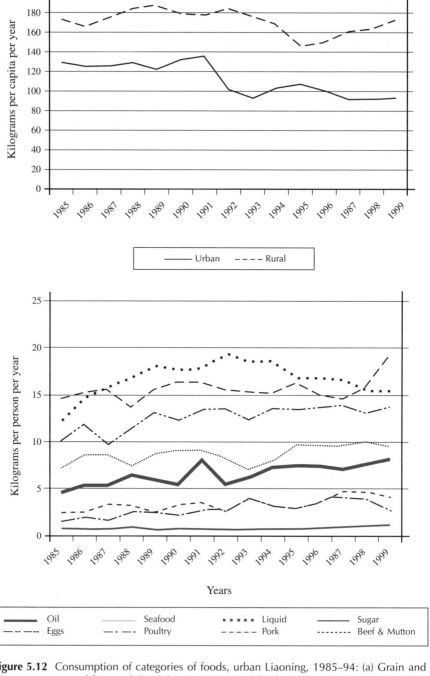

Figure 5.12 Consumption of categories of foods, urban Liaoning, 1985–94: (a) Grain and vegetables, and (b) Other categories of foods. Source: Liaoning Statistical Yearbooks.

of meat's fat content, especially because meat in China is not trimmed.) Vegetable consumption also climbed, replacing some of the more expensive items in the food basket. Liquor, interestingly, continued to increase in popularity. Urban per capita incomes kept pace with food inflation, but consumption statistics show that families made some changes in their menus.

In 1990, in Liaoning, as in China as a whole, the government took steps to control rising prices. Details of these measures are outside the scope of this book, but the important point here is that inflation slowed, rising only 2% for food over all in urban areas. Grain prices actually declined. Taking advantage of such a bargain, families ate a little more grain, and their consumption of pork and seafood rose again. Use of more pork could replace some of the cooking oil, which then declined. Consumption of vegetables also declined, now replaced by other ingredients in *cai*.

The next period of rapid price increases came in 1993 to 1994. In general, food inflation, was over 9% in 1992, 16% in 1993, and almost 30% in 1994; in those same years, grain rose between about 30% and almost 50% (Table 5.4). In 1992 and 1993, with per capita incomes more than keeping up with the rise in prices, the Engel's ratio declined (Figure 5.10), as did the consumption of grain. In fact, the sharpest decline in per capita grain consumption was in 1991 and 1992. People were eating fewer vegetables, and, except for liquor and eggs, less of almost everything else. Consumption of eggs held steady, and oil, after a spike in 1991, returned to its previous level.

Table 5.4. Indexes of increases in incomes and prices, Liaoning,
1985–1994 (prior year = 100)

Year	Urban			Rural		
	Income	Food prices	Grain prices	Income	Food prices	Grain prices
1985	na	116.3*	103.5*	na	116.3*	103.5*
1986	125.0	107.9*	104.7*	109.8	107.9*	104.7*
1987	112.4	111.2*	105.9*	112.4	111.2*	105.9*
1988	121.2	120.6*	109.9*	116.7	120.6*	109.9*
1989	117.8	116.2*	119.6*	105.8	116.2*	119.6*
1990	109.3	102.0	93.8	104.9	101.1	89.2
1991	110.0	105.6	na	115.5	99.6	na
1992	113.4	109.4	143.2	111.0	101.7	97.5
1993	118.7	116.2	129.1	116.7	107.9	108.9
1994	132.3	129.7	146.5	122.6	129.7	147.4

Notes: na = data not available
* figures for province as a whole
Source: Liaoning Statistical Bureau, *Liaoning Tongji Nianjian 1991, 1993* to *1995* (*Liaoning Statistical Yearbook 1991, 1993* to *1995*) (Beijing: Statistical Publishing House, 1991, 1993-1995), and calculations by the author.

In 1994, overall food prices continued to rise at a slower pace than per capita incomes, but grain prices rose faster. Engel's ratio rose, fueled by that price rise, as well as by greater consumption of other foods. Grain, after all, is not as large a component of urban diets as it is of those in rural areas, but, in 1994, urban people did increase their consumption of grain, as everything else also had become more expensive (the Giffen effect). They ate fewer vegetables, about the same amount of pork, more eggs, more seafood, and more oil. Beef and mutton consumption declined; liquor, which had declined in 1992 from 1991, remained almost the same. Thus, as prices rose in general, people did sacrifice dietary quality to the extent of eating more grain, but the rapid rise in the price of that commodity meant that their overall food bill, as a proportion of income, still went up. Engel did not take rampant inflation into account in his "law," nor did Bennett.

Across income groups in urban areas (Figure 5.13), the pattern of consumption is somewhat uneven. Consumption of grain does not follow Bennett's Law exactly: the medium-low income group, not the lowest group, actually has the highest consumption. Furthermore, the high-income group has a higher consumption than the two groups below it. Reasons for this pattern are unclear, but may have to do with the dietary preferences of the people surveyed. Similarly, the consumption of vegetables rises with income until the highest 10% group, whose consumption is lower than the group

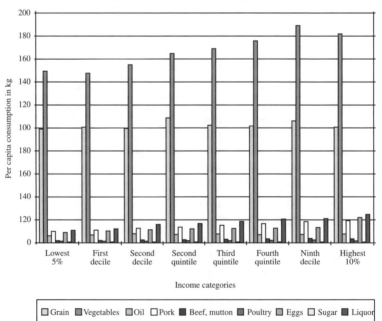

Figure 5.13 Consumption of categories of foods by income group, urban residents, Liaoning, 1994. Source: Liaoning Statistical Bureau, 1995: 123.

below it. To some extent, this marks the shift to other foods in the *cai* portion of meals; the increase in the use of eggs should be noted especially.

Contrary to China as a whole, the Engel's ratio for rural areas in Liaoning (Figure 5.10) was *lower* than that for urban areas until 1993. It had begun to decline slightly between 1985 and 1988, when the effect of the Dengist reforms was greatest; in 1988, the trend turned upward, despite rising incomes.

In line with Bennett's Law, grain consumption began to decline with the Dengist reforms, and the consumption of everything else rose, including vegetables (Figure 5.14). (Consumption of sugar remained about the same.) The increases then leveled off, and, with the high inflation rates of the late 1980s, consumption declined. Significantly, grain consumption rose again in those years (Figure 5.14a), and the rapid rise in its price — well above the rise in incomes — drove the Engel's ratio upward. Grain prices declined in the countryside in 1990, even more than they did in the cities; in general, food prices rose less than incomes, but the Engel's ratio stayed even, as consumption of grain rose and other foods remained the same. People evidently felt they had not been getting enough grain in the inflationary years and now took advantage of lower prices to eat their fill. In 1991 and 1992, they reduced their intake of grain and ate more of other foods, especially meat (Figure 5.14b).

In 1994, inflation in food prices, particularly grain prices, outpaced the rise in incomes. Meat consumption declined; oil consumption increased again, following a drop in 1993, as did other protein foods and vegetables. The consumption of grain also increased, despite a rise in price of nearly 50%, (the Giffen effect again), as everything else was even more expensive. The Engel's ratio took another step upward. Furthermore, the proportion of grain that is considered fine grain (rice and wheat) had risen dramatically in the early years of the Dengist reforms and had continued to climb, although more slowly, since 1985 (Figure 5.15). In 1993 and 1994, it declined, reflecting consumption of more poor, coarse grains (millet, corn, and sorghum) — an economy measure and a reduction in the quality of the diet.

People in Liaoning, as in all of China, show a marked difference in dietary composition between those in the city and those in the countryside (Figure 5.16). Rural Liaoning residents eat almost three times as much grain per capita per year as urban residents; unlike Chinese in general, they also eat more vegetables. Urban people in Liaoning, as all urban Chinese, however, eat more oil, meat, eggs, seafood, liquor, and sugar. In general, they exhibit Bennett's Law: those with higher incomes eat less grain. Rapid inflation in the price of food, specifically grain, however, has produced examples of the Giffen effect: it has driven people to consume more grain because everything else is so much more expensive. Even so, in inflation-driven violation of Engel's Law, the proportion of income that goes for food has risen because of high prices, despite higher incomes.

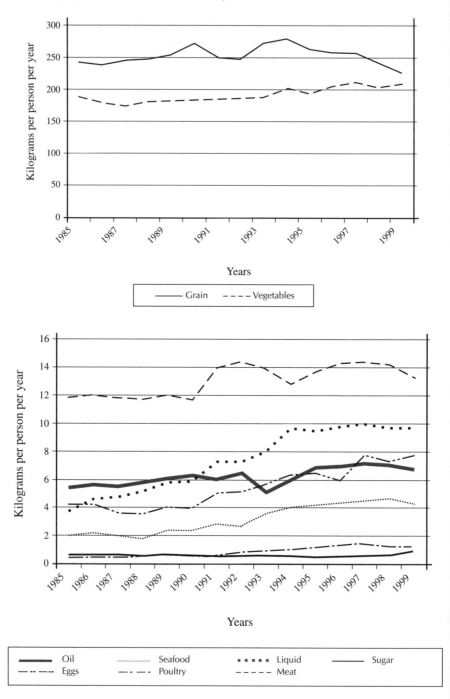

Figure 5.14 Consumption of categories of foods, rural Liaoning, 1978-94: (a) Grain and vegetables; and (b) Other foods. Source: Liaoning Statistical Yearbooks.

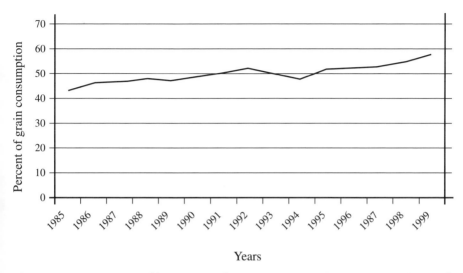

Years

Figure 5.15 Consumption of fine grain, rural Liaoning, 1978-94. Source: Liaoning Statistical Yearbooks, and calculations by the author.

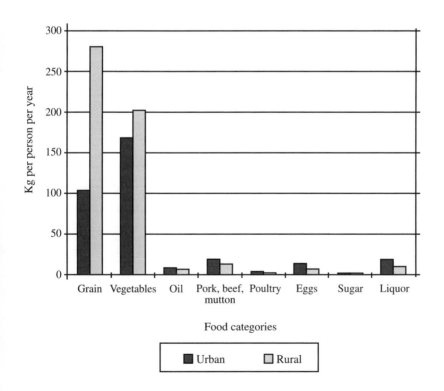

Food categories

■ Urban   □ Rural

Figure 5.16 Urban and rural consumption of categories of food, Liaoning, 1994. Source: Liaoning Statistical Yearbook, 1995.

6

Meals in the Households of Liaoning

As we have seen, on the national and provincial scale, China indeed displays a rural/urban contrast in economic aspects of diet. But what do Chinese people really eat? What is Chinese food like in China? Are Chinese tastes really changing in line with the preferred foods among better-off citizens? For that information, we must look at food and nutrition at a very local scale by asking the people themselves. The sample of individual households from whom this information came represents places of varying economic development and urbanization levels, as Terry McGee (1989, 1991a) described in his model. Thus, these households represent not just a rural/urban divide, but several levels of economic development and urbanization within the rural areas. In the McGee model, which is based on economic factors, these different kinds of regions form a continuum between the city and the least developed, sparsely populated frontier. Does this continuum also apply to food, nutrition, and foodways?

In the first section, we look at the task of collecting the data set itself. The second section uses this information to examine the intake of a selection of nutrients, and, the third section, to see variations in the specific foods that households choose to eat. An examination of the cultural trait of assigned eating-related tasks follows, and the chapter concludes with a summary of dietary regimes.

The Field Study

Fieldwork with individual households was the only way to see what Chinese people really eat on a day-to-day basis (Quandt, 1987; Wan, 1996; Zhai, 1996). Throughout China, the individual household is the unit of food consumption, and since the reforms that began in 1978, it is the unit of production as well. The household is also the unit of dietary decision making at several levels:

what to grow, what to buy, and what to cook for any given meal. Furthermore, on-site visits to the people and their homes offered an invaluable dimension in understanding their lives and culture, which have a great impact on their foodways (Quandt, 1987; Wilson, 1977). The field survey was designed to gather information on specific choices of foods for individual meals and snacks. It consisted of interviews to collect general information about the family and its situation (Wilson, 1977: 64) and food diaries (Quandt, 1987; Wilson, 1977) in which a member of the household recorded what foods were eaten at each meal over a specific time period.

The Choice of Liaoning

To measure the degree of cultural change, as reflected in foodways that are related to economic development in China, requires information about an area that has undergone this process, at least in some places. Liaoning Province was among the first parts of China to be industrialized, although the building of industry was the work of foreigners (Chapter 5). It formed a major base of heavy industry for the People's Republic. More recently, under the Dengist reforms, it has benefited from its coastal location in attracting investment both from China and abroad. Consequently, McGee (1991a) found south-central Liaoning to be an example of *desakotadesasi* (*zhenxianghua*) development, and Zhou (1991) cited it as an interlocking metropolitan region.

The Choices of Research Sites

Research sites specifically were chosen to illustrate the types of regions in McGee's (1989, 1991a) *zhenxiang* model of development and urbanization in East Asia. If, indeed, there exists a rural-urban cultural continuum, there should be distinct differences in nutritional levels and food choices in the various areas of this spatial model.

Based on maps of social and economic indicators (Chapter 5), an administrative unit was chosen to represent each of the types of regions in McGee's *zhenxianghua* spatial model. The following places were included (Figure 6.1).

Region 1, Shenyang, a large, pre-existing city.

Region 2, peri-urban zones. The suburban districts around Shenyang met the criteria of a location within a convenient commuting distance of the city and with economic ties to it.

Region 3, the *zhenxianghua* region. Dengta County, on the main rail line and superhighway between Shenyang and Dalian, displays the dense rural population and mixed land use characteristics of this type of region.

Population density is 368 persons per km² (Figure 5.3), and only 15% of the population is officially non-agricultural (Figure 5.4). Yet, primary activities contribute only 22% of the gross domestic product (GDP) (Figure 5.6); the secondary sector contributes 55% (Figure 5.7). The per capita national income of 4,850 yuan reflects the growth of manufacturing and the shift of the labor force into the area(Figure 5.5).

Region 4, the densely populated rural region. Beizhen County has highways, but no rail transportation and is outside the main rice-growing area. Population density is less than 300 per km² (Figure 5.3), reflecting the dominance of grain crops other than rice, and the non-agricultural population is 18% (Figure 5.4). Primary activities contribute 55% of GDP (Figure 5.6) and secondary activities only 25% (Figure 5.7).

Region 5, the sparsely populated frontier. The counties in northern Liaoning that border Inner Mongolia display similar economic and social characteristics: population density (Figure 5.3) is low, there are fewer than 150 persons per km², and the non-agricultural population (Figure 5.4) comprises less than 20% of the total. Primary production (Figure 5.6) contributes more than 60% of the GDP, while secondary production (Figure 5.7) contributes less than 20%. National income per capita (Figure 5.5) is less than 2,000 yuan. Of these counties, Kangping was chosen for this study because its government was under the jurisdiction of the city of Shenyang, which eased the logistics of arranging fieldwork.

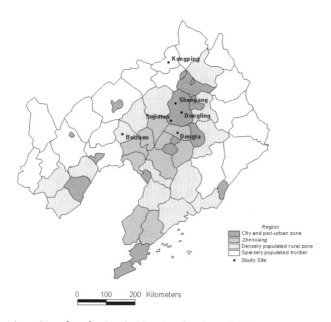

Figure 6.1 Location of study sites in Liaoning Province, 1994.

In order to give each household in all of the regions a theoretically equal chance to be included, the sample was weighted according to the proportion of the total population that the administrative area represented. The number of families by region is shown in Table 6.1.

Table 6.1. Sample size by region

McGee Model	Liaoning Example	Population (1993)		Number of Families in Sample
		Number	Percent	
1. Major city	Shenyang	3,139,335	50	125
2. Peri-urban	Shenyang suburbs	1,469,260	26	65
3. *Zhenxiang*	Dengta County	493,159	9	2
4. Densely populated rural	Beizhen County	529,967	9	23
5. Sparsely populated rural	Kangping County	319,944	6	15
TOTALS		5,663,715	100	250

In Shenyang (Region 1), families were recruited by colleagues and their friends, relatives, and acquaintances. These people, in turn, asked colleagues in their work units to participate. By specific request, a portion of the sample consisted of workers in the state-owned factories that are such an important base to Shenyang's economy.

In the non-city regions, contact with local officials was made through the Shenyang Foreign Affairs Office and its provincial counterpart; these officials selected the specific villages and families. A cross-section of varying economic and family situations was requested, with the stipulation that at least one member of each family had to be literate in order to complete a food diary.

In the Shenyang suburbs (Region 2), families were drawn from two districts. In Sujiatun, they lived in Bayizhen (August 1 Township, formerly August 1 Commune. August 1 is the anniversary of the founding of the People's Liberation Army), which recently has shifted from dry-field farming to paddy rice (Hsu and Hsu, 1977: 312) and, according to its vice-mayor, produces the best rice in China. It is about 24 kilometers from Shenyang.

In the other suburban district of Shenyang, Dongling, Xiashen was the village that was chosen. It is a model village about an hour by bicycle from Shenyang. Its agricultural products include rice, vegetables, and livestock. It also has small factories; one packs chickens, and another makes fishhooks. Because it is a model village, it has an agricultural extension service office. A new middle (high) school was built in 1994, and the village is very proud of the fact that all its roads are paved.

In Dengta County (Region 3), families were drawn from two villages:

Lüfangshi and Pangoucun. They represented the mixture of economic activities that McGee (1989, 1991a) described for such a region. A few families from the county town of Dengta also participated.

The village of Hewacun in Beizhen County, representing region 4, is close to the county town, at the base of Lü Shan Scenic Area. Virtually all of the villagers operate restaurants to serve the tourists who, following the example of several Qing emperors, come to climb Lü Shan. The other village in that county, Xiaguan in Changxing Township, is south of the county town, about 45 minutes by car, off the main highway over incredibly bumpy, rutted roads. It specializes in raising fruit, especially apples, pears, and grapes. Thus, both villages in Beizhen County, while outside the area where the combination of paddy rice agriculture and good transportation have spurred industrial development, were involved in commercial activities that served the urban market: tourism and specialty agriculture. Beizhen County is a Manchu Autonomous County, although the Manchu people now are assimilated thoroughly into Chinese culture, and no one speaks the Manchu language anymore (Li Fuquan, 1994).

In Kangping County, representing region 5, is Liangjiazi village, in the township of the same name. It is an hour's drive north of Kangping town. Once a commune headquarters, it still has the storage buildings that had been constructed at that time. Its streets are unpaved, pigs have the run of the village, and fields are devoted to dry-field crops, including corn, millet, and sorghum. Even a jeep cannot reach the more distant fields. What little manufacturing there is involves processing wood from nearby forests. Xiuliwohao and Daolantaohai villages in Shengli ("Victory") Township are geographically closer to the county town, but their economic life is similar. Even among three villages, it was difficult to find 15 families in which at least one member was literate. The national "Hope" project, which funds education for poor children, is active in Kangping County, in an effort to raise the educational level of the population.

The process of gathering data from all of these households involved two phases: an interview with a questionnaire and the recording in food diaries. The information in each part complemented each other. The questions in the questionnaire were designed to provide background information about the family and its food habits, which could then be used along with the data about daily meals and menus in the diaries. Two versions were prepared: one for holders of urban household registration and one for holders of rural household registration. Because of differences in the sources of food for families in the two categories, certain questions varied, for example, those regarding fields, vegetable gardens, and self-produced versus purchased foods. The two versions (with English translations) are in Appendix B. Each family received the food diary forms that included a cover sheet and pages for fourteen days of recording.

Pretesting

Families of a class of thermal engineering students from the Liaoning Branch of Northeastern University in Shenyang provided the population for pretesting the questionnaires and food diaries. The Branch University is comprised of students who pay their own fees because their scores on the university entrance examination are not sufficient to win them scholarships. Although they are in separate classes and live in separate dormitories, they study the same course as other students. They all are from Liaoning Province, but their family situations are quite varied, and they come from all parts of the province. Taking me home on weekends, they served as interpreters, which gave them valuable practice in English (part of their curriculum). Students in China regard taking a foreign teacher home to be a great privilege. They also got a free trip home, a good meal, and a visit with their families. Their parents had an opportunity to see that the money being spent on their education was worthwhile. The responses of this group of households are not included in the statistical tabulations, but some of the descriptive material is used.

Main Data Collection

Data collection for the study itself began in the spring. Late winter and spring in an agricultural society are the low-food seasons, in terms of both quantity and variety of foods available. Visits were made to each of the five areas. In rural areas, each family was interviewed in Mandarin Chinese at home. Accompanying me was a student research assistant, a graduating senior in geology whose advanced computer skills exempted him from class work for the semester, so that he was free to travel. In each of the regions, we were accompanied in the field by assorted local cadres, who chose the families to be included and, occasionally, did some of the interviewing. Heads of household also were permitted to write the answers to the questions directly on the questionnaires, if they preferred. Each family then was provided with a food diary and detailed instructions about the kind of information to be recorded, together with a stamped, self-addressed envelope to return it to me.

During the early summer of 1994, above-average rainfall (Table 5.1) produced flooding in the Liao River valley, as well as in other farming regions of China. Liaozhong, Tai'an, Panshan, and Dawa counties, in the heavily rice-growing region of the lower Liao and Hun river valleys, were the hardest hit in Liaoning's worst flood in 30 years (Jiang, 1994).

Coupled with the end of rationing and accompanying price controls, the flood-caused reduction in food supplies aggravated an already serious inflation in the cost of food. In September, the Liaoning Provincial Government, in order to provide some relief from price increases, re-opened state grain shops that had been closed for more than a year. The government provided grain from its stores, and private grain trading was prohibited (*China Daily*, September 20, 1994). Urban households were issued coupons entitling them to purchase a certain quantity of rice and cooking oil at controlled prices. While the amounts were insufficient to provide all of a family's needs (Wu, 1994), being able to buy a portion of the groceries at controlled prices helped the families' budgets. The measures were deemed effective in controlling prices (*China Daily*, September 20, 1994).

In the fall of 1994, in order to gather data for foods consumed during harvest time when quantity and variety would be at their height, a fresh set of diaries was distributed to the same households who had participated in the spring. The interviews, of course, were not repeated. Again, stamped, addressed envelopes were provided to return the diaries. The response in the fall was much lower. Apparently, the first time around, people thought that being part of the foreigner's research was a real status symbol. The second time, it was just tedious work. Especially in the countryside, what is eaten may depend greatly on what is available, and available foods are subject to variation, depending on the time in the agricultural cycle. Consequently, it was not possible to ask those families, who initially had not returned diaries, to complete them at a later time.

Resulting Data

As must be expected, families varied in the care and attention they gave to completing diaries. Furthermore, the keeping of such records focuses unusual attention on foods eaten and can have the effect of skewing choices to items that are easy to remember and to record (Wilson, 1977: 64). For this reason, the interview questionnaire asked what the family had eaten the day before; comparison with the content of the diaries gave assurance that the diaries reflected a realistic sample of family menus. Thus, the basic data are generally thought to be consistent and reliable; the main variation was in the amount of detail.

Economically, these families, especially the rural ones, are probably somewhat better off than the average. No per capita income statistics are available for any unit smaller than the province as a whole, so no statistical test of this comparison was possible. This conclusion, thus, flows from observation and from certain realities of doing field research in China (Morgan, 2000).

Although food choices themselves are not a political issue, levels of nutrition and diet are because they measure economic well-being. China is very proud (and rightly so) of the progress that the Dengist reforms have brought about and the rising living standards that have resulted; the Chinese are sensitive to possible reports to the contrary. Officials in Beizhen County expressed concern about bringing the study to their county: "If the American doctor goes back to America and says that the food in Beizhen is good, that's nice. But if she goes back and says it's awful, we all lose face." When it was pointed out that my coming to Beizhen County was in line with the Opening to the World policy, the apprehension disappeared. Nevertheless, the villages that the local officials chose to be included had developed high-value specialities — tourist restaurants and fruit-growing.

Similarly, the inclusion of a model village in the suburban district would tend to raise the level of economic well-being above the average. In Kangping County, the necessity that at least one member of each household be literate (in order to keep the food diary) made a number of potential participants ineligible, and they were probably among the least prosperous. For purposes of this study, however, a sample that excludes the poorest stratum of society can still provide important results. Because it examines cultural change, which is more likely to occur first in the upper classes, their adoption or non-adoption of change is telling.

Nutrition Levels

Because the spring data collection was more successful than the autumn collection, the spring diaries will be used for the basic analysis, and the fall diaries will be examined for seasonal variations.

Food Energy

The most basic measure of adequacy of food intake is the amount of energy that the food provides, measured in kilocalories, or Calories with a capital "C." Chinese nutritionists recommend a higher level of Calorie intake than do authorities in the United States, in part, to sustain higher activity levels. Most Chinese, especially workers and farmers, still do heavy manual labor, and almost everyone travels by bicycle. Early morning and mid-morning exercise is an ongoing tradition, augmented today by aerobics. The U.S. recommendation (National Research Council, 1989: 33) is 2,900 Calories per day for an adult male under age 50 and 2,300 thereafter; for females, the recommendation is 2,200 under age 50 and 1,900 thereafter. The corresponding Chinese recommendations (Chinese Academy of Preventive Medicine, 1991: 130) further subdivide by activity level. An adult male under age 45 should consume 2,400 Calories per day for very light work, 2,600 for light work, 3,000 for moderate work, 3,400 for heavy work, and 4,000 for very heavy work. For females, the recommendations are 2,100 for very light work,

2,300 for light work, 2,700 for moderate work, and 3,000 for heavy work. Recommended minimums drop at age 45, and again at age 60 and age 70, for both men and women. Not only must China provide food for a huge population, it also must provide high caloric intake per person to sustain the hard physical labor that most workers need to perform.

The difference in Calorie consumption between residents of the city of Shenyang and rural areas in the study is striking (Table 6.2). While Shenyang residents consumed, on average, one-third more Calories than the recommended minimum, all rural areas show less than 100%. The deficit however, is small; only in the suburban districts is it greater than 10%. The data, thus, confirm the published reports that, on average, Chinese consume sufficient Calories. The rural/urban divide in the amounts consumed, however, remains: city residents are better fed than rural residents.

Table 6.2. **Mean daily Calorie consumption**

Region	Mean daily Calories (percent of recommendation)
1. Shenyang	133.10
2. Suburbs	81.68
3. Dengta County	99.93
4. Beizhen County	97.62
5. Kangping County	94.29

Source: Field data.

Protein

Because protein is such an important "building block" for the body, adequate amounts of this nutrient are vital to good health and the growth and development of children. The most efficient source of protein is animal foods because they contain all nine essential amino acids, but combined plant foods, especially grains, also can supply adequate protein, if chosen with care and eaten in sufficient amounts. The Chinese diet traditionally contains little meat and less dairy food; protein has come from the combination of grain (rice or wheat) and soybean products, especially the various forms of tofu.

Among the regions in this study, Beizhen and Kangping counties, the least urbanized and developed areas, show the highest protein consumption. The sample of returned diaries from Beizhen was too small to be very reliable, but visits revealed elements in the economic activities of the families that would increase their consumption of animal foods. In one village, the families operated restaurants that served visitors to a nearby scenic attraction (Mount

Lü), giving them access to a wider variety of foods and more luxury foods. In the other village, families included the commercial raising of pigs and chickens as part of their farming activities.

Similarly, Kangping County is in the far north of the province and borders Inner Mongolia. With insufficient water for paddy rice growing, dry farming with large fields is the norm, and more land is available for grazing animals. The tradition of animal raising is also stronger in this borderland of the Mongolian grasslands.

On the other hand, the Shenyang suburbs, and even more markedly Dengta, are dominantly rice-growing. While a few animals are pastured on wasteland under highway overpasses and on the islands in rivers, and dairying is found in the suburban districts, raising large animals for meat is neither the tradition nor the most economical use of valuable land.

Data from the food diaries on the frequency of consumption of the various animal foods supports these conclusions. In the spring, all families in Shenyang (Table 6.3) reported eating meat at least once in the two weeks they kept their diaries; they averaged 20 servings of meat during those 14 days, or 49% of all meals (some meals were meatless, and other meals included more than one meat dish). All rural areas, except Beizhen from which the sample is too small to be reliable, showed less meat consumption, although the number of families that ate no meat at all is small. The average number of servings, however, declines in rural areas, especially in Dengta.

Table 6.3. Meat consumption

(a) Spring

Region	Households reporting meat		Frequency	
	Number	Percent	Average number of servings	Percent of meals
1. Shenyang	62	100.0	20.4	49.0
2. Suburbs	32	97.0	13.5	32.0
3. Dengta	18	94.7	9.2	22.0
4. Beizhen	7	100.0	17.7	42.0
5. Kangping	13	92.9	11.2	27.0

(b) Fall

1. Shenyang	23	100.0	26.5	41.0
2. Suburbs	23	100.0	14.7	37.3
3. Dengta	20	90.9	4.6	11.0
5. Kangping	14	100.0	13.4	31.9

Source (a) & (b): Field data.

Egg consumption is also very common, reaching 100% of families in the small sample from Beizhen, where the daughters in one household proudly showed me a huge chicken house. The average number of servings of eggs, however, peaks in the suburbs, with 9.5 in a two-week period; one family reported that most of its eggs come from ducks, which they raised. Dengta was the second consumer of eggs, in terms of number of servings. In both areas, small animals, such as chickens, are easier to keep than large meat-producing animals because they require less land. Chickens are also scavengers, so that in the suburban districts and Dengta they consume little of the field crop. Those in Beizhen, where rice is not grown, mostly are fed locally grown corn.

Milk has more consumers in the city of Shenyang, with 75% of families drinking it at least once, most often for breakfast. The numbers of families in rural areas that consume milk are much lower; only two families in Dengta (10%) and Beizhen (29%) drank it. The number rises to four (29%) in Kangping, where, as mentioned, the keeping of large animals and the consumption of dairy products has a slightly stronger tradition because of the nearby Mongolian grasslands. Kangping also had the only household to report the drinking of yogurt, although that form of milk is widely available on city streets in China. Kangping families appear to enjoy yogurt, consuming it ten times in the spring and six times in the fall. Because it is often drunk as a snack, more Shenyang families may have consumed it than reported it.

Although the number of families in the suburbs who drank milk is less than one-quarter as great as in Shenyang, those who were milk-drinkers drank it more often: almost ten servings in the suburbs versus only five in the city. This may reflect the presence of dairy cows in the suburbs, where people drank some of their own cows' production. In suburban districts, dairying supplies the milk-drinkers in the nearby city, but, in other rural districts with no tradition of large grazing animals or milk consumption, milk is little used.

The problem of obtaining sufficient protein for good health, as defined by Chinese nutritionists, persists for Chinese who follow the traditional diet. As consumption of meat, eggs, and dairy products continues to increase, at least in cities, protein consumption probably will reach more satisfactory levels. However, because meat is expensive, pockets of protein deficiency will remain a problem in times of rapid price rises and income disparities.

Another measure of dietary quality in the Chinese diet is the ratio of carbohydrates (primarily derived from grain and starches) to fats (primarily derived from animal products and cooking oil). In stir-frying, oil is used very sparingly. Although meat is sold untrimmed and only whole milk is available, these foods comprise such a small proportion of the diet that the amount of fat they contribute is small. Most Chinese eat very little fat; lack of body fat storage may have been one reason why the protesting students in Tiananmen Square in Beijing in 1989 fainted so quickly when they went on a hunger strike.

Because urban residents consume more meat and milk, and, consequently, rely less on grain than rural residents, the ratio of carbohydrates to fat would be expected to be lower. In Shenyang, it is 3.38; in the suburbs, 4.06; in Dengta, 6.76; and in Kangping, 7.59. (The small sample from Beizhen shows 2.84.) Both sides of the equation contribute: throughout the regions, Calories from carbohydrates rise, while Calories from fat drop. These findings agree with the published statistical data for China and Liaoning, showing much higher grain consumption and lower meat consumption in rural areas than in cities (Chapter 5).

Calcium is vital to healthy teeth and bones; the richest sources of calcium are dairy foods, but tofu and green vegetables also contain this mineral. Although a diet that is low in protein requires less calcium, the traditional lack of calcium in the Chinese diet shows in the poor quality of many people's teeth and the stooped posture (from osteoporosis) of the elderly, especially women. In none of the regions surveyed did people consume anywhere near the recommended amount of calcium; the closest was 65% in Shenyang, where milk drinking is more common. (The small sample in Beizhen recorded 66%.) It was less than 50% elsewhere. This issue will become more important as life spans in China increase and people live long enough to suffer the effects of insufficient calcium in the diet.

Vitamins

Vegetables and fruits are the main sources of Vitamin A and Vitamin C, respectively. Green vegetables and tomatoes (botanically, a fruit) also contain Vitamin C. In the city of Shenyang, as meat replaces vegetables in the *cai* portion of meals, Vitamin A consumption suffers. Families, on average, consumed only 85% of the recommended amount. The suburban families, many of whom grow vegetables for the urban market but yet do not eat much meat, enjoy healthy quantities of Vitamin A, consuming just over the minimum recommendation (102%). (Vitamin A is fat-soluble, so over-consumption is not recommended.) In Dengta and Kangping, where some families eat very little *cai*, Vitamin A consumption is deficient, averaging 77% and 74%, respectively. The small sample in Beizhen recorded 95% of the recommended amount.

Fruit, the best source of Vitamin C, traditionally is a luxury in China, and it remains comparatively expensive; however, tomatoes are a very common vegetable. Consumption of Vitamin C is more than adequate everywhere, reaching 273% of the minimum recommendation in Shenyang. (Vitamin C is water soluble, so over-consumption is not a threat.) In rural areas, it ranges from 221% in the suburbs to 190% in Dengta, 185% in Beizhen (where one village specializes in fruit growing), and 112% in Kangping.

Food Variety

Nutritionists' first recommendation for adequate nutrient consumption is to eat a variety of foods. Because a greater variety is available in a market than any one farmer can possibly grow, city residents, who purchase their food, eat more of these different foods than rural residents, who grow their own. Furthermore, urban markets have more variety than rural markets because they can draw on more sources of supply and serve a larger clientele. While the statistical correlation between the percentage of food that is self-produced and the number of different foods reported is not statistically significant, urban residents do eat a more varied diet than rural residents (Table 6.4). Urban residents also enjoy higher incomes, although the correlation between per capita income and number of foods reported is not statistically significant.

Table 6.4. Mean number of different foods, Spring

Region	Mean number of foods
1. Shenyang	38.52
2. Suburbs	32.38
3. Dengta County	26.32
4. Beizhen County	28.14
5. Kangping County	26.36

Source: Field data.

Seasonal Variation in Nutrition Levels

In a subsistence agricultural society, the quantity and variety of food available is greatest at harvest time and least available in late winter, just before the new growing season begins. Consequently, nutritional levels would be expected to rise in the fall and decline in the early spring. This variation would be greatest in the countryside, where households depend more on their own production, than in the city, where markets are supplied from a much broader geographical region. With increasing use of greenhouses to supply winter vegetables, and more and better transportation of foods from elsewhere, the days are long gone when Shenyang subsisted on nothing but cabbage all winter.

Because fewer households completed and returned diaries in the fall than in the spring, and because many diaries were written less carefully, the fall-season sample is smaller and less reliable than that from the spring. No families in Beizhen County returned diaries in the fall. Nevertheless, the evidence shows seasonal variations for only a few nutrients. For some nutrients, probably because of poor record-keeping, consumption in the fall shows a decline, rather than the expected increase.

Shenyang

As expected, the seasonal variation for most measures of nutrition for the city of Shenyang was too small to be statistically significant, although the power of the statistical tests was also low. Only the consumption of Vitamin A showed a statistically significant change.[1] With a greater abundance of fresh vegetables available in the fall, and lower prices as a result, greater consumption of Vitamin A is as expected.

The only other measure to show a statistically significant change was protein consumption.[2] A decline in consumption of meat would agree with an increase in the consumption of vegetables because these foods tend to replace each other in the *cai* portion of meals. In addition, consumption of eggs and milk also was reported to be lower in the fall.

Suburbs

In the suburban districts, the only measure to show a statistically significant change from spring to fall is the ratio of Calories from carbohydrates to Calories from fats.[3] The change in the ratio came from an increase in the consumption of carbohydrates, which was significant.[4] At harvest time, suburban families enjoyed at least some of their own grains.

Dengta

Dengta households recorded statistically significant declines in several measures of nutritional levels in the fall.[5] Consumption of protein, Vitamin C, and Vitamin A declined, as did overall Calorie intake and the ratio of carbohydrates to fats. It is counterintuitive that all of these measures would decline at harvest time, despite inroads of urbanization and development. Dengta was not affected by the flooding that hit some parts of the province in the summer of 1994. Close examination of the diaries themselves suggests that, although most households returned diaries in the fall, they recorded their food intake less carefully, and probably more foods were consumed than were reported.

Kangping

In Kangping, the percentage of recommended Calorie consumption also declined in the fall.[6] The change seems to have come from a decline in the consumption of carbohydrates in some of the households that had eaten the most of this nutrient in the spring.

Consumption of protein also declined in the fall, with the mean falling to 75% of the recommendation; however, the reasons for this are unclear. Although meat consumption rose slightly, with everyone now eating it at least once and an average of 13 (versus 11) times, consumption of eggs and milk (including yogurt) declined. Consumption of Vitamin A showed a statistically insignificant change, indicating little change in the consumption of vegetables.

This sample of households, from places that exhibit different levels of development and urbanization, clearly shows varying levels of nutrition that relate to levels of economic development. Although most Chinese now consume adequate energy (Calories), by all measures, city residents enjoy better nutrition and less seasonal variation than rural residents. Although they produce little or no food for themselves, higher incomes and the availability of a greater variety of food in the markets enable them to maintain adequate or better consumption of food energy and most nutrients.

Several characteristics of the sample, resulting from the logistical constraints of conducting field research in China, probably decrease, on average, the calculated difference between urban and rural nutritional levels, beyond the contrast in the entire population. Several households in the villages in Kangping County were eliminated from the study because of the necessity for at least one member of each household to be literate. Consequently, the sample of rural households did not include the poorest stratum of the population. Illiteracy is not a problem in the city, and the method of drawing the sample, using personal networks that reached low-income factory workers, probably gave a better spread in the city, even if "floating" migrants were not included. If a sample that included a broader spectrum of the city population still shows higher nutritional levels than a more restricted one in the countryside, the perceived differences become even more reliable.

Food Choices

Having established that nutritional levels are higher in the city than in the countryside, we turn to the question of whether the cultural divide, posited by Robert Redfield and his followers and applied to China by Leon Stover, is demonstrated in other ways in China. This cultural divide should be evident in families' choices of individual food items and menus. This section first examines the choice of grain for the *fan* portion of the meal, then the choices of meats, followed by the use of milk and new, non-traditional foods. Then we turn to seasonal variations in the choices of foods and to foods consumed for China's most important holiday, Spring Festival (Chinese New Year). Finally, we look at patterns of breakfast menus.

Grain and Grain/Meat Combinations

The most important part of a Chinese meal, the *zhushi* or *fan*, consists of grain, traditionally rice in the south and wheat in the north. These two grains are reported as "fine grain" (*xiliang*) in the statistics; millet, corn, and sorghum are "coarse grains." The former are much preferred.

Liaoning lies in the part of China where wheat, millet, sorghum, and corn are the traditional grains (Kariel, 1966: 74–5). Since 1950, construction of irrigation works in the Liao River valley has made possible increased production of rice; the flat land does not even require terracing. The growing season permits one crop of fast-maturing rice.

Outside of the rice-producing region, wheat, sorghum, corn, and millet are grown by rain-fed agriculture. Corn, which came to China with the Columbian Exchange, has found a real niche in Liaoning. At the beginning of the Deng Xiaoping period, it was the major staple of most people's diet. The continued immigration of Han Chinese, however, raised the preference for rice, once it became available.

Rice

All of the families in the study reported the eating of rice; however, the frequency with which they ate it varied by region (Figure 6.2). In Shenyang, where diets are more varied, it formed part of 57% of all meals. In the suburban districts and Dengta, where rice is grown, its use rises to 77% and 74%, respectively. The small sample in Beizhen County reported 54% of meals, and in Kangping County, it was served at 39%. Thus, as might be expected, rice was used more intensively in places where it is grown.

All of the regions also showed statistically significant variations between spring and fall. In Shenyang, the average meals with rice rose to 68%,[7] probably as a result of the issuance of emergency coupons for purchase at subsidized prices; this measure was designed to combat rapid inflation in the market price after summer floods destroyed part of the crop.

In the suburbs, on the other hand, the consumption of rice, in the fall, took a statistically significant drop to an average of 66% of meals.[8] This change may be related to the same phenomenon: farmers could get a sufficiently high price for their rice by selling it, thereby reducing the amount they consumed. People who purchased their food, unless they held urban household registration, would have to pay higher market prices for rice, leading them to consider alternatives. By contrast, Dengta, the other rice-growing region in the study but located farther from urban markets, showed no statistically significant change in consumption.

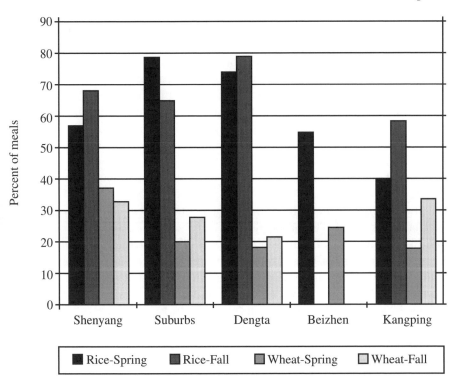

Figure 6.2 Rice and wheat use. Source: Field data.

Rice consumption rose to almost 60% of meals in Kangping County. The reasons for this rise[9] are unclear because Kangping County does not produce rice and, thus, the people must buy it.

Wheat

Only in Beizhen County was there a family that did not eat wheat at some point. Wheat, however, was part of fewer meals than rice everywhere, and the decline in its use followed the urban hierarchy of the regions (Figure 6.2). In Shenyang, it was served in some form at 37% of meals; in the suburban districts, almost 20%; in Dengta County, 18%; and in Kangping County, 17.5 %. (The small sample from Beizhen County reported 24%.)

The seasonal change in use of wheat was statistically significant only in the suburban districts and Kangping. In the suburbs, it increased[10] because it replaced some rice in the diet. Rice contains more protein than wheat, so, as reported above, the decline in rice consumption also decreases the amount of protein in the diet.

In Kangping County, wheat consumption also increased.[11] It appears to have been replacing coarse grains in the diet and, thus, marks an improvement, possibly reflecting the bounty of harvest time.

Wheat can appear in the diet in several forms, all of them based on wheat flour. In this study, the most common form was pancakes (*bing*). Pancakes are most popular in the city (95% of Shenyang households ate them at 41% of their meals), but less popular in the countryside. In the suburbs, 76% of families consumed them at 33% of meals; in Dengta County, 68% ate them at 44% of meals; and in Kangping County, 22% ate them at 35% of meals. (All of the small sample from Beizhen County reported eating them; they appeared at 19% of meals.)

The traditional bread in China is steamed (*mantou*). More city families (92%) ate this bread. The proportion in the countryside was considerably less: 70% in the suburbs; 74% in Dengta County; 71% in Kangping County; and the small sample in Beizhen all reported its use. The intensity of use, measured as the percent of meals containing wheat that consisted of steamed bread, however, was lower in the city, at 30%. In the suburbs, it was 41%; in Dengta County, 50%; and in Kangping County, 40%. (In Beizhen, it was 33%.)

Western yeast bread (*mianbao*) also is known in China, but, because most families have no ovens, it must be purchased. Its use is overwhelmingly urban, with 68% of Shenyang families reporting it, but only 9% of suburban families, 16% of Dengta County families, and 14% of Kangping County families. No one in Beizhen County reported it. The two families in Kangping County who used it had it at 55% of all meals that contained wheat, by far, the highest proportion. In Shenyang, it comprised 19% of meals with wheat; in Dengta County, 17%; and in the suburbs 12%.

Noodles, as described in Chapter 3, are an ancient traditional food in China. Not surprisingly, the percentage of families reporting noodles in their meals was uniformly high, with between 80% and 90% of families in all regions reporting them. The proportion of meals comprised of noodles ranged from 25% to 50%, with no strong urban/rural distinction.

Coarse Grains

The use of millet, corn, and sorghum would seem to decline with increasing prosperity, and these grains are certainly more common in the far rural countryside than elsewhere (Figure 6.3). As with whole-grain bread in the West, however, they have enjoyed a certain degree of renewed popularity in the city, primarily to add variety and to satisfy nostalgia.

In the spring, ten Shenyang families (16% of the total) reported using millet at 4% of their meals. Four suburban families and four Dengta County families used it slightly more frequently, at 5% of meals. It is in Kangping

County, where rice cannot be grown, that its use jumps noticeably: 85% of families used it at 10% of meals. (No one in the small Beizhen County sample reported using millet.)

In the fall, nine Shenyang families used millet, but less frequently; it was part of only 3% of meals; use in the suburbs was similar in the fall, with three families reporting millet, but at only 2% of their meals. No one in Dengta reported millet in the fall, but nine families (64% of the total) in Kangping County ate it at 7% of their meals.

In the cities, maize (corn), which was the staple food before the Dengist reforms, enjoys renewed interest. Corn pancakes are made and sold in markets, and some families make dumplings with cornbread. In Shenyang in the spring, 15% of families reported eating corn as grain at 5% of their meals. No one in the suburbs or in Beizhen County reported it, and only one family in Dengta ate it at 2% of their meals. In the suburbs and in Dengta County, rice is by far the dominant grain; corn probably would have appeared in Beizhen County if more families had returned their food diaries, because it still is grown widely there. Kangping County, again, has the largest proportion of families eating corn (5 families or 36%), who ate it at 17% of their meals.

In the fall, Kangping County also had the most eaters of corn (seven families or 50%), but they ate it at only 3% of meals. Two families in Dengta County ate corn at 6%; five families in Shenyang, at 1%; and no one in the suburbs reported it.

According to Li Fuqi (1994), when he was a child in Beizhen County, sorghum was used mostly for pigs or poor people. Nevertheless, two Shenyang families reported it at 4% of meals, and three families in the suburbs and Beizhen County reported it at 2% and 28%, respectively. In Kangping County, everyone ate sorghum for an average of 20% of their meals.

In the fall, Kangping County again showed the greatest use of sorghum, although only 50% of families reported it at an average of 10% of their meals. Only one family each in Shenyang, the suburbs, and Dengta County reported using sorghum in the fall, for an average of 2%. Thus, sorghum shows a distinct pattern of greater use with increasing distance from large urban areas and decreasing levels of urbanization and development.

Grain/Meat Combinations

The *fan* and *cai* portions of a meal can be combined and eaten together by wrapping meat-vegetable filling in some form of wheat-flour covering. The most common forms are dumplings (*jiaozi*), stuffed buns (*baozi*), filled pancakes (*xianbing*), and wonton soup (*huntun*). Eggrolls (*chunjuan* or spring rolls in Chinese) are also this kind of combination, but they do not appear in any of these food diaries.

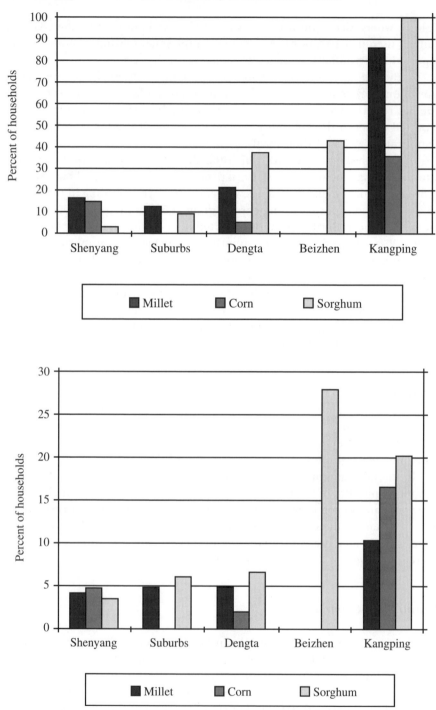

Figure 6.3   Use of coarse grains: (a) Households, and (b) Meals. (Source: Field data.)

Such combinations are very popular. In the spring, the smallest proportion of families who had included them was found in the suburban districts with 73%; Dengta showed 79%, and the other areas between 90% and 100%. In the fall, Dengta still showed the smallest percentage (77%), but, elsewhere, it was between 95% and 100% of families.

By far, the most common form of grain/meat combination is dumplings (*jiaozi*). Its frequent recording in the diaries as *bao jiaozi* (literally, "pack dumplings") shows that its social role, a family activity with any guests participating, is part of the appeal of the dish. As will be evident later, it is the traditional food in northern China for Spring Festival (Chinese New Year) and, by extension, has come to be associated with happy occasions in general. In the spring, among families who reported eating meat/grain combinations, the percentage who ate some as dumplings ranged from 58% in the suburbs to 100% in Kangping. In the fall in Dengta, only one-half of the families who ate combinations ate some of them in the form of dumplings; elsewhere, the percentages ranged from 95% to 100%. For the families who ate dumplings, the proportion of combination meals that included them in the spring ranged from 58% in Shenyang to 85% in Kangping County. In the fall, the range was from 47% in Shenyang to 96% in Dengta County; although fewer families ate dumplings, they tended to do so more frequently. Again, in the city, meals are more varied with less likelihood that one food will dominate the menu.

Stuffed buns (*baozi*) are second in popularity. In the spring, 71% of Shenyang families ate them, but in the countryside the proportions were much less, ranging from 21% in Dengta County to 36% in Kangping County (Beizhen County reported 57%). With dumplings dominating the grain/meat combinations in rural areas, it is not surprising that the highest proportion who ate stuffed buns was in Shenyang (58%). Suburban districts followed with 49%; Dengta County was lowest with 8%; and Kangping County had 24% (Beizhen County registered 29%). In the fall, the proportion of families eating stuffed buns and their frequency of use remained very similar, except that, in Dengta County, stuffed buns now comprised 90% of meals with grain/meat combinations.

Filled pancakes actually had the most popularity in Kangping County with 29% of families who ate grain/meat combinations in the spring eating these pancakes. Elsewhere, the percentage of families was less than 20, but the three suburban families who ate them made them part of 47% of their meals. (No families in Beizhen County reported eating them.) In the fall, the highest percentage of families was in Shenyang (30%), but Dengta County (at 100%) was the only place where they comprised more than 30% of meals.

Wonton soup (a corruption of the Chinese *hundun*) is made with small *jiaozi*-like dumplings. It is not very popular. In the spring, only nine Shenyang families and two suburban families ate it, at 27% and 32%, respectively, of meals with combinations. In the fall, five Shenyang and four suburban families ate it at 27% and 18%, respectively; one Kangping County family ate it at 20%. Apparently, if one is going to the effort of making dumplings, the preferred way of eating them is as dumplings, not as an ingredient in soup. (The water in which dumplings are cooked, however, quite commonly is drunk as soup at the end of the meal.)

Meat

As previously discussed in connection with protein consumption, urban residents in China eat more meat than do rural people (Figure 6.4).

Pork

By far, the most common meat in China is pork. In fact, the word for "meat" (*rou*), unless modified, is understood to mean "pork." The cultural-ecological reasons for the importance of pork are discussed in Chapter 3.

In the spring, all families in Shenyang and Kangping reported eating pork: in the suburbs, 97%; and in Kangping, 94%. (Everyone in the small sample from Beizhen County ate pork.) Those in Shenyang also ate more servings of pork (13 in the two-week period), but because they ate more meat in total, the proportion that was pork was lower than elsewhere (62%), indicating greater variety in the diet. In the suburbs, the average number of servings was nine, comprising 68% of meals with meat; in Dengta, seven servings comprised 80% ; and, in Kangping, ten servings comprised 85%. In other words, the variety declines from city to countryside along with the total number of servings of meat. (In Beizhen, the average number of servings was 13, comprising 75% of meals with meat.) In Dengta, people eat less meat to begin with, so the lower frequency of pork still comprises a higher proportion of what they do eat.

The pattern for the fall was very similar. Only in Dengta were there families who did not eat pork at all. In Shenyang, it was served an average of 18 times or 68% of meals with meat; in the suburbs, an average of ten servings or 68%; in Dengta,with lower meat consumption, two servings or 39%; and, in Kangping, ten servings or 74%.

Beef

Beef is not traditional among the crop-farming people of China. The beef that is available today is usually tough. In contrast to the United States, beef is not the expected meat dish for the main meal of the day. Even in Shenyang, less than 60% of families ate it; in the suburbs, 21%; in Dengta, 16%; and, in

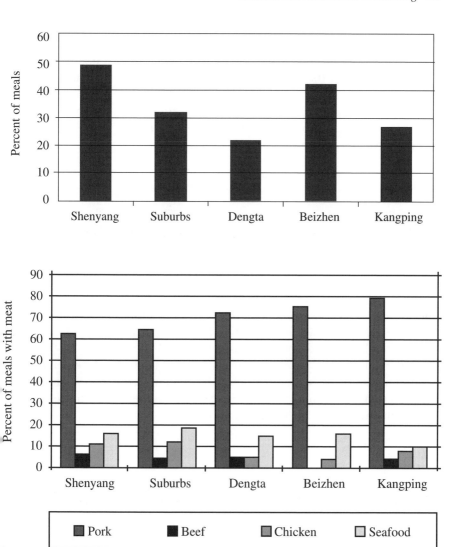

Figure 6.4 Meat use, spring: (a) Meals with meat, and (b) Meat choices. (Source: Field data.)

Kangping, 29%. (No families in Beizhen ate it.) Again, Dengta, where neither economics nor cultural tradition favors the raising of large meat animals, shows the smallest use of beef. Among the families that ate beef, it comprised only 3% of meals with meat. In the suburbs, with higher incomes and development levels in general, beef comprised 19% of meals with meat; and, in Kangping, near the Mongolian grasslands, almost 16% contained beef.

However, in the fall, no Kangping County families reported eating beef. In Shenyang, a higher percentage of families (87%) did eat it at 9% of their meals with meat. In the fall, its use rose in the suburbs (26% of families at 14%) and in Dengta (41% of families at 24%) . The reasons for the differences are unclear. The greater use in Kangping County in the spring may have related to a local decision to slaughter one or more beef cattle, whereas in the fall, no such local supply was available.

Chicken

Chinese like chicken, as the popularity of Kentucky Fried Chicken attests, but it traditionally has been expensive. Consumption generally followed the urban hierarchy in terms of numbers of families. In the spring in Shenyang, 73% of families ate chicken, comprising 12% of their meals with meat. Fewer families (58%) in the suburbs ate it, but it made up more of their meat meals (21%). Among Dengta County families, it was less popular (44%) and comprised 14% of meals; chickens seem to be kept for eggs, rather than meat. In Kangping County, 55 % of families used it for 17% of meat meals. (Among the small sample from Beizhen County, 29% used it for 14%.)

In the fall, everyone in the Shenyang sample ate chicken; the percentage in the suburbs rose to 70% and, in Kangping County, it fell to 21%. In Dengta County, it remained almost the same. The intensity of use (percentage of meat meals containing chicken) remained very similar.

Fish

With better transportation and the construction of fish ponds, aquatic products are becoming more widely available in Liaoning Province. Kangping County also has a large natural lake. Ocean fish are more expensive than freshwater fish, so probably most of the fish consumed was freshwater, although it usually was recorded just as "fish." In Shenyang, 95% of families ate fish, which made up 17% of their meals. In Sujiatun District in the suburbs, there is a large artificial fish pond, and 70% of families ate fish, comprising 25% of their meals with meat. In Dengta County, the percentage of families eating fish drops to 53%. Land animals are less popular in Dengta County than elsewhere, and fish comprised 30% of meals with meat. In Kangping County 43% of families ate fish for 24%, (In Beizhen County, 71% of families ate it an average of four times or 23% of their meals.)

In the fall, the proportion of families in Shenyang who ate fish remains unchanged, but they ate it less frequently (12% of meals). In the suburbs, the proportion of families rises to 91%, but the intensity of use is the same. Use in Dengta is unchanged; in Kangping, more families (57%) ate it, but at fewer meals (22%).

Other meats

As expected, the greatest variety of other meats reported came from Shenyang. In the spring, 15 families reported eating lamb, which is the favorite meat of Muslims and, thus, widely available (none of the families in the study were Muslim). Dog was reported by two families. Shrimp is a luxury food and was particularly expensive in 1994 because of disease problems in the shrimp beds. Nevertheless, 20 families reported eating it at least once in the spring, and six families ate it in the fall. Shellfish were reported by eight families in the spring. In the fall, three families reported the eating of ham, three reported duck, and two reported rabbit. In the fall, two Shenyang families reported eating silkworm cocoons.

In the suburbs, the variety drops greatly. In the spring, three families ate dog and two ate ham; in the fall, three ate ham, two ate shrimp, and one ate lamb.

In Dengta, ham and lamb were reported by one family each in the spring; in the fall, one family reported shrimp and one reported ham. Kangping County was the only place to show the eating of donkey meat. That four families ate it (usually as an ingredient in dumplings) in the spring and six in the fall indicates that someone slaughtered a donkey and the meat was distributed around the village. Other meats reported in Kangping County were lamb (one family in spring and four in fall), goose, and dog (two families each in the fall).

Again, the consumption of meat and the choices of which meats to eat show the clear distinction between city and countryside that persists in China. Urban people eat much more meat, and they eat a greater variety of meat as reflected in their level of protein consumption and the ratio of Calories from carbohydrates to Calories from fat. No one kind, even pork, dominates all their meals. Because it is not sold in markets, but rather becomes available as a farm animal is slaughtered, donkey meat is found only in the most rural areas. Likewise, large grazing animals, such as cattle, are more commonly eaten closer to the grasslands for both economic (cultural-ecological) and cultural reasons.

Beverages and Treats

Tea, of course, is the beverage traditionally associated with China; however, it rarely was recorded, probably because it generally is not regarded as a "food." For example, the menu in the foreigners' diningroom at Northeastern University did not list tea, although it was available on request.

Alcoholic beverages occasionally were recorded. More may have been consumed than appeared in the diaries, not because people are ashamed of drinking alcohol, but because it generally is not regarded as "food." In Shenyang in the spring, 14 families (23% of the sample) recorded drinking beer, an average of just over two times. Two families reported drinking *baijiu* (distilled liquor) once. In the spring, 11 families reported drinking beer, an average of just under two times; one family reported *baijiu* three times.

In the suburbs in the spring, five families reported beer just under five times each, and three reported *baijiu* five times. Elsewhere, only in Beizhen did a family report alcohol; one family drank beer once, and one drank *baijiu* twice. In the fall, only *baijiu* is reported by one family four times. Again, the difference between city and countryside is clear in reported alcohol consumption.

Chinese traditionally consume little sugar or sweets; however, in the hot weather of early summer, popsicles were quite popular, and more may have been consumed than reported because they are a snack food. In Shenyang in the spring, 11 families reported them an average of three times, and, in the suburbs, five families reported them an average of two times. Three families in Kangping County reported them three times; in Dengta, one family reported them once. (In Beizhen County, one family reported popsicles four times.) Nobody reporting eating popsicles in the fall, when the weather was colder.

Consumption of Coca-Cola will be considered later in the chapter, but China has native varieties of soda, or carbonated fruit-flavored beverages. These are also popular in hot weather, and it is now possible to buy them chilled. Three families in Shenyang, five in the suburbs, and three in Kangping reported sodas three times each. (One family in Beizhen County reported soda 11 times.) In the fall, the popularity declines with the onset of colder weather. Only two Shenyang families and two Kangping County families reported one soda each.

Candy is increasingly consumed in China, primarily by the spoiled children of the one couple/one child generation. While bewailing candy's effect on dental health, parents indulge their children anyway. Its consumption probably exceeds its reporting, again, because it is not regarded as "food." Five families in Shenyang reported it in the spring (once each), and one family in the suburbs reported it once. In the fall, one suburban family reported it once, and one Kangping County family reported it three times.

Chinese have a festival celebrating the full moon in September, called Moon Festival or Mid-Autumn Festival, and it is marked by eating fruit and mooncake, a very rich filled cake. Mooncakes appear in the diaries of three Shenyang families and one Dengta family in the fall.

Baked cakes and cookies are widely available in China. Like yeast bread, they generally must be purchased because most Chinese have no ovens. As expected, more urban than rural families eat cake and cookies; cake appears frequently on urban breakfast menus (discussed later in the chapter). In Shenyang in spring, 50% of families ate such foods an average of almost four times. Four suburban families, three families in Dengta County, and four in Kangping County ate cakes and cookies. While fewer rural families reported these foods, their frequency was similar to that of city families. (One family in Beizhen County reported eating them twice.) In the fall, fewer city families reported cake and cookies (mooncakes replaced some of them) and a few more were reported in Kangping County.

New Foods

As expected, more urban than rural families ate foods that traditionally are not part of the Chinese diet. The most common is strawberry jam, which they spread on either steamed or yeast bread, usually for breakfast. Four Shenyang families in the spring and one suburban family in the fall reported using it.

As mentioned above, beef is used less commonly in China than pork, and beefsteak is even less common. Two Shenyang families ate beef steak in the spring and one in the fall. One Shenyang family reported curried chicken in the fall.

Despite its frequent use in Chinese restaurants in the West, broccoli is not a traditional food in China. In the spring, one Dengta County family reported it; in the fall, one suburban family did. These families probably grow it for sale in urban markets and occasionally eat some of their own production.

Orange juice can be made at home from oranges, which are traditional, although rarely available in the Northeast before modern marketing and transportation. In the spring, one family in each of Shenyang, the suburbs, and Kangping County reported drinking orange juice. One Kangping County family reported drinking cocoa.

Ice cream was reported only in the spring; colder weather in the fall makes it less appealing. One family in Shenyang and one in the suburbs reported it. Because it is usually a snack, more may have been eaten than reported.

In Shenyang in the spring, three families reported using honey, one reported eating chocolate, and one each drank Coca-Cola and coffee. These two beverages are still very expensive by Chinese standards.

Thus, a total of 11 Shenyang families reported a new, non-traditional food in the spring, and three families reported such foods in the fall. Only three suburban families reported non-traditional foods in each season; one Dengta County family did so in the spring and one in the fall, and one Kangping County family reported these foods in the spring. (No families in Beizhen County reported such foods.) Only honey was reported more than twice for the same family. Thus, as expected, newly introduced foods gain popularity in and around cities first.

Holiday Foods

Food for major holidays and festivals is slower to change than everyday foods. The last major festival in China before the families kept their food diaries was Spring Festival (Chinese New Year), the biggest holiday of the year.

The traditional food for this festival in northern China is dumplings; the shape is similar to a purse, thus symbolizing wealth. Typical of holiday foods, they are also time-consuming to make and require ingredients that are traditionally expensive. Of the households who answered the question about foods for Spring Festival, the following reported eating dumplings: 48% in Shenyang;, 63% in the suburbs; 67% in Dengta County; 43% in Beizhen County; and 100% in Kangping County.

Meats are also an important part of the celebration. Meat consumption is still low in China because it is expensive, but Spring Festival is such a special occasion that families make an effort to include it in the menu. Furthermore, pork fades from its usual dominant position; only in the suburbs did more families eat pork than other meats. In Shenyang and Beizhen County, fish was the most popular meat; it was the second choice in the suburbs. Chicken was also a common choice.

The major variation between city and countryside in Spring Festival meals was the number of different foods eaten. In addition to dumplings and meats, Shenyang families reported 14 other foods, suburban families 12, Dengta County families 9, Beizhen County families (some of them restaurant owners) 16, and Kangping County families only 2.

As expected, city families have retained holiday traditions regarding foods, but they have added more new foods to the menu. Higher incomes, more exposure to new ideas, and availability of a greater variety of foods influence holiday meals, as well as everyday diet. Most rural families, especially in Kangping County, stick more closely to the traditional holiday foods.

Breakfast

In the West, breakfast tends to be composed of foods that differ from the rest of the day's meals and is more resistant to change. While almost all Chinese regularly eat breakfast, as did all of the families in this study, the menu for the first meal of the day varies greatly between city and countryside.

For purposes of tallying, breakfasts were categorized into four types:
1. Gruel with steamed or stuffed buns (the typical breakfast served to tourists in Chinese hotels).
2. Pancakes or fried breadsticks with some food made from beans, frequently a flavored tofu.

3. *Fan* plus *cai*, that is, a menu similar to any other meal of the day. Breakfasts consisting of dumplings fell into this category.
4. Milk plus yeast bread or cake.

Breakfasts in the city are much more varied than those in the countryside (Figure 6.5). No one menu dominates in either season. In the spring, menus 1, 3, and 4 appeared in 80% of families; menu 2 was the least common, with only 74%. In the fall, every family ate at least one breakfast of menu 1; menu 2 was again the least common with 57%.

Everywhere in the countryside, menu 3 was dominant both seasons; all rural families ate it. In fact, in Dengta and Kangping counties in the spring, no one ate menu 2.

Menu 4 most closely resembles the Western breakfast. In the spring, 80% of Shenyang families ate this kind of breakfast; in the fall, 78% did. In the spring, only two families from the suburbs ate it, and, in the fall, six families did; in Dengta County, the numbers were three and four, respectively, and, in Kangping County, only one family reported it in both seasons. The popularity of a more Western type of breakfast shows the same urban/rural divide as other Western foods and eating patterns.

Because of the greater variety of breakfasts in the city of Shenyang, no one menu dominates the total breakfasts eaten (Figure 6.6). Menu 1, which all families ate at least once, comprised not quite 25% of all breakfasts in the spring, followed by menu 3 with 29%. Least popular was menu 2, with 17%, while menu 4 was 28%.

In the countryside, although all families ate menu 3 at least once, they did not eat it every day. In the spring, it comprised 80% of all breakfasts in the suburbs; 82% in Dengta County; and 98% in Kangping County. (In Beizhen County, 88% of breakfasts were of this type.) The distribution in the fall was virtually the same.

Food-Related Chores

Like many preindustrial societies, traditional China assigned to women the work of the household, including food preparation. Since 1949, urban women have joined the labor force in large numbers, a move that the Communist party encouraged in order to increase the labor force without increasing the number of urban families it had to support with subsidies. Chinese housewives, like their counterparts in the United States, complain that, in addition to their outside jobs, they are still responsible for the running of homes.

Among these families, however, work related to food is being shared more than it was in the past. The father, as head of the household, is responsible for: planning menus, 29% of families; shopping, 47%; cooking, 22%; and

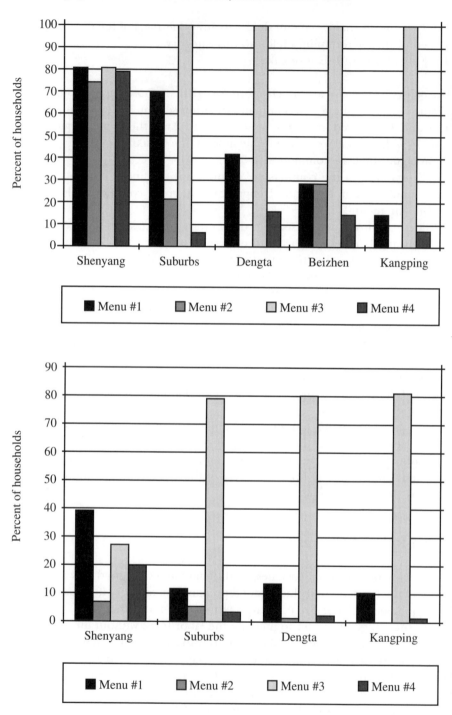

Figure 6.5 Breakfast menus by households: (a) Spring, and (b) Fall. (Source: Field data.)

dishwashing, 10%. Mothers do menu planning in almost the same proportion (27%), and 16% of families reported that "everyone" has a say in what to eat. In 4% of the families, the father and mother decide together. Shopping is the work of 29% of the mothers, a slightly smaller proportion than the men. The women however, still dominate in the kitchen: 45% do the cooking and dishwashing. In 8% of families, however, everyone shares these tasks; in 12%, the father and mother share cooking; and, in 8%, they share dishwashing. Children help plan menus in 4% of families; an adult daughter does shopping in 2%; and children do the dishes in 10%. Sons do dishes in 4% of homes, which is a real break from the past. Only one Shenyang family reported having a vegetable garden, and the father decided what to grow in it.

The suburbs show a very different pattern of work assignments. While 15% of male heads of household still plan menus, 62% of mothers have this responsibility. Shopping is now dominated by women (44% versus 23%), and cooking (67% versus 13%) and dishwashing (69% versus 10%) are overwhelmingly women's work. In 15% of families, everyone helps decide what to eat; in 18%, everyone does grocery shopping. Everyone helps cook in only 8%, and everyone helps with dishwashing in 10%. Father and mother share work in the following ways: in three families, menu planning; in two families, shopping; in three families, cooking; and, in four families, dishwashing. In one family, adult daughters plan menus, grocery shop, and cook; in two families, they wash dishes. One son shops and one son washes dishes with his mother, but no other sons do any food-related chores. Deciding what to raise in the vegetable garden is more equally divided between the father and mother (18% and 15%, respectively); in two families, everyone helps decide; and, in one family, the father and mother decide together.

In Dengta County, the mother has overwhelming responsibility for most food chores: menu planning, 63%; deciding what to grow in the vegetable garden, 47%; shopping, 37%; cooking, 89%; and dishwashing, 74%. Only as shoppers do men carry anywhere near an equal load(32%). A son in only one family shops, and one daughter shops and one washes dishes. Everyone has a say in menu planning in only three families, and everyone participates in shopping, cooking, or dishwashing in one. In two families, the father and mother together decide the menus.

In Beizhen County, for which there were more questionnaires than food diaries, fathers take more responsibility for deciding what to grow in vegetable gardens (33%) and for shopping (62%). They plan menus in 29% of families (versus 52% of mothers), but they do no cooking or dishwashing; those tasks are women's work (81% and 67% of families, respectively). In two families, the grandfather plans menus; in one, he decides what to grow in the vegetable garden, and, in the other, he does the shopping. Adult sons plan the garden and shop in one household each; adult daughters shop and cook in one family each, and wash dishes in two families. In one family, everyone helps with dishes;

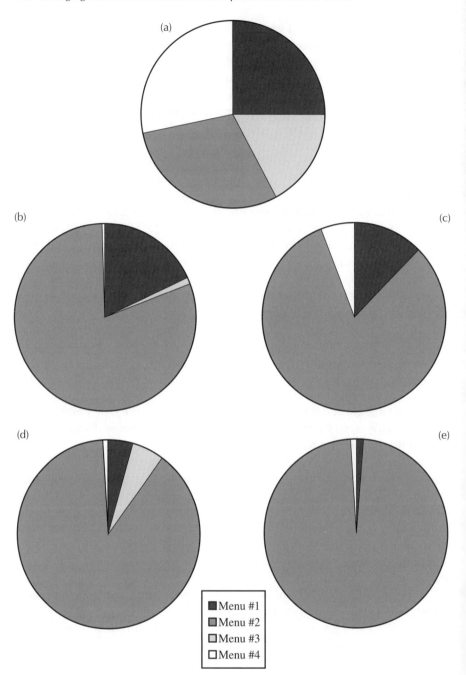

Figure 6.6 Breakfast menus by proportion of total breakfasts, spring: (a) Shenyang, (b) Suburbs, (c) Dengta County, (d) Beizhen County, and (e) Kangping County. (Source: Field data.)

in one family each, both the father and mother plan the vegetable garden and menus, and do dishes; and, in two families, both parents cook. In one family, mother and son wash dishes.

In Kangping County, the mother plans the garden in 43% of families and the menus in 50%; everyone participates in these decisions in 21% and 29%, respectively. Shopping is the father's job in 50% of families,; in one family, two adult daughters shop. In 93% of families, the mother does the cooking; in 86%, she washes the dishes. One adult daughter does the dishwashing. In one family, the father and mother together cook and wash dishes.

Thus, assignment of food-related chores follows the urban hierarchy. Only in the city do men share in the traditional women's work of cooking and dishwashing to any degree. The public activity of shopping and the decision-making chore of planning menus are the most common food-related chores for rural fathers to assume, but, even here, women still dominate and, thus, remain the "gatekeepers" for what appears on the family table. Because women carry so much responsibility for choosing, procuring, and preparing food for their families, especially in the countryside, this area's persisting problem of illiteracy is a distinct hindrance in any effort to raise nutritional levels. In general, illiteracy points to low educational levels. Poorly educated people have not studied health and nutrition as a subject, and they are handicapped in obtaining further information once they establish their own households. Along with the related problem of low incomes, low education levels translate into low nutritional levels.

In dietary regimes, as in nutritional levels, the contrast between city and countryside remains in China. In both measures, the biggest change comes between Shenyang and its suburbs; the suburban districts are more similar to the rest of the countryside than they are to the nearby city, although some suburban residents have non-farming jobs.

In all regions, grain (*fan*) is the main part of the meal, but more coarse grains are used in the countryside. Similarly, pork dominates the meat selection everywhere, but by a greater degree in rural than urban areas. In the city, there is also a greater variety of foods that combine grain and meat, in holiday foods, and in breakfast menus. Food-related chores are shared more equally between men and women in the city. Urban families continue to have higher incomes and a greater variety of foods available, and they are more venturesome in planning their menus. With more food security for a longer time, they are more willing to risk trying new and different foods.

The Geography of Dietary Regimes in Liaoning

Having examined the nutritional levels and the use of specific foods across the spatial continuum, we can now put this information together into a dietary regime for each of these regions.

Shenyang

As mentioned, the people of Shenyang eat the greatest variety of food. The Han Chinese heritage of most residents of Shenyang is expressed in the preference for rice as the *fan* in meals, especially now that it is readily available from local growers. So important is rice in the diet of Shenyang residents that when flood-induced shortages and general inflation drove the price too high in 1994, the government stepped in with a ration of subsidized rice for each urban-registered family. The northern Chinese preference for wheat also finds expression in Shenyang, and this grain, in its various forms, is second in importance. Pancakes are the most popular way to eat wheat, followed by steamed bread (*mantou*), noodles, and yeast bread.

Coarse grains — millet, corn, and sorghum — have recovered somewhat from their association with poverty and are eaten occasionally for variety and nostalgia. As memories of the terrible famine that followed the Great Leap Forward begin to fade, sweet potatoes are also popular as a street snack. City residents have had food security for a sufficiently long enough time that their perception of such foods has improved, and they now eat them by choice. This use, however, is as a secondary food, not a staple food.

Fan can also combine wheat (less frequently corn) and meat and/or vegetables. Dumplings (*jiaozi*) and filled buns (*baozi*) are the most popular, even occasionally appearing at the same meal, followed by filled pancakes and wonton soup. Usually such meals will not include additional rice or other wheat preparations.

Accompanying the *fan* in all other urban meals is some kind of meat, or vegetables, or both. Each meal includes, on average, two such dishes; meals for guests or special occasions increase the number of dishes. Almost half of all meals contain meat, most frequently pork, followed by fish, chicken, and beef. Tofu is the vegetarian source of protein and is used occasionally, if only for variety. Eggs may constitute part of any meal. Stir-frying is, by far, the most common way of preparing *cai*, although steaming (especially for fish) and deep-fat frying also are used.

Vegetables are the other principal ingredient of *cai*, and the variety is almost endless, with city markets drawing on local greenhouse agriculture and transportation from regions with different environmental conditions. Cabbage and onions still are eaten widely, but they are supplemented with many varieties of green beans, peppers, cauliflower, cucumbers, squash, eggplants, tomatoes, carrots, turnips, radishes, celery, parsley, garlic (including stems), spinach, potatoes, and others.

Supplementing the *fan* and *cai* are beverages, snacks, and treats. City families now eat fruit quite regularly, usually before a meal, rather than as dessert. Apples, pears, bananas, oranges, strawberries, kiwi fruit, peaches, plums, litchi, and grapes are widely available. Other snacks include cookies, cake, soda, popsicles, ice cream, and candy. Beer and other alcoholic beverages also accompany meals, and no particular social scorn is attached to drinking them. Tea is rather expensive, but, at least, is served regularly to guests.

Most of the time, breakfast tends to be different from other meals. It may consist of rice porridge and steamed bread, sometimes accompanied by pickles, cucumber, and/or peanuts and milk; milk with cake or yeast bread spread with strawberry jam or honey; or pancakes or fried breadsticks with some form of tofu. It also may follow the same *fan/cai* pattern of other meals.

As the Chinese have done throughout their history, Shenyang families are incorporating newly introduced foods into their menus. The basic *fan/cai* meal plan allows such additions without changing the basic organization of menus. Broccoli, Western bread, soft drinks, coffee, jams and jellies, and chocolate now have a definite following in cities. They are supplementary foods — even "junk" foods — that serve purely as treats, so they are the kind most easily adopted because they leave the basic traditional dietary regime intact.

Nutritionally, the urban dietary regime provides adequate Calories and most other nutrients, except for calcium, which suffers from low dairy consumption. The addition of broccoli is a nutritional advantage, but the other newly introduced foods add little nutrition. The dietary regime in Shenyang retains the traditional pattern of the importance of grain, with meat and vegetables added for nutrition and flavor. It features a wide variety of grains, meats, and vegetables, a key to providing good nutrition.

Suburbs

Suburban meals resemble those of other rural areas more than they do those of the city. Grain's position as the main element in the meal remains, but the proportion represented by rice increases. Rice is grown locally, whereas wheat, millet, sorghum, and corn must be purchased from elsewhere, and, consequently, they decline in importance. Among the foods made from wheat, noodles are the most common, followed by steamed bread (*mantou*) and pancakes. Yeast bread, the Western import, is uncommon.

Grain and meat and/or vegetables can be combined in the same food; among such foods, dumplings (*jiaozi*) are, by far, the most common, followed by stuffed buns, filled pancakes, and wonton soup. It is rare to serve grain with a meal that contains a combination food.

Suburban residents eat less meat than city people, and most of that is pork. Cows, which can graze on wasteland and serve the urban demand for milk, increase the use of beef. Few suburban residents, however, drink milk. Chickens, which are scavengers, supply meat and eggs to the diet, and local aquaculture supplies fish.

On average, only one dish is served as a *cai* dish at each meal in the suburbs, so the variety of foods also declines. Cabbage and onions are still common, of course, supplemented by the same kinds of vegetables as city people eat, but each family's variety is smaller because more families are producing more of their own food. While they have a wide choice in what to grow, no one family can grow everything, so their diets are more repetitive.

Treats and snacks are also less varied. Suburban families do not grow much fruit, so they eat little of it. Soda and popsicles are popular snacks in hot weather, but newly introduced foods, such as ice cream, Coca-cola, or chocolate are rare.

Breakfast menus in the suburbs follow the same basic meal plan as any other meal of the day: a grain plus some kind of vegetable or meat accompaniment. Breakfasts show little variety.

The dietary regime of the Shenyang suburbs is quite different from that of the city; it shows definite rural qualities. The locally produced grain — rice — is, by far, the most common because rural people rely on locally grown food. Fewer foods accompany the grain, and they are less varied. They also are produced locally. These foods may serve the urban market, for example, cows produce milk, but suburban residents most frequently use cows in the traditional way. In other words, they will eat beef more readily than they will drink milk. Other ingredients of *cai* — chickens and pigs — fill the traditional ecological niche in the Chinese farming system.

Treats and snacks are extra luxuries that most families seldom can afford. Likewise, they seldom are venturesome or prosperous enough to experiment with newly introduced foods, which tend to be expensive. Primarily relying on their own production, they tend to be conservative.

With less variety and less high-quality protein food in the diet than urban residents, suburban residents' nutrition barely meets most of the nutritional recommendations. Calcium is the most deficient; vegetables rich in Vitamin C make up for the lack of fruit in the diet.

Dengta County

Dengta County, as the Shenyang suburbs, is a rice-growing region and relies on rice for most of its grain consumption. Wheat, millet, and corn constitute a very small part, but sorghum use is higher than it is in the city or the suburbs. It provides an inexpensive supplement to rice.

Among the various ways of preparing wheat, steamed bread (*mantou*) is the most common, and yeast (Western) bread, by far, the least. Among the foods that combine grain and meat or vegetables in one food, dumplings (*jiaozi*) are the most popular, followed by stuffed buns and filled pancakes. Wonton soup is not part of the dietary regime of this region.

Dengta County has the lowest meat consumption of any of the regions, and a high percentage of that is pork. Without a large city nearby to provide a market for milk, and with land intensively farmed in rice paddies and vegetable crops, the grazing of cows is not an economical proposition. Even chickens are uncommon; pigs are the main scavengers. Dengta County represents the very traditional rice-growing horticulture for which China is famous.

Vegetables are the main ingredient in *cai*, and there is an average of only one such dish per meal. The assortment of possible vegetables is the same as it is in the suburbs, but, again, the variety that any one family can grow is limited. With families primarily dependent on self-produced food, meals are more repetitive, and the number of different foods is relatively small. Similarly, few families eat fruit, sweets, or baked goods. Most breakfasts follow the same meal plan as any other meal of the day: grain plus some kind of meat or vegetable accompaniment.

Beizhen County

Because so few families from Beizhen County returned food diaries, the impression of the dietary regime in that region is somewhat less certain. Available evidence is that rice, which is not grown locally, is still the majority grain, although not by much. Wheat is used more, with noodles the most common form, followed by steamed bread and pancakes. Western (yeast) bread is not eaten. Grain and meat combination foods are popular, especially dumplings and stuffed buns.

Coarse grains have a visible presence in Beizhen County, especially sorghum. Corn probably has an important place in the dietary regime here because the county produces so much of it, and rural families tend to rely on locally produced food.

Meat is certainly a favorite food, and ownership of restaurants makes it possible for that segment of the population to indulge this desire. Pork, fish, and chicken, in that order, are the preferred meats; Beizhen County is famous for blackened chicken. Eggs also are eaten very commonly. Beef is much less common. Agriculture is sufficiently intensive, even without rice paddies, that pastureland is seen as wasteful. No nearby urban market exists for milk, although the Manchu people of the county are not lactose intolerant and some of them drink milk. It is an indication of their assimilation into Chinese culture that so few do.

Vegetables are the other ingredient in the *cai* portion of meals, which, again, averages one dish per meal. The assortment of vegetables is the same as elsewhere in the province. Fruit is eaten more commonly in Beizhen County because it has developed as a commercial specialty to serve urban markets, and people eat some of their own production.

Kangping County

Rice is the favorite grain in Kangping County, and wheat is second. Everyone eats both, but rice is served at more meals. Coarse grains, however, which are grown locally, are eaten more commonly in Kangping County than elsewhere. Because they are locally produced and less favored, they are less expensive, supplementing the more expensive grains that must be imported. Everyone eats them some of the time.

Meat is too expensive for most Kangping County families to eat very often, but it is served more frequently than in Dengta County, with its intensive horticultural agriculture. Kangping County, which borders Inner Mongolia, has the cultural tradition and the extensive farmland to devote more land to pasturing animals. Consequently, beef is second only to pork as the meat of choice, although pork comprises a higher proportion of meat here than anywhere. Milk (and yogurt) also have more consumers here than in other rural areas. Chicken comprises little of the diet, although eggs are sometimes eaten; the fish portion comes from a local lake. Other meats depend on local availability, especially the appearance from time to time of donkey meat.

Vegetables generally come from household gardens or fields, and the same assortment that prevails throughout the province is found here. Some fruit is grown, so Kangping County residents actually eat more of it than Dengta County, with its emphasis on rice and horticultural farming.

Breakfast menus, as those in other rural areas, are similar to the menu for any other meal. It was in Kangping that I was served dumplings (*jiaozi*) for breakfast, as a special treat. *Jiaozi* are highly prized and show up in their position as the most popular dish combining meat and grain.

Thus, the dietary regimes of the different parts of Liaoning Province reflect the degree of urbanization and the local cultural ecology. The primary distinction, however, remains that between city and countryside. The variations from one type of region to another still illustrate the basic dichotomy that urban areas have more variety and more new foods, while rural areas show a greater adherence to local conditions and agriculture.

In the city of Shenyang, local production certainly is reflected in the preference for rice, which now is grown nearby. This also works however, the other way around: the preference for rice in the urban market drives the local farmers to grow it. The urban market is the dog that wags the tail of the farmer's choice of crops. On a larger scale, urban needs and preferences set the priorities in national economic (including agricultural) plans.

This impact of the urban market also is seen in the production of vegetables, eggs, milk, and meat in the suburbs and is especially noticeable in the profusion of plastic-covered greenhouses for winter vegetables. The city also can import foods from a wider area, further increasing the variety, especially in winter. Urban people, exposed to new ideas about food, as well as other things, and enjoying a relatively long period of dependable food supplies, want a variety of foods and are ready and willing to add new items to their diets. Nevertheless, they still follow the age-old basic plan of grain plus meat and vegetables. Even highly educated people, unless they have lived or traveled in the West, have no idea how to put together a Western meal. But adding new ingredients to the traditional Chinese diet is easy and itself has a long history.

In the past decade, the trend of distinction between city and countryside continues and, in fact, has increased. Western-style supermarkets and fast-food restaurants have appeared in Shenyang, which now boasts a McDonald's, a Kentucky Fried Chicken, and a Pizza Hut. Rural towns have no such outlets, so rural residents only rarely eat such foods, if at all. They also lack ready access to the kinds of prepackaged and manufactured foods that supermarkets offer.

For many reasons, rural diets are more conservative. First of all, the people are more dependent on their own production. Thus, the greatest dependence on rice is in the areas that produce it. These same areas have little space or incentive to keep large grazing animals, so most of their meat comes from pigs, thereby turning potentially useless garbage into food for people and fertilizer for the fields. Chickens are also scavengers, but they are smaller, so they produce less meat per animal. Chicken and duck eggs, however, are a common food.

Areas that lack water and are unsuitable for rice depend more on coarse grains because that is what they can grow locally. It is a reflection of increased marketing of foods under the Dengist reforms that they eat any rice or wheat at all. Their interest in wanting to eat these grains, of course, is a reflection of the migration and increased Han Chinese presence in Liaoning Province.

In such areas, pigs still serve as living garbage cans, but land is farmed less intensively, leaving room for grazing animals. Especially in Kangping County, there also is a stronger cultural tradition of such animals from the nearby Mongolian grasslands. Work animals, such as donkeys, that have outlived their usefulness on the farm, are a supplementary source of meat.

All cultures change; some just change faster. Foodways generally are persistent and most likely to change when other parts of the culture undergo substantial change. Certainly the Dengist reforms have been such a change, although, in a sense, they simply returned Chinese agricultural organization to an earlier system: land is farmed by individual households, who owe a portion of the production to the landlord, which is now the government.

Liaoning has seen some changes in its diet, most importantly, the availability of rice, following construction of irrigation works and the freedom, under the Dengist reforms, to respond to the dietary preferences of the Han Chinese. In that sense, then, the rise of rice eating in the province was not so much a shift in dietary preferences as it was a decision to comply with those preferences. In this way, southern Liaoning Province shifted from Kariel's

(1966) Class 17 pattern — northern and Northeastern China (millet, sorghum, and wheat) — to his Class 9 pattern — East China (Yangtze River Valley) with its rice (dominant) and maize (secondary). Farther from areas where rice can be grown, even with the application of irrigation technology, the dependence on rice is less.

Possibilities for further minor changes in the diets of rural people also are related to the demands of the urban market. As rural farmers produce to meet those demands, and, as they continue to depend on their own production for their food, they are likely to eat some of those new foods themselves. This phenomenon already has shown up in the consumption of broccoli and increased eating of fruit because these crops are grown commercially. Cows kept to supply urban markets with milk may tempt a few rural people to drink milk, but slaughtering them, from time to time, increases the amount of beef in the diet.

Processed and manufactured foods are being marketed in rural areas, as well as in cities. To date, they have less of a following among rural people. Rural people's food security has a much shorter history, and their incomes are lower; consequently, they tend to be more conservative in their diets, especially when trying new foods that involve direct cash expenditure. Nevertheless, some rural families occasionally eat such foods as ice cream, orange juice, soda, and popsicles. While such foods increase people's pleasure, many are nutritionally inferior to traditional foods. If they replace grain, vegetables, and meat in the diet, as they have tended to do in the West, the nutrition of the Chinese will suffer, rather than benefit. Whether the few families that have begun to use these foods will form the necessary critical mass of adopters of such new ideas that make the new foods a regular part of the Chinese diet, will depend on continued economic improvement and cultural influences from outside — in other words, continued economic development.

7

China's Changing Rice Bowl

China's last great famine was from 1958 to1961, the result of the failed campaign of the Great Leap Forward. The next major political upheaval, the Cultural Revolution (1966–76) did not produce widespread starvation, although diets were terribly unbalanced and lacked important nutrients. In promoting economic development and unleashing the energies of China's farmers, the Dengist reforms undoubtedly improved the quantity and variety of food available to the Chinese people.

After nearly two decades of Deng's reform, development and modernization programs — both Engel's and Bennett's laws — operate in China with two exceptions: first, government intervention in food markets (rationing and subsidies) and, second, the restrictions on crops that farmers can grow. Engel's Law and Bennett's Law also are violated in times of prolonged inflation. Such conditions begin to impact Bennett's Law when families economize by reducing their consumption of expensive foods. After such "fat" is trimmed from the diet, if inflation persists, the household has little choice but to increase the proportion of income that is spent on food, so this percentage increases although incomes are rising.

The McGee (1989; 1991a) spatial model, based on levels of urbanization with an emerging regional urban hierarchy, posits a hierarchy of city and rural areas in regions of dense pre-existing agricultural populations in East Asia, as they evolve in response to forces of economic development and industrialization. Life-style or *genre de vie* cultural factors, such as diet, were not applied in the creation of McGee's model. As we have seen, clear and striking differences in nutritional levels and food choices are evident within the same province in China, and more between cities and the countryside than among rural regions. The Dengist Opening to the World has brought in Western supermarkets and fast-food outlets, further differentiating urban and rural diets.

Nutrition, Economic Development, and Culture in China

Long ago, China developed a dietary regime and a farming system — a cultural ecology — that is capable of feeding a large population on a small amount of land. In the Chinese conceptual scheme or conceptual map of food, the centerpiece of a Chinese meal is grain, which is lower on the food chain than meat that Westerners regard as the main dish. The Chinese staple grain of choice — rice — requires tremendous amounts of labor, but it feeds those laborers by providing high levels of nutrition per unit of land. In lands that are too dry for paddy rice, wheat produces abundant Calories and protein. Millet, sorghum, and maize, following its introduction in the Columbian Exchange, provide supplements.

Grain in a Chinese meal is supplemented and enhanced by vegetables and small amounts of meat. The most common meat is pork. Pigs contribute to the Chinese farming system by consuming what otherwise would be discarded as waste, and turning it into food in the form of pork and ham. Chickens and ducks perform a similar function because they produce not only meat but also eggs; however, because they are smaller, they provide less meat per animal than pigs. The traditional Chinese attitude that large herd animals are "barbarian," coupled with the Chinese lactose intolerance, reduces the cultural desire to allocate large amounts of land to pasture. A great variety and large quantity of vegetables are produced on small garden plots and in greenhouses, and fruits occupy some of the land that is unsuited to rice and vegetable farming.

This pattern of the central role of grain (*fan*), with vegetables and meat as a condiment, has persisted in China over hundreds of years. Rice became the dominant grain, especially in the south, before the Song dynasty was confined to rice-growing regions by the Mongol conquests in the north. The agriculture that supplies this dietary regime has been amenable to intensification, most recently under the reforms of Deng Xiaoping.

New foods have been added to the Chinese diet throughout this long history. Wheat itself was an early import, but most of the additions have been supplementary, rather than staple, foods. Maize is an exception. Nevertheless, although it can form *fan* in a meal, it is not favored in this role. Once the Dengist reforms and technological improvements made rice available in Liaoning Province, corn declined greatly in importance as a staple food, in favor of more traditionally used grains. Supplementary foods, such as tomatoes, peanuts, chili peppers, and, more recently, Coca-Cola and ice cream, have enjoyed considerably more success. They enter the system at a less basic point and, therefore, one that is more amenable to change. Furthermore, their acceptance has been primarily urban, where Western products and ideas are prestigious in the new Opening to the World and developmental policies of the Dengist era: "To get rich is glorious." To consume these products symbolizes prosperity and "modernness," as does dining at a fast-food outlet.

Nutrition in China

These findings in Northeast China confirm the conventional knowledge and research in medicine and anthropology (Croll, 1983; Morgan, 2000; Piazza, 1986; Shen, Habicht, and Chang, 1996) that nutritional levels remain higher in the city than in the countryside by virtually every measure, just as they have for hundreds of years. The major divide is between city and countryside; suburbs are more similar to other rural areas than they are to the city. McGee's (1989; 1991a) model dealt with economic matters. The regions it sets out are determined on the basis of demographic and economic measures. In terms of nutrition and food, however, there are only two regions: city and countryside.

Although on average, rural Chinese consume adequate Calories (energy), urban people eat as much as one-third more than the minimum daily recommendation. National and provincial statistics and results of the field study confirm that rural Chinese still eat much more grain than urban people and much less meat, eggs, and other high-protein food. While still less than the recommendation, protein and calcium consumption in urban areas is higher than that in the countryside. Both deficiencies relate to the small quantities of meat in the diet and even smaller amounts of dairy foods.

Because of heavy consumption of vegetables and fruits, vitamin consumption in urban and rural China is generally adequate, but fats are still very low because stir-frying requires so little oil and people eat so little meat. Most Calories come from carbohydrates (mostly grain), with the ratio of Calories from carbohydrates to Calories from fat following the urban hierarchy; the highest ratios are in the most rural areas.

Urban families eat a greater variety of foods than do rural families, making the provision of complete nutrition more certain. The more varied diet is partly the result of the purchasing of food in the market, which offers a greater variety than a farm family can produce by growing its own food. It is also a result of a greater willingness to try new and different foods. In terms of Maslow's Hierarchy of Human Needs (1954), urban families have had basic food security for a much longer time than rural families because the government has provided their food at subsidized prices. They have reached the level in the hierarchy where they can use food for self-expression and be creative with a wider variety of foods, including foods that are not traditional to China.

Economic Development and Nutrition

According to Todaro's (1989: 87) definition, economic development includes an increase in the well-being of ordinary people. Because food is a basic need for survival and good health, it is a very important component of well-being. Economic development should bring improvements in nutrition.

Popkin's (1993) Nutrition Transition (Chapter 4), was based on the Western, especially European, experience. The "fit" with Chinese history and China's current situation is less certain. Nevertheless, urban and rural China clearly exhibit different patterns. Rural China, as indicated by national and provincial statistics and the data from the food diaries, is in Pattern 3, Receding Famine, in which better technology and transportation make a wider variety of foods available, and rising incomes enable people to purchase them. This assessment considers the Dengist reforms to be the "Industrial Revoluion" because previous efforts to industrialize China affected only limited areas or precipitated such major disasters as the Great Leap Forward. Since China began embarking on widespread development under Deng, the conditions for Pattern 3 have penetrated the countryside: a greater variety of foods, rising cash incomes to purchase them, new food-processing technology, and improved cooking technology. Nutritional deficiency diseases have decreased, and life spans have lengthened. The Chinese population control policies have reduced the population explosion that accompanied this pattern in the West, increasing the aging of the population because fewer babies are born.

Urban China is entering Pattern 4, Degenerative Diseases, as people are starting to eat more meat and, thus, more fat, along with more processed foods, including Western fast foods. Although the Chinese have remained more active than most Westerners, even in cities, fewer urban Chinese do heavy manual work, and more and more of them enjoy the convenience of home appliances. Obesity, especially in children, is appearing.

These transitions involve a reduction in the amount of grain consumed in favor of other foods: meat, vegetables, and fruits. China has followed Bennett's Law (1941), and the urban-rural contrast demonstrates it. National and provincial statistics clearly show much greater grain consumption in the countryside than in cities, and the field data confirm this difference. Rural people obtain a much higher proportion of their Calorie intake from grain and less from fat than do urban residents. Consequently, a rapid increase in the price of grain can force rural families to spend an increasing proportion of their income on food despite rising incomes, which violates Engel's Law. It also can prompt them to purchase more grain (less favored than vegetables and meat) despite rising incomes and rising prices — the Giffen effect. Because urban families are less dependent on grain, a rise in its cost is less likely to increase their food expenditure as a proportion of income or to produce the Giffen effect. In fact, in 1994, the Liaoning government sold grain to urban residents at subsidized prices to avoid this effect from the flood-induced inflation of that year and the social unrest that it feared such sacrifices might provoke.

Although Mao Zedong's oratory glorified the peasants of China, and his revolution depended on their support, he also used the countryside to supply the needs of the favored city residents, in line with Mintz's (1979; 1996) description of capitalists. The household registration system, which gave urban residents subsidized food (and housing and other services), actually increased the disparities between urban and rural areas. The Chinese leadership was and remains urban. Urban people even speak rather disparagingly of peasants — at best, they are child-like individuals who must be looked after — and Chinese who have left the countryside for the city have no desire to return. Deng's economic reforms have increased the status of the city, as is evident in the large number of illegal migrants who flock to urban areas. As imperial China, Socialist China is ruled by urban people from cities. Cities still have the political and economic clout to draw what they need from the countryside, which is required to produce food to feed the cities. The countryside receives technology, as well as fertilizer in the form of night soil in return, but the terms of trade are still uneven. City residents, on average, still eat and live better.

Culture and Nutrition

Each culture makes choices about which substances will be considered appropriate as food. Initially, such choices involve foods that naturally occur in the environment; with farming and animal husbandry, the application of technology ensures that the chosen foods will be available and increases the inventory of potential foods.

The impact of technology is readily apparent in the dietary regime of the people of Liaoning. Millet and sorghum were the initial staple grains; they later were supplanted by maize and, most recently, by wheat and rice. The latter development has depended upon large-scale irrigation works, but answers a strong cultural demand of Han Chinese migrants to the region, for whom rice was symbolic of adequate food in general. Increased rice consumption has improved the nutritional status of the people of the region, especially as the population density has increased. Today, a few urban families eat maize as a nostalgia and variety food; millet and sorghum are almost exclusively rural foods because they symbolize poverty. Thus, cultural preference of in-migrants has prompted the application of technology to change the dominant grain in the diet and impose an inferior status on formerly dominant grains. Wheat, the staple grain of Western Europe and North America, has long been a staple in northern China as well, but its use lags behind rice.

Meat choices continue to be more traditional everywhere, although urban families eat more meat in total and a greater variety than rural families. Pork is still, by far, the meat of choice. As China faces greater challenges in providing food for its people, pork probably will retain its importance because of its cultural-ecological niche in the Chinese farming system and its consequent symbolic importance as a sign of prosperity and well-being. The necessity to free land that is suitable for rice growing, because of its high per-land-unit

Calorie production, may promote more raising of animals that are fed from fields in areas that are not suitable for rice cultivation. It is uncertain whether this government-supported trend will lead to an increase in consumption of such range-fed animals as beef and lamb. At present, it is minuscule in both urban and rural areas. Such animals are still symbolic of what the Han agriculturalists regard as an inferior culture, that of nomadic-herding "barbarians."

Similar to pigs, chickens and ducks are scavengers, but, because they are small, they are less efficient as meat-producers and, thus, are valued mostly for their eggs. Turkeys, despite their larger size, are not raised in China, but ducks and geese are and, occasionally, are eaten.

Chinese eat fish, but much of China is far from the sea. Improved transportation and storage for fish has made seafood more widely available, and aquaculture in inland areas is increasing the supply of freshwater fish. Fish are used interchangeably with other animal foods. Neither chicken nor fish shows distinct urban-rural differences.

Combinations of meat and grain, including dumplings, filled buns and pancakes, and wonton soup, are traditional foods in China. Because they use meat, the popularity they enjoy in the countryside today is probably recent. As casseroles in the West, they provide an economical way of serving meat because the filling is made from ground or very finely chopped meat, which can start as an inexpensive part of the animal. There is no great rural-urban divide in the use of these foods.

The greater reliance on grain and lower consumption of meat in rural areas, as compared with urban areas in China, is partly economic: meat costs more than grain. It may be cultural as well. Rural people have grown up with the cultural food concept that meals should be based on grain and that meat is an expensive luxury to be savored only occasionally. Rural people tend to be conservative, bred by centuries of isolation, a precarious existence, and resulting reluctance to take great risks.

Even in the countryside, however, culture does change. Most likely, diet changes in times of large-scale innovations in other areas of life. Certainly, the changes in Deng Xiaoping's China have been momentous, and they have affected the countryside greatly; in fact, the first reforms were rural. Agriculture is the first of the Four Modernizations. As with all the other campaigns and movements that have affected the Chinese countryside since 1949, the current economic reform is directed cultural change (Naylor, 1996). It has been directed by city people, down the hierarchy of urban areas, to rural areas. As far as food is concerned, the main official thrust of the reforms has been to produce more of it, but efforts of government health workers and educators also have been directed toward getting peasants to eat better. And they probably, on average, eat better than at any previous time in Chinese history. They, however, have not enjoyed food security for a sufficiently long time, so many of them are unwilling to venture into major changes in their diet, that is, to change the basic map of the concept of food. A persisting barrier of low educational levels, particularly among women, hinders dietary change because women do most of the food-related chores and, thus, are the main "gatekeepers" in the channels through which food reaches the family table.

The choice of foods to be eaten on specific occasions also shows a marked rural-urban divide. Urban families retain the traditional foods for Chinese New Year, but they also add more foods, many of them luxury foods that are a treat for the holiday. Rural families, whose diet is generally less imaginative and, hence, less risky, stick with the "tried and true."

Similarly, urban families' breakfasts show a much greater variety and the acceptance of a more Western-style menu of milk and yeast bread or cake, at least some of the time. Most rural families overwhelmingly eat the same foods for breakfast that they do for any other meal.

As economic development — including urbanization — proceeds, farmers become more commercial. They produce crops to sell in the market (primarily in cities) and purchase their food in stores like non-farmers. Chinese farmers still rely on their own production for a major portion of their needs, but they are developing more commercial specialties, such as fruits, diary cows, and new kinds of vegetables. Because they eat some of their own crop, these specialities change their diets, and urban food preferences, thus, spread to rural people.

Advertising is another form of directed cultural change by which urban preferences penetrate the countryside. As time goes on and rising incomes permit, the few rural families in the field study who ate newly introduced foods may be the beginning of the necessary nucleus of innovators from whom changes in diet will spread to others. Of course, if the foods that are being adopted are mostly candy and ice cream, nutritional levels will not benefit, but such choices do signal cultural change and are in line with the shift to Pattern 4 of Popkin's (1993) Nutrition Transition.

Economic Development and Culture in China

Deng Xiaoping's reforms, especially the household responsibility system that returned land to the control of individual peasant households, has brought great changes to the Chinese countryside. Once they meet the terms of their contracts, households have the freedom, to grow what they want to eat and what they know will sell well in the market. They are enjoying unprecedented prosperity, and their diets reflect this improvement in their lives in general.

Nevertheless, farmers still make a living supplying what city residents want. As John Lossing Buck (1937) described before the establishment of the People's Republic, Chinese peasants sell a high-value product in the market and purchase something else for their own use.

Living standards in urban areas remain much higher than they are in rural areas, and the gap is growing. Urban nutritional levels and dietary quality and variety remain better than those in the countryside. Urban families have higher incomes, and they purchase their foods in markets that can and do offer more choices than any one farmer can grow.

The divide between city and countryside is more than purely economic, however. Urban areas, by nature (Wirth, 1938), bring together a variety of people, who rub shoulders and generate new ideas. Although China's cities historically have been centers of conservatism compared to Western cities (Murphey, 1954), they drew people and ideas from a much broader area and range of interests than a rural village. In Stover's (1974) terms, they were and remain part of the elite.

Urban areas also amass both economic and political power, which they can use to influence what goes on in the countryside. They are the market for rural production, and the market determines what will be produced. In this way, at a minimum, ideas from the city will be felt in the countryside.

The countryside may have to produce for the city, but rural people are traditionally conservative. They are isolated by distance and (historically) by illiteracy and lack of mass communications. Their world is local and circumscribed — Stover's (1974) Green Circle. Life is precarious; any new innovation may produce disaster, a belief that the Great Leap Forward did nothing to dispel. Therefore, although the current life is spartan, it is relatively assured. Life has always been the way it is now, and, as far as anyone knows, it probably will never be any better. And because it could get worse — much worse — no one dares to make changes, lest they lead to starvation. Although Mao Zedong's government reached the level of the villages and the peasants, probably for the first time in Chinese history, his most enduring effect was to bleed the countryside, just as his imperial predecessors did. His first priority was the development of heavy industry. The famine of the Great Leap Forward hardly made peasants want to take major risks!

The Dengist reforms have brought urban functions and landscape features to the countryside in a way that is somewhat unique to East Asia (McGee, 1989; 1991a). Because the agricultural population is already dense, manufacturing concerns take advantage of available labor and locate along transportation routes in rural areas, leading to rural urbanization (Zhao, 1994). Away from these corridors, development and urbanization are less, declining to almost none in the regions farthest from cities and transportation.

Economic development, with its attendant opportunities for manufacturing and service employment, brings changes in ways of life. Farmers, or members of their families, are employed for cash wages, rather than working the land to produce food directly. In many Chinese families, one or more members work off the farm, while others continue to work the land. Some of these families do continue to produce their own food, but more and more families are buying, rather than growing, their food. Similar to families in the cities, they are now buying food in the market, using cash and enjoying a greater variety of choices.

Diet, however, has remained rather resistant to change. Staple foods are especially persistent. Even families whose lifestyle becomes more urban-like, due to livelihoods shifting to manufacturing or services, may continue to eat the same dietary regime. National and provincial statistics and the food diaries indicate that this is happening in China. Although the government of the People's Republic has reached the local village and changed many aspects of peasants' lives several times, it has not changed one of the most fundamental, central parts of their culture: their dietary regime — their conceptual map of food. The same dietary regime continues to symbolize well-being. In terms of nutrition and diet, the main divide remains between city and countryside.

Despite the enormous changes that the People's Republic has wrought in the countryside and despite rhetoric that China must "walk on two legs," and that the city and countryside are equal, there remains a great difference between the two types of regions. The real contrast is between the city and the countryside, rather than among the rural areas. In other words, the suburbs are more similar to other rural areas than to the city. Robert Redfield's folk-urban continuum, as applied to China by Stover, is alive and well in Liaoning Province.

The persistence of this rural-urban contrast, despite government efforts to develop the countryside, shows that culture is a force that runs deeply in the people who hold it. The dietary regime, which is especially central to the Chinese, is particularly resistant to change, and, even more so, in the rural population, which tends to be conservative. Whether rural residents will become more venturesome in their food choices will depend on China's ability to continue to supply its citizens with adequate amounts of food and, thus, to provide food security. With a growing population and land being converted to urban and industrial uses, food supply in China remains a challenge.

If the rural Chinese do begin to adopt a conceptual map of food that bears a greater resemblance to urban choices, including Western additions, the change will have great implications for China's — and the world's — economy. It will mean satisfying a greatly increased demand for meat, which is higher on the food chain and, thus, more costly in terms of capital and of land to produce. Use of more processed and manufactured foods will divert resources into their production without necessarily improving nutritional levels in China or anywhere else. Because China's population is so large and its rapid economic growth is giving its people more purchasing power, what its people choose to eat can have a great impact on the entire world.

Notes

CHAPTER 2

1. The classic fictional account is Pearl S. Buck's Nobel Prize-winning novel, *The Good Earth* (1930).
2. Overeating is also a form of malnutrition — over-nutrition.

CHAPTER 3

1. The first record of its cultivation in the United States, where it was regarded as a botanical curiosity, was in Savannah, Georgia, by Samuel Bowen in 1765 (Wittwer et al., 1987: 184).

CHAPTER 4

1. Promotion of *agriculture*, not manufacturing — the "Food First Hypothesis" — leads to development in the form of better nutrition. See Cheng, 1989.
2. The Four Modernizations are, in order of priority, Agriculture, Industry, Science and Technology, and the Military.

CHAPTER 5

1. A *jin* is a little more than a pound; 2 *jin* equal 1 kilogram.

CHAPTER 6

1. According to the Wilcoxon Signed Rank Test (used because of non-normal distribution), with W = 153.0, T+ = 203.0, and T– = –50.0. In other words, the changes in households that increased consumption totaled 203, the changes in those that decreased consumption totaled 50, and the total change was 153. Testing variation by season does not appear in the literature of foodways and nutritional studies. Because the paired-*t* test examines changes before and after some intervention to see whether the intervention had a significant effect, it was chosen for this purpose in cases where the data were normally distributed. Specifically, this test calculates changes resulting from a "treatment"; here, the "treatment" is

the change of seasons. Examining the changes, rather than the values themselves, removes the differences that result from individual responses, producing a more sensitive and powerful test. The *t*-test statistic is a ratio of the mean difference of the subjects (households in this case) before (in the spring) and after (in the fall), divided by the standard error of the mean difference (a measure of the approximation with which the mean computed from the sample approximates the true population mean).

If the data were not normally distributed, a Wilcoxon signed ranks test was used in place of the paired-*t* test. The Wilcoxon test statistic *W* is computed by ranking all of the differences before and after the treatment (in this case, the change of seasons) based on their absolute value, then attaching the signs of the difference to the corresponding ranks. The signed ranks are then summed and compared. A large *W* statistic indicates that there was a significant change because all of the changes were in one direction. By the same token, a small *W* statistic indicates that there was a mixture of positive and negative changes, and they cancelled each other out.

2. The paired-*t* test (t = 2.95) shows a decline. The power of the test with alpha at .05, however, is slightly below the level needed to give complete confidence to the results.

3. Using the paired-*t* test ($t = 3.52$).

4. The paired-*t* test shows $t = 2.8$; however, the power of that test with alpha .05 was lower than desired for full confidence in the results.

5. The paired-*t* test for the percentage of the recommended consumption of protein was $t = 3.26$, with a power high enough to lend confidence to the results. By the same test, Vitamin C consumption also declined ($t = 2.13$), but the power of the test was too low to be used with confidence. The change in the consumption of Vitamin A was even greater ($t = 4.89$), and the power of the test was high enough to be used with confidence. Because of non-normal distributions, the change in percentage of recommended Calorie consumption was tested using the Wilcoxon Signed Rank Test, with W = –186, T+ = 2.00, and T– = –188. Likewise, the Wilcoxon Signed Rank Test was used for the ratio of carbohydrates to fats, with W = –104, T+ = 43, and T– = 147.

6. According to the paired-*t* test, the change was statistically significant ($t = 3.54$), with a power high enough to be used with confidence. Because the distribution is non-normal, the Wilcoxon Signed Rank Test was used to compare the ratio of Calories from carbohydrates to Calories from fats and showed a statistically significant change: W = –89, T+ = 8, and T– = –97. The change in Calories from fats in this equation was too small to be statistically significant, but Calories from carbohydrates declined significantly ($t = -1.59$), although the power of the test is low, requiring caution in the interpretation. For protein consumption, $t = 3.33$ with a power to allow confidence in the results.

7. ($t = -2.76$); the power of the test is low, requiring caution in interpretation.

8. ($t = 4.51$).

9. ($t = -2.31$). The power of the test, however, is also low enough to require caution in interpretation.

10. ($t = -3.32$).

11. ($t = -4.49$).

References

Abler, Ronald, John S. Adams, and Peter Gould. 1971. *Spatial Organization: The Geographer's View of the World*. Englewood Cliffs, NJ: Prentice-Hall.

Abrams, H. Leon, Jr. 1987. The preference for animal protein and fat: A cross-cultural survey, in *Food and Evolution: Toward a Theory of Human Food Habits*, eds. Marvin Harris and Eric B. Ross, pp. 207–23. Philadelphia: Temple University Press.

Aebi, H.E. 1981. Food acceptance and nutrition: Experiences, intentions and responsibilities. An introductory paper, in *Criteria of Food Acceptance: How Man Chooses What He Eats*, eds. J. Solms and R. L. Hall, pp. 3–11. Zurich, Switzerland: Forster Verlag.

Alexander, J.W. 1985. Immunity, nutrition, and trauma: An overview, *Acta Chirurgica Scandinavica* 522: 141–50.

Allport, Susan. 2000. *The Primal Feast: Food, Foraging, and Love*. New York: Harmony Books.

Alfin-Slater, R. B., and L. Aftergood. 1968. Essential fatty acids reinvestigated, *Physiological Reviews* 48: 758–84.

American Cancer Society Advisory Committee on Diet, Nutrition, and Cancer Prevention. 1996. American Cancer Society guidelines on diet, nutrition, and cancer prevention: Reducing the risk of cancer with healthy food choices and physical activity, *CA—A Cancer Journal for Clinicians* 46(6): 325–41.

Anderson, E.N. 1988. *The Food of China*. New Haven, CT: Yale University Press.

Anderson, E.N., Jr., and Marja L. Anderson. 1977. Modern China: South, in *Food in Chinese Culture*, ed. K.C. Chang, pp. 317–82. New Haven, CT: Yale University Press.

Andersson, J. Gunnar. 1934. *The Children of the Yellow Earth: Studies in Prehistoric China*. London: Kegan, Paul, Trench, Trubner & Co., Ltd.; reprinted ed. 1973, Cambridge, MA: M.I.T. Press,.

Antolini, Piers, and The Lian Tjo. 1990. *The Great Book of Chinese Cooking*. New York: International Culinary Society.

Arnaud, Claude D., and Sarah D. Sanchez. 1990. Calcium and phosphorous, in *Present Knowledge in Nutrition*, 6th ed., ed. Myrtle L. Brown, pp. 212–23. Washington, DC: International Life Sciences Institute Nutrition Foundation.

Ashton, Basil, Kenneth Hill, Alan Piazza, and Robin Zeitz. 1984. Famine in China, 1958–61, *Population and Development Review* 10, no. 4 (December): 613–45.

Atkins, Peter, and Ian Bowler. 2001. *Food in Society: Economy, Culture, Geography*. London: Arnold.

Atkinson, P. 1978. From honey to vinegar: Lévi-Strauss in Vermont, in *Culture and Curing: Anthropological Perspectives on Traditional Medical Beliefs and Practices*, eds. Peter Morley and Roy Wallis, pp. 168–88. London: Owen

_____. 1980. The symbolic significance of health foods, in *Nutrition and Lifestyles*, ed. Michael Turner, pp. 79–89. London: Applied Science Publishers.

_____. 1983. Eating virtue, in *The Sociology of Food and Eating: Essays on the Sociological Significance of Food*, ed. Anne Murcott, pp. 9–17. Aldershot, England: Gower.

Aubert, Claude. 1988. China's food take-off? in *Transforming China's Economy in the Eighties*, Vol. I: *The Rural Sector Welfare and Employment*, eds. Stephan Feuchtwang, Athar Hussain, and Thierry Pairault, pp. 101–46. Boulder, CO: Westview Press.

Back, Kurt W. 1977. Food, sex, and theory, in *Nutrition and Anthropology in Action*, ed. Thomas K. Fitzgerald, pp. 24–34. Amsterdam: van Gorcum, Assen.

Banister, Judith. 1987. *China's Changing Population*. Stanford, CA: Stanford University Press.

Barthes, Roland. 1961. Vers une psycho-sociologie de l'alimentation moderne, *Annales: Économies, Sociétés, Civilisations* 5: 977–86; reprinted in English in *Food and Culture: A Reader*, eds. Carole Counihan and Penny Van Esterik, 1997, pp. 20–8. New York: Routledge.

Banpo Museum. 1987. *Banpo Yizi Huace [Banpo Ruins Illustrated Handbook]*. Xi'an: Shaanxi People's Art Publishing Company.

Basta, Samir S. 1977. Nutrition and health in low income urban areas of the Third World, *Ecology of Food and Nutrition* 6: 113–24.

Beck, Melinda A., Peter C. Kolbeck, Lisa H. Rohr, Qing Shi, Virginia C. Morris, and Orville A. Levander. 1994a. Benign human enterovirus becomes virulent in selenium-deficient mice, *Journal of Medical Virology* 43: 166–70.

_____. 1994b. Vitamin E deficiency intensifies the myocardial injury of coxsackievirus B3 infection of mice, *Journal of Nutrition* 124: 345–58.

Beck, Melinda A., Peter C. Kolbeck, Qing Shi, Lisa H. Rohr, Virginia C. Morris, and Orville A. Levander. 1994. Increased virulence of a human enterovirus (Coxsackievirus B3) in selenium-deficient mice, *Journal of Infectious Diseases* 170: 351–7.

Becker, Jasper. 1997. *Hungry Ghosts: Mao's Secret Famine*. New York: Free Press.

Beijing Review. 2000. China will make new and greater contributions to the world food security, *Beijing Review* April 10, p. 29.

Bell, David, and Gill Valentine. 1997. *Consuming Geographies: We Are Where We Eat*. London: Routledge.

Bell, Michael M. 1992. The fruit of difference: The rural-urban continuum as a system of identity, *Rural Sociology* 57(1): 65–82.

Bennett, John W. 1946. An interpretation of the scope and implications of social scientific research in human subsistence, *American Anthropologist* 48: 553–73.

Bennett, Merrill K. 1941. International contrasts in food consumption, *Geographical Review* 31(3): 365–76.

Bergman, Edward F. 1995. *Human Geography: Cultures, Connections, and Landscapes*. Englewood Cliffs, NJ: Prentice Hall.

Berry, Brian J.L. 1962. Some relations of urbanization and basic patterns of economic development, in *Urban Systems and Economic Development*, ed. Forrest R. Pitts, pp. 1–15. Eugene, OR: School of Business Administration, University of Oregon.

_____. 1969a. Policy implications of an urban location model for the Kanpur region, in *Regional Perspective of Industrial and Urban Growth: The Case of Kanpur*, eds. P. B. Desai et al., pp. 203–19. Bombay: Macmillan and Company.

_____. 1969b. Relationships between regional economic development and the urban system: The case of Chile, *Tijdschrift voor Economische en Sociale Geografie* 60: 283–307.

Booth, D.A. 1981. Momentary acceptance of particular foods and processes that change it, in *Criteria of Food Acceptance: How Man Chooses What He Eats*, ed. J. Solms and R. L. Hall, pp. 49–68. Zurich, Switzerland: Forster Verlag.

Bourdieu, Pierre. 1984. *Distinction: A Social Critique of the Judgement of Taste*. Cambridge, MA: Harvard University Press.

Bloch, M.R. 1963. The social influence of salt, *Scientific American* 209 (July): 88–98.

Bray, Francesca. 1984. Agriculture. Part II of Vol. 6: Biology and Biological Technology, in *Science and Civilisation in China*, ed. Joseph Needham. Cambridge: Cambridge University Press.

_____. 1994. Agriculture for developing nations, *Scientific American* 271 (July): 30–7.

Brody, Jane E. 1984. Garlic may mend your ailments, *Lancaster* [Pa.] *Intelligencer-Journal*, November 8, p. 15.

_____. 1990. Huge study of diet indicts fat and meat, *New York Times*, May 8, pp. 1

Brown, Lester R. 1995. *Who Will Feed China? A Wake-up Call for a Small Planet*. New York: W.W. Norton.

_____ and Christopher Flavin. 1996. China's Challenge to the United States and to the Earth, *World Watch* 9, No. 5 (September/October): 10–13.

Brown, Myrtle L. 1990. Thiamin, in *Present Knowledge in Nutrition*, 6th ed., ed. Myrtle L. Brown, pp. 142–5. Washington, DC: International Life Sciences Institute Nutrition Foundation.

Bryant, Carol A., Anita Courtney, Barbara A. Markesbery, and Kathleen M. DeWalt. 1985. *The Cultural Feast: An Introduction to Food and Society*. St. Paul, MN: West Publishing Company.

Buck, David D. 1978. *Urban Change in China: Politics and Development in Tsinan, Shantung, 1890–1949*. Madison: University of Wisconsin Press.

_____. 1981. Politics favoring the growth of smaller urban places in the People's Republic of China, 1949–1979, in *Urban Development in Modern China*, eds. Laurence J.C. Ma and Edward W. Hanten, pp. 114–46. Boulder, CO: Westview Press.

Buck, John Lossing. 1937. *Land Utilization in China*. Chicago: University of Chicago Press.

Buttrick, John. 1960. Toward a theory of economic growth: The neoclassical contribution, in *Theories of Economic Growth*, eds. Bert F. Hoselitz et al., pp. 155–92. Glencoe, IL: Free Press of Glencoe.

Cai, Yan. 1991. A better diet off the menu until 2000, *China Daily*, October 25.

_____. 1993. No more coupon books to buy the rice of life ... , *China Daily*, Nov. 29, p. 6.

Campbell, T. Colin, Chen Junshi, Thierry Brun, Banoo Parpia, Qu Yinsheng, Chen Chumming, and Catherine Geissler. 1992. China: From diseases of poverty to diseases of affluence. Policy implications of the epidemiological transition, *Ecology of Food and Nutrition* 27: 133–44.

Caplan, Pat. 1997. Approaches to the study of food, health and identity, in *Food, Health and Identity*, ed. Pat Caplan, pp. 1–31. London: Routledge.

Carter, Colin A. 1997. The urban-rural income gap in China: Implications for global food markets, *American Journal of Agricultural Economics* No. 5: 1410–8.

Chang, K.C. 1977a. Ancient China, in *Food in Chinese Culture: Anthropological and Historical Perspectives*, ed. K.C. Chang, pp. 22–52. New Haven, CT: Yale University Press.

_____. 1977b. Introduction, in *Food in Chinese Culture: Anthropological and Historical Perspectives*, ed K.C. Chang, pp. 1–21. New Haven, CT: Yale University Press.

Chang, Kwang-chih. 1977c. *The Archaeology of Ancient China*, 3rd ed. New Haven, CT: Yale University Press.

Chang, Sen-dou. 1963. The historical trend of Chinese urbanization, *Annals of the Association of American Geographers* 53, No. 2(June): 109–43.

Chao, Kang. 1986. *Man and Land in Chinese History: An Economic Analysis*. Stanford, CA: Stanford University Press.

Chee, Bernadine W.L. 2000. Eating snacks and biting pleasure: Only children in Beijing, in *Feeding China's Little Emperors: Food, Children, and Social Change*, ed. Jun Jing, pp. 48–70. Stanford, CA: Stanford University Press.

Chen, C.-S. 1973. Population growth and urbanization in China, *Geographical Review* 63: 55–72.

Chen, Junshi, T. Colin Campbell, Li Junyao, and Richard Peto. 1990. *Diet, Life-style and Mortality in China: A Study of the Characteristics of 65 Chinese Counties*. Oxford: Oxford University Press.

Chen, Xiangming. 1991. China's city hierarchy, urban policy and spatial development in the 1980s, *Urban Studies* 28, No. 3: 341–61.

Chen, Xiaoshu, Guangqi Yang, Junshi Chen, Xuecun Chen, Zhimei Wen, and Keyou Ge. 1980. Studies on the relations of selenium and Keshan disease, *Biological Trace Element Research* 2: 91–107.

Chenery, Hollis B., and M. Syrquin. 1975. *Patterns of Development, 1950–1970*. London: Oxford University Press.

Cheng, Wei-Yuan. 1989. Testing the food-first hypothesis: A cross-national study of dependency, sectoral growth and food intake in less developed countries, *World Development* 17, No. 1(January): 17–27.

Childe, V. Gordon. 1983. *Man Makes Himself*. New York: New American Library (orig. published 1936, rev. 1951).

China Academy of Preventive Medicine, Institute of Nutrition and Food Hygiene. 1991. *Shiwu Chengfen Biao (Quanguohua Biao Zhen)* [*Food Component Tables (Entire Country Values)*]. Beijing: People's Hygiene Publishing Company.

China Daily. 1991. Rural unemployed siphon city resources, *China Daily*, October 24.

Chiu, T.N. 1980. Urbanization processes and national development, in *China: Urbanization and National Development*, Paper No. 196, eds. C. K. Leung and Norton Ginsburg, pp. 89–107. Chicago: Department of Geography Research, University of Chicago.

Christian Science Monitor. 1993. Prosperity reduces popularity of Chinese cabbage, *Christian Science Monitor*, February 18; reprinted in *China News Digest*, February 22, 1993.

Chu, Godwin C., and Francis L. K. Hsu. 1979. *Moving a Mountain: Cultural Change in China*. Honolulu: University Press of Hawaii.

Chu, Godwin C., and Yanan Ju. 1993. *The Great Wall in Ruins: Communication and Cultural Change in China*. Albany: State University of New York Press.

Clark, Colin. 1957. *The Conditions of Economic Progress*, 3rd ed. London: Macmillan Company.

Cousins, Robert J., and James M. Hempe. 1990. Zinc, in *Present Knowledge in Nutrition*, 6th ed., ed. Myrtle L. Brown, pp. 251–60. Washington, DC: International Life Sciences Institute Nutrition Foundation.

Cressey, George Babcock. 1934. *China's Geographic Foundations: A Survey of the Land and Its People*. New York: McGraw-Hill.

Critser, Greg. 2003. *Fat Land: How Americans Became the Fattest People in the World*. Houghton Mifflin.

Croll, Elisabeth. 1983. *The Family Rice Bowl: Food and the Domestic Economy in China*. London: Zed Press.

_____. 1988. The new peasant economy in China, in *Transforming China's Economy in the Eighties*, Vol. I: *The Rural Sector, Welfare and Employment*, eds. Stephan Feuchtwang, Athar Hussain, and Tierry Pairault, pp. 77–100. Boulder, CO: Westview Press.

Crosby, Alfred W., Jr. 1972. *The Columbian Exchange: Biological and Cultural Consequences of 1492*. Westport, CT: Greenwood Press.

_____. 1991. Metamorphosis of the Americas, in *Seeds of Change: A Quincentennial Commemoration*, eds. Herman J. Viola and Carolyn Margolis, pp. 70–89. Washington, DC: Smithsonian Institution Press.

Crouch, Mira, and Grant O'Neill. 2000. Sustaining identities? Prolegomena for inquiry into contemporary foodways, *Social Science Information* 39(1): 181–92.

Dallman, Peter R. 1990. Iron, in *Present Knowledge in Nutrition*, 6th ed., ed. Myrtle L. Brown, pp. 241–50. Washington, DC: International Life Sciences Institute Nutrition Foundation.

Dando, William A. 1980. *The Geography of Famine*. New York: V. H. Winston & Sons, John Wiley.

Davis, C. 1928. Self-selection of diets by newly-weaned infants, *American Journal of Diseases of Children* 36: 351–79.

Davis, Kingsley. 1950. *Human Society*. New York: Macmillan.

de Blij, Harm J. 1993. *Human Geography: Culture, Society, and Space*, 4th ed. New York: John Wiley.

Dekker, M. 1995. Tea-producing countries, *Food Reviews International* 11(3): 381–2.

DeMaeyer, E., M. Adiels-Tegman, and E. Rayston. 1985. The prevalence of anemia in the world, *World Health Statistical Quarterly* 38: 302–16.

Dennett, Glenn, and John Connell. 1988. Acculturation and health in the highlands of Papua New Guinea, *Current Anthropology* 29(2): 273–99.

Dernberger, Robert F. 1980. Introduction: Quantitative measures and analysis of China's contemporary evolution: Problems and prospects, in *Quantitative Measures of China's Economic Output,* ed. Alexander Eckstein, pp. 1–43. Ann Arbor: University of Michigan Press.

Develin, John T., and Edward S. Horton. 1990. Energy requirements, in *Present Knowledge in Nutrition*, 6th ed., ed. Myrtle L. Brown, pp. 1–6. Washington, DC: International Life Sciences Institute Nutrition Foundation.

DeWalt, K.M., P.B. Kelly, and G.H. Pelto. 1980. Nutritional correlates of economic microdifferentiation in a Highland Mexican community, in *Nutritional Anthropology: Contemporary Approaches to Diet and Culture*, eds. Norge W. Jerome, Randy F. Kandel, and Gretel H. Pelto, pp. 205–21. Pleasantville, NY: Redgrave Publishing Company.

Dewey, Richard. 1960. The rural-urban continuum: Real but relatively unimportant, *American Journal of Sociology* 66: 60–6.

Ding, Xueyong. 1994. Personal interview, Shenyang, Liaoning, China, March 26.

Douglas, Mary. 1966. *Purity and Danger: An Analysis of Concepts of Pollution and Taboo.* London: Routledge & Kegan Paul.

_____. 1972. Deciphering a meal, *Daedalus* 101: 61–81.

_____. 1976–77. Structures of gastronomy, in *The Future and the Past: Annual Report*, ed. Mary Douglas. New York: Russell Sage Foundation.

Durkheim, Emile. 1933. *De la division de travail social*, trans. George Simpson as *Émile Durkheim on the Division of Labor in Society.* New York: Macmillan.

Eckstein, Alexander, ed. 1980. *Quantitative Measures of China's Economic Output.* Ann Arbor: University of Michigan Press.

Economist Intelligence Unit. 1991. EIU Country Report—China, No. 1, p. 28.

Elvin, Mark. 1973. *The Pattern of the Chinese Past: A Social and Economic Interpretation.* Stanford, CA: Stanford University Press.

Evans, John C. 1972. *Tea in China: The History of China's National Drink.* Westport, CT: Greenwood Press.

Ewald, Ursula. 1977. The von Thünen principle and agricultural zonation in colonial Mexico, *Journal of Historical Geography* 3: 123–33.

Farb, Peter, and George Armelagos. 1980. *Consuming Passions: The Anthropology of Eating.* New York: Washington Square Press.

Farnsworth, Elizabeth. 1997. Interview with Cara de Silva, author of *Memory's Kitchen. The News Hour with Jim Lehrer*, PBS, February 17.

Fei, Hsiao-Tung. 1953. *China's Gentry*, rev. & ed. by Margaret Redfield. Reprinted 1980. Chicago: University of Chicago Press,

Fernández-Armesto, Felipe. 2002. *Near a Thousand Tables: A History of Food.* New York: The Free Press.

_____. 1989. *Rural Development in China: Prospect and Retrospect.* Chicago: University of Chicago Press.

Field, Robert Michael. 1988. Trends in the value of agricultural output, 1978–86, *China Quarterly* No. 116: 556–91.

Fieldhouse, Paul. 1986. *Food and Nutrition: Customs and Culture.* London: Croom Helm.

Fischler, Claude. 1988a. Cuisines and food selection, in *Food Acceptability*, ed. David M. H. Thomson, pp. 193–206. London: Elsevier Applied Science.

_____. 1988b. Food, self, and identity, *Social Science Information* 27(2): 275–92.

Fisher, Allen. 1939. Production, primary, secondary, and tertiary, *Economic Record* 15 (June): 24–38.

Fitzgerald, Thomas K. 1986. Dietary change among Cook Islanders in New Zealand, in *Shared Wealth and Symbol: Food, Culture and Society in Oceania and Southeast Asia*, ed. Lenore Manderson, pp. 67–86. Cambridge: Cambridge University Press.

Foster, George M. 1953. What is folk culture? *American Anthropologist* 55(2, pt. 1): 159–73.

_____. 1962. *Traditional Cultures and the Impact of Technological Change.* New York: Harper & Row.

Frank, André Gunder. 1967. *Capitalism and Underdevelopment in Latin America: Historical Studies of Chile and Brazil.* New York: Monthly Review Press.

Freeman, Michael. 1977. Sung, in *Food in Chinese Culture: Anthropological and Historical Perspectives*, ed. K.C. Chang, pp. 141–76. New Haven, CT: Yale University Press.

Friedmann, John. 1966. *Regional Development Policy: A Case Study of Venezuela.* Cambridge, MA: M.I.T. Press.

Gamble, Sidney D. 1933. *How Chinese Families Live in Peiping.* New York: Funk and Wagnalls.

_____. 1954. *Ting Hsien: A North China Rural Community.* Stanford, CA: Stanford University Press.

Garnault, Ross, and Guonan Ma. 1993. How rich is China? Evidence from the food economy, *Australian Journal of Chinese Affairs* No. 30(July): 121–46.

Gauntt, Charles, and Steven Tracy. 1995. Deficient diet evokes nasty heart virus, *Nature Medicine* 1(1): 405–6.

Gillie, R. Bruce. 1971. Endemic goiter, *Scientific American* 224(June): 93–101.

Gillis, Malcolm, Dwight H. Perkins, Michael Roemer, and Donald R. Snodgrass. 1983. *Economics of Development.* New York: W. W. Norton.

Ginsburg, Norton. 1991. Extended metropolitan regions in Asia: A new spatial paradigm, in *The Extended Metropolis: Settlement Transition in Asia,* eds. Norton Ginsburg, Bruce Koppel, and T. G. McGee, pp. 27–46. Honolulu: University of Hawaii Press.

Glover, Ian C., and Charles F.W. Higham. 1996. New Evidence for early rice cultivation in South, Southeast and East Asia, in *The Origins and Spread of Agriculture and Pastoralism in Eurasia,* ed. David R. Harris, pp. 413–41. Washington, DC: Smithsonian Institution Press.

Goldstein, Sidney, and Alice Goldstein. 1984. Population movement, labor force absorption, and urbanization in China, *Annals of the American Academy of Political and Social Science* 476(November): 90–110.

Goody, J. 1982. *Cooking, Cuisine and Class: A Study in Comparative Sociology.* Cambridge: Cambridge University Press.

Gottmann, Jean. 1961. *Megalopolis.* New York: Twentieth Century Fund.

Greene, Felix. 1961. *Awakened China: The Country Americans Don't Know.* Westport, CT: Greenwood Press.

Griffin, Ernst. 1973. Testing the von Thünen theory in Uruguay, *Geographical Review* 636: 500–16.

Grigg, David. 1995. The Nutrition Transition in Western Europe, *Journal of Historical Geography* 21(3): 247–61.

Grilo, Carlos M., and Kelly D. Brownell. 1994. Weight cycling, *Weight Control Digest,* July/August, n.p.

Grivetti, Louis Evan, and Marie B. Paquette. 1978. Non-traditional ethnic food choices among first generation Chinese in California, *Journal of Nutrition Education* 10(3): 109–12.

Gu, Boqi. 1983. Pathology of Keshan disease, *Chinese Medical Journal* 96: 251–61.

Guldan, Georgia S. 1999. Obesity–a new challenge to health in China. Heinz Institute of Nutritional Sciences 12th Annual Symposium on Maternal and Infant Nutrition, Nanjing, China, 11 to 12 November 1998, *Australian Journal of Nutrition and Dietetics* 56(1): 43.

_____. 2000. Paradoxes of plenty: China's infant- and child-feeding transition, in *Feeding China's Little Emperors: Food, Children and Social Change,* ed. Jun Jing, pp. 27–47. Stanford, CA: Stanford University Press.

Guo, Xuguang, Barry M. Popkin, and Fengying Zhai. 1999. Patterns of change in food consumption and dietary fat intake in Chinese adults, 1989–1993, *Food and Nutrition Bulletin* 20(3): 344–53.

Hall, P. 1982. *Urban and Regional Planning.* London: Allen and Unwin.

Hallberg, L., M. Brune, and L. Rossander-Hulthén. 1987. Is there a physiological role of Vitamin C in iron absorption?, in *Third Conference on Vitamin C. Annals of the New York Academy of Sciences* 498, eds. J. J. Burns, J. M. Rivers, and L. J. Machlin, pp. 324–32. New York: New York Academy of Sciences.

Harris, David. R. 1996. The origins and spread of agriculture and pastoralism in Eurasia: An overview, in *The Origins and Spread of Agriculture and Pastoralism in Eurasia*, ed. David R. Harris, pp. 552–73. Washington, DC: Smithsonian Institution Press.

Harris, Marvin. 1979a. *Cultural Materialism: The Struggle for a Science of Culture.* New York: Random House.

_____. 1979b. Our pound of flesh, *Natural History* 88(7): 30–6.

_____. 1986. *Good to Eat: Riddles of Food and Culture.* London: Allen and Unwin.

Harriss, Barbara. 1989. Commercialisation, distribution and consumption: Rural-urban grain and resource transfers in peasant society, in *The Geography of Urban-Rural Interaction in Developing Countries: Essays for Alan Mountjoy*, eds. Robert B. Potter and Tim Unwin, pp. 204–32. London: Routledge.

Heilig, Gerhard K. 1999. China's changing land: Population, food demand and land use in China, *Options* (Summer): 18–20; reprinted in *Geography 00/01*, 15ᵗʰ edition, ed. Gerald R. Pitzl, pp. 218–20. Annual Editions. Guilford, CT: Dushkin/McGraw-Hill.

Henderson, Zorika Petic. 1994. To your health: A plant-based diet, *Human Ecology Forum* 22(3): 6–8.

Herbert, D.T. 1982. The changing face of the city, in *The Changing Geography of the United Kingdom*, eds. R. J. Johnston and J. C. Doornkamp, pp. 227–55. London: Methuen.

Hiebert, Paul G. 1976. *Cultural Anthropology.* Philadelphia: J. B. Lippincott.

Hilker, D.M., and J.C. Somogyi. 1982. Anti-thiamins of plant origin: Their chemical nature and mode of action, *Annals of the New York Academy of Science* 378: 137–45.

Hilliard, Sam Bowers. 1972. *Hog Meat and Hoecake: Food Supply in the Old South, 1840–1860.* Carbondale: Southern Illinois University Press.

Hirschman, Albert O. 1988. *The Strategy of Economic Development.* Boulder, CO: Westview Press.

Ho, Peter. 2003. Mao's war against nature? The environmental impact of the grain-first campaign in China, *The China Journal* No. 50: 37–59.

Ho, Ping-ti. 1955. The introduction of American food plants into China, *American Anthropologist* 57: 191–201.

_____. 1969. The loess and the origin of Chinese agriculture, *American Historical Review* 75(1): 1–36.

_____. 1975. *The Cradle of the East: An Inquiry into the Indigenous Origins of Techniques and Ideas of Neolithic and Early Historic China, 5000–1000 B.C.* Hong Kong: The Chinese University of Hong Kong.

Hodder, Robert. 1994. State, collective and private industry in China's evolving economy, in *China: The Next Decade*, ed. Denis Dwyer, pp. 116–27. Harlow, Essex: Longman Scientific and Technical.

Hoebel, E. Adamson. 1972. *Anthropology: The Study of Man*, 4th ed. New York: McGraw-Hill Book Company.

Hom, Ken. 1990a. *Ken Hom's Quick and Easy Chinese Cooking.* San Francisco: Chronicle Books.

_____. 1990b. *The Taste of China.* New York: Simon and Schuster.

Hornig, D. 1975. Metabolism of ascorbic acid, *World Review of Nutrition and Dietetics* 23: 225–58.

Horvath, Ronald J. 1969. Von Thünen's isolated state and the area around Addis Ababa, Ethiopia, *Annals of the Association of American Geographers* 59: 308–23.

Horwitt, M.K., E. Liebert, O. Kreisler, and P. Wittman. 1948. *Investigation of Human Requirements for B-Complex Vitamins*, Bulletin of the National Research Council, No. 116. Report of the Committee on Nutritional Aspects of Ageing, Food and Nutrition Board, Division of Biology and Agriculture. Washington, DC: National Academy of Sciences.

Howard, Maurice. 1990. Industry, energy and transport: Problems and policies, in *The Geography of Contemporary China: The Impact of Deng Xiaoping's Decade*, eds. Terry Cannon and Alan Jenkins, pp. 168–202. London: Routledge.

Hoyt, Elizabeth E. 1961. Integration of culture: A review of concepts, *Current Anthropology* 2(5): 407–26.

Hsu, Cho-yun. 1980. *Han Agriculture*. Seattle: University of Washington Press.

Hsu, Mei-Ling. 1985. Growth and control of population in China: The urban-rural contrast, *Annals of the Association of American Geographers* 75: 241–57.

Hsu, Shin-yi. 1981. The ecology of Chinese Neolithic agricultural expansion, *China Geographer* No. 11: 1–26.

Hsu, Vera Y.N., and Francis L.K. Hsu. 1977. Modern China: North, in *Food in Chinese Culture: Anthropological and Historical Perspectives*, ed. K.C. Chang, pp. 295–316. New Haven, CT: Yale University Press.

Hunter, John M. 1973. Geophagy in Africa and in the United States: A culture-nutrition hypothesis, *Geographical Review* 63(2): 170–224.

Hussain, Athar, and Stephan Feuchtwang. 1988. The people's livelihood and the incidence of poverty, in *Transforming China's Economy in the Eighties*, Vol. I: *The Rural Sector, Welfare and Employment*, eds. Stephen Feuchtwang, Athar Hussain, and Thieray Pairault, pp. 36–76. Boulder, CO: Westview Press.

Inouye, K., and E. Katsura. 1965. Etiology and pathology of beriberi, in *Review of Japanese Literature on Beriberi and Thiamine*, eds. N. Shimazono and E. Katsura. Vitamin B Research Committee of Japan. Tokyo: Igaku Shoin.

Jacob, Robert A., and Marian E. Swendseid. 1990. Niacin, in *Present Knowledge in Nutrition*, 6th ed., ed. Myrtle L. Brown, pp. 163–69. Washington, DC: International Life Sciences Institute Nutrition Foundation.

Jerome, N.W. 1980. Diet and acculturation: The case of Black-American in-migrants, in *Nutritional Anthropology: Contemporary Approaches*, eds. Norge W. Jerome, Randy F. Kandel, and Gretel H. Pelto, pp. 275–325. Pleasantville, NY: Redgrave Publishing Company.

———, Randy F. Kandel, and Gretel H. Pelto, ed. 1980. *Nutritional Anthropology: Contemporary Approaches to Diet and Culture*. Pleasantville, NY: Redgrave Publishing Company.

Jerome, Norge W., G.H. Pelto, and R.F. Kandel. 1980. An ecological approach to nutritional anthropology, in *Nutritional Anthropology: Contemporary Approaches*, eds. Norge W. Jerome, Randy F. Kandel, and Gretel H. Pelto, pp. 13–45. Pleasantville, NY: Redgrave Publishing Company.

Jiang, Changqing. 1994. Take immediate actions and win a victory in the battle of providing for and helping oneself by engaging in production, *Liaoning Ribao* [*Liaoning Daily*], August 20, p. 1, in FBIS-CHI-94-174, September 8 , pp. 68–9.

Jiang, Zhongyi. 1988. The form of basic food subsidies needs to be reformed urgently, *Jingji Ribao* [*Economic Daily*], FBIS-CHI, April 12, pp. 58–9.

Jones, Jeff A. 1992. Personal communication.

Jussaume, Raymond A., Jr. 2001. Factors associated with modern urban Chinese food consumption patterns, *Journal of Contemporary China* 10(27): 219–32.

Kandel, R.F., and G.H. Pelto. 1980. The health food movement: Social revitalization or alternative health maintenance system?, in *Nutritional Anthropology: Contemporary Approaches to Diet and Culture*, eds. Norge W. Jerome, Randy F. Kandel, and Gretel H. Pelto, pp. 327–63. Pleasantville, NY: Redgrave Publishing Company.

Kantha, Sachi Sri. 1990. Nutrition and health in China, 1949 to 1989, *Progress in Food and Nutrition Science* 14: 93–137.

Kariel, Herbert G. 1966. A proposed classification of diet, *Annals of the Association of American Geographers* 56: 68–79.

Katz, Solomon H. 1987. Food and biocultural evolution: A model for the investigation of modern nutritional problems, in *Nutritional Anthropology*, ed. Francis E. Johnston, pp. 41–63. New York: Alan R. Liss.

Keen, Carl L., and Sheri Zidenberg-Cherr. 1990. Manganese, in *Present Knowledge in Nutrition*, 6th ed., ed. Myrtle L. Brown, pp. 279–86. Washington, DC: International Life Sciences Institute Nutrition Foundation.

Keesing, Felix M. 1958. *Cultural Anthropology: The Science of Custom*. New York: Holt, Rinehart and Winston.

Keshan Disease Research Group. 1979a. Epidemiologic studies of the etiologic relationship of selenium and Keshan disease, *China Medical Journal* 92: 477–82.

_____. 1979b. Observations on the effect of sodium selenite in prevention of Keshan disease, *China Medical Journal* 92: 471–76.

Keys, Ancel, Josef Brožek, Austin Henschel, Olaf Mickelsen, Henry Longstreet Taylor, et al. 1950. *The Biology of Human Starvation*, 2 vols. Minneapolis: University of Minnesota Press.

Kirkby, R.J.R. 1985. *Urbanization in China: Town and Country in a Developing Economy 1949–2000 A.D.* New York: Columbia University Press.

Kretchmer, Norman. 1972. Lactose and lactase, *Scientific American* 227(4): 71–8.

Kroeber, A., and C. Kluckholn. 1952. Culture: A critical review of concepts and definitions, *Papers of the Peabody Museum of American Archaeology and Ethnology* 47.

Kueh, Y.Y. 1988. Food consumption and peasant incomes in the post-Mao era, *China Quarterly* No. 116: 634–70.

_____. 1989. The Maoist legacy and China's new industrialization strategy, *China Quarterly* No. 119: 420–47.

Kurlansky, Mark. 2002. *Salt: A World History*. New York: Walker and Company.

Kuznets, Simon. 1966. *Modern Economic Growth: Rate, Structure, and Spread*. New Haven, CT: Yale University Press.

Kwok, D.W.Y. 1991. The pleasures of the Chinese palate, *Free China Review* 41, No. 9 (September): 46–51.

Lan, Yong. 1996. 2000 nian lai Zhongguo xingliao kouwei yinshi wenhuaquande skikong tezheng ji huanjing chengyin [Characteristics of the space-time continuum and environmental contributing factors of 2000 years of China's hot-bitter flavored food and drink culture], paper presented at the International Historical Geography Conference, Beijing, July.

Lardy, Nicholas R. 1983. *Agriculture in China's Modern Economic Development*. Cambridge: Cambridge University Press.

_____. 1984. Consumption and living standards in China, 1978–83, *China Quarterly*, No. 100: 849–65.

Latham, Michael C. 1990. Protein-energy malnutrition, in *Present Knowledge in Nutrition*, 6th ed., ed. Myrtle L. Brown, pp. 39–46. Washington, DC: International Life Sciences Institute Nutrition Foundation.

Leeming, Frank. 1985. *Rural China Today.* London: Longman.

_____. 1989. Rural change and agricultural development, *Geography* 74, no. 325(October): 348–50.

_____. 1993. *The Changing Geography of China.* Oxford: Blackwell.

_____. 1994. Necessity, policy and opportunity in the Chinese countryside, in *China: The Next Decades*, ed. Denis Dwyer, pp. 77–94. Harlow, Essex: Longman Scientific and Technical.

Leppman, Elizabeth J. 1999. Urban-rural contrasts in diet: The case of China, *Urban Geography* 20, No. 6(December): 567–79.

_____. 2002. Breakfast in Liaoning Province, China, *Journal of Cultural Geography* 20(1): 77–90.

Levander, O.A. 1987. A global view of human selenium nutrition, *Annual Review of Nutrition* 7: 227–50.

_____, Arba L. Ager, Jr., and Melinda A. Beck. 1995. Vitamin E and selenium: Contrasting and interacting nutritional determinants of host resistance to parasitic and viral infections, *Proceedings of the Nutrition Society* 54: 475–87.

Levenson, S.M., G. Manner, and E. Seifter. 1971. Aspects of the adverse effects of dysnutrition on wound healing, in *Progress in Human Nutrition*, Vol. 1, ed. S. Margen, pp. 132–56. Westport, CT: AVI Publishing.

Lévi-Strauss, Claude. 1963a. *Structural Anthropology*, trans. Claire Jacobson and Brooke Grundfest Schoepf. New York: Basic Books.

_____. 1963b. *Totemism*, trans. R. Needham. Boston: Beacon.

_____. 1970. *The Raw and the Cooked*, trans. J. and D. Wrightman. New York: Harper & Row.

_____ and Didier Eribon. 1991. *Conversations with Lévi-Strauss,* trans. Paula Wissing. Chicago: University of Chicago Press.

Lewin, Kurt. 1943. Forces behind food habits and methods of change, in *The Problem of Changing Food Habits*, eds. National Academy of Sciences, National Research Council. Report of the Committee on Food Habits, 1941–43, National Research Council Bulletin No. 108, pp. 35–65. Washington, DC: National Academy of Sciences.

Lewis, Oscar. 1951. *Life in a Mexican Village: Tepoztlán Revisited.* Urbana, IL: University of Illinois Press.

Lewis, W. Arthur. 1955. *The Theory of Economic Growth.* Homewood, IL: Richard Irwin.

Li, Fuqi. 1994. Personal interview, Shenyang, Liaoning, May 5.

Li, Fuquan. 1994. Personal interview, Beizhen, Liaoning, May 15.

Li, Zhuoyan. 1992. Guangdong acts to scrap grain rations, *China Daily*, April 18, p. 3.

Liang, Zhenhua. 1995. Pork production and sales and factors contributing to its price increase analyzed, *Nongye Jingji Wenti* [*Problems of Agricultural Economy*], November 23; reprinted and trans. as *Pork Sales, Production, Price Trend Analyzed*, FBIS-CHI–95–037, February 24, pp. 70–3.

Liaoning Education College. 1983. *Liaoning Dili* [*Liaoning Geography*]. Shenyang: Liaoning Education College.

Liaoning Statistical Bureau. 1995. *Liaoning Statistical Yearbook 1995.* Beijing: China Statistical Publishing House.

Lieberman, Leslie Sue. 1987. Biocultural consequences of animals versus plants as sources of fats, proteins, and other nutrients, in *Food and Evolution: Toward a Theory of Human Food Habits*, eds. Marvin Harris and Eric B. Ross, pp. 225–58. Philadelphia: Temple University Press.

Life Sciences Research Office. 1987. *Physiological Effects and Health Consequences of Dietary Fiber.* Bethesda, MD: Federation of American Societies for Experimental Biology.

Lin, Justin Yifu. 1988. The household responsibility system in China's agricultural reform: A theoretical and empirical study, *Economic Development and Cultural Change* 36, No. 3, Supplement(April): S200–S24.

———. 1990. Collectivization and China's agricultural crisis in 1959–1961, *Journal of Political Economy* 98, No. 6(December): 1228–52.

Lin, Piao. 1965. Long live the victory of the People's War, *Peking Review* 3: 9–30.

Lin, Yutang. 1935. *My Country and My People.* New York: Regnal & Hitchcock.

Lippitt, Victor D. 1987. *The Economic Development of China.* Armonk, NY: M.E. Sharpe.

Lo, Chor-Pang. 1990. The geography of rural regional inequality in Mainland China, *Transactions of the Institute of British Geographers* N.S. 15: 466–86.

———, Clifton W. Pannell, and Roy Welch. 1977. Land use changes and city planning in Shenyang and Canton, *Geographical Review* 67, No. 3(July): 268–83.

Lockitch, G., G.P. Taylor, L.T.K. Wong, A.G.F. Davidson, P.J. Dison, D. Riddell, and B. Massing. 1990. Cardiomyopathy associated with nonendemic selenium deficiency in a Caucasian adolescent, *American Journal of Clinical Nutrition* 52: 572–7.

Loomis, W.F. 1970. Rickets, *Scientific American* 223 (December), pp. 76–910.

Loveland, Carol J., Thomas H. Furst, and Georgia C. Lauritzen. 1989. Geophagia in human populations, *Food and Foodways* 3, No. 4: 333–56.

Lozada, Eriberto P., Jr. 2000. Globalized Childhood?: Kentucky Fried Chicken in Beijing, in *Feeding China's Little Emperors: Food, Children, and Social Change* ed. Jun Jing, pp. 114–34. Stanford, CA: Stanford University Press.

Lozoff, B., and G.M. Brittenham. 1986. Behavioral aspects of iron deficiency, *Progress in Haematology* 14: 23–53.

Luo, Yu, and Clifton W. Pannell. 1991. The changing pattern of city and industry in post-reform China, in *The Uneven Landscape*, ed. Gregory Veeck, pp. 29–51. Geoscience and Man, Vol. 30. Baton Rouge: Department of Geography and Anthropology, Louisiana State University.

Lupton, Deborah. 1996. *Food, the Body and the Self.* London: Sage Publications.

Ma, Guansheng. 1998. Nutrition knowledge, attitude, food practices and changes in China, *Australian Journal of Nutrition and Dietetics* 55(1)Supplement: S9–S11.

Ma, Haijiang, and Barry M. Popkin. 1995. Income and food-consumption behaviour in China: A structural shift analysis, *Food and Nutrition Bulletin* 16(2): 155–65.

Ma, Laurence J.C., and Gonghao Cui. 1987. Administrative changes and urban population in China, *Annals of the Association of American Geographers* 77, No. 3(September): 373–95.

Ma, Rong. 1992. The development of small towns and their role in the modernization of China, in *Urbanizing China*, ed. Gregory Elihu Guldin, pp. 119–53. Westport, CT: Greenwood Press.

Mallory, Walter H. 1926. *China: Land of Famine.* American Geographical Society Special Publication No. 6. New York: American Geographical Society.

Mangelsdorf, Paul C. 1953. Wheat, *Scientific American* 189: 50–9.

Mansfield, Edwin. 1988. *Microeconomics: Theory and Applications*, 6th ed. New York: W. W. Norton.

Maslow, Abraham H. 1954. *Motivation and Personality.* New York: Harper & Row.

Maus, Norbert, and Volker Pudel. 1988. Psychological determinants of food intake, in *Food Acceptability*, ed. David M.H. Thomson, pp. 181–92. London: Elsevier Applied Science.

May, Jacques M. 1961. *The Ecology of Malnutrition in the Far and Near East.* New York: Hafner Publishing Company.

May, Jon. 1996. "A little taste of something more exotic": The imaginative geographies of everyday life, *Geography* 81: 57–64.

Maynard, Leonard A., and Wen-Yuh Swen. 1937. Nutrition, in *Land Utilization in China* by John Lossing Buck, pp. 400–36. Chicago: University of Chicago Press.

Mazlish, Bruce. 1991. The breakdown of connections and modern development, *World Development* 19(1): 31–44.

McColl, Robert, and Youguan Kou. 1990. Feeding China's millions, *Geographical Review* 80, No. 4: 434–43.

McCracken, R.D. 1971. Lactase deficiency: An example of dietary evolution, *Current Anthropology* 12: 479–517.

McGee, Terry G. 1971. *The Urbanization Process in the Third World: Explorations in Search of a Theory.* London: G. Bell & Sons.

_____. 1989. Urbanisasi or kotadesasi? Evolving patterns of urbanization in Asia, in *Urbanization in Asia: Spatial Dimensions and Policy Issues*, eds. Frank J. Costa, Ashok K. Dutt, Laurence J. C. Ma, and Allen G. Noble, pp. 98–108. Honolulu: University of Hawaii Press.

_____. 1991a. The emergence of *desakota* regions in Asia: Expanding a hypothesis, in *The Extended Metropolis: Settlement Transition in Asia*, eds. Norton Ginsburg, Bruce Koppel, and T. G. McGee, pp. 3–26. Honolulu: University of Hawaii Press.

_____. 1991b. Eurocentrism in geography—The case of Asian urbanization, *Canadian Geographer* 35, No. 4(Winter): 332–44.

McIntosh, William Alex, and Mary Zey. 1989. Women as gatekeepers of food consumption: A sociological critique, *Food and Foodways* 3(4): 317–332.

McMillan, John, John Whalley, an Lijing Zhu. 1989. The impact of China's economic reforms on agricultural productivity growth, *Journal of Political Economy* 97, No. 4: 781–807.

McNeill, William H. 1991. American food crops in the Old World, in *Seeds of Change: A Quincentennial Commemoration*, eds. Herman J. Viola and Carolyn Margolis, pp. 43–59. Washington, DC: Smithsonian Institution Press.

Mennell, S. 1985. *All Manners of Food: Eating and Taste in England and France from the Middle Ages to the Present.* Oxford: Blackwell.

Messer, Ellen. 1984. Anthropological perspectives on diet, *Annual Review of Anthropology* 13: 205–49.

Miner, Horace. 1952. The folk-urban continuum, *American Sociological Review* 17(5): 529–37.

Mingione, Enzo, and Enrico Pugliese. 1988. The urban/rural question: Between theoretical mastery and problems of uncertain limits, *Critica Sociologica* 85: 27–50.

Mintz, Sidney. 1979. Time, sugar, and sweetness, *Marxist Perspectives* 2(4): 56–73.

_____. 1996. *Tasting Food, Tasting Freedom.* Boston: Beacon Press.

Morgan, Stephen L. 2000. Richer and taller: Stature and living standards in China, 1979–1995, *The China Journal* No. 44(July): 1–39.

Mote, Frederick W. 1977. Yüan and Ming, in *Food in Chinese Culture: Anthropological and*

Historical Perspectives, ed. K.C. Chang, pp. 193–257. New Haven, CT: Yale University Press.

Murcott, Anne. 1988. Sociological and social anthropological approaches to food and eating, *World Review of Nutrition and Dietetics,* Vol. 55: *Sociological and Medical Aspects of Nutrition,* ed. Geoffrey H. Bourne. Basil: Karger.

Murphey, Rhoads. 1954. The city as a center of change: Western Europe and China, *Annals of the Association of American Geographers* 44(4): 349–62.

_____. 1969. Traditionalism and colonialism: Changing urban roles in Asia, *Journal of Asian Studies* 29(1): 67–84.

_____. 1970. *The Treaty Ports and China's Modernization: What Went Wrong?* Michigan Papers in Chinese Studies No. 7. Ann Arbor: University of Michigan Center for Chinese Studies.

_____. 1974. The treaty ports and China's modernization, in *The Chinese City Between Two Worlds,* eds. Mark Elvin and G. William Skinner, pp. 17–71. Stanford, CA: Stanford University Press.

_____. 1980. *The Fading of the Maoist Vision: City and Country in China's Development.* New York: Methuen.

Myrdal, Gunnar. 1957. *Economic Theory and Underdeveloped Regions.* London: Gerald Duckworth & Co.

National Research Council, Food and Nutrition Board, Commission on Life Sciences. 1989. *Recommended Daily Allowances,* 10th ed. Washington, DC: National Academy Press.

Naughton, Barry. 1988. The Third Front: Defence industrialization in the Chinese interior, *China Quarterly,* No. 115: 351–86.

Naylor, Larry L. 1996. *Culture and Change: An Introduction.* Westport, CT: Bergin & Garvey.

Newman, James L. 1995. From definition, to geography, to action, to reaction: The case of protein-energy malnutrition, *Annals of the Association of American Geographers* 85(2): 233–45.

Nielsen, Forrest. 1990. Other trace elements, in *Present Knowledge in Nutrition,* 6th ed., ed Myrtle L. Brown, pp.294–307. Washington, DC: International Life Sciences Institute Nutrition Foundation.

Nolan, Peter, and Gordon White. 1984. Urban bias, rural bias or state bias? Urban-rural relations in post-revolutionary China, *Journal of Development Studies* 20(3): 52–81.

O'Dell, Boyd L. 1990. Copper, in *Present Knowledge in Nutrition,* 6th ed., ed. Myrtle L. Brown, pp. 261–67. Washington, DC: International Life Sciences Institute Nutrition Foundation.

Oi, Jean C. 1989. *State and Peasant in Contemporary China: The Political Economy of Village Government.* Berkeley: University of California Press.

Olson, James A. 1990. Vitamin A, in *Present Knowledge in Nutrition,* 6th ed., ed. Myrtle L. Brown, pp. 96–107. Washington, DC: International Life Sciences Institute Nutrition Foundation.

Omran, Abdel R. 1971. The epidemiologic transition: A theory of the epidemiology of population change, *Millbank Memorial Fund Quarterly* 49: 509–38.

Ophaug, Robert. 1990. Fluouride, in *Present Knowledge in Nutrition,* 6th ed., ed. Myrtle L. Brown, pp. 274–278. Washington, DC: International Life Sciences Institute Nutrition Foundation.

Orleans, L.A. 1959. Recent growth of China's urban population, *Geographical Review* 49: 43–57.

———. 1982. China's urban population: Concepts, conglomerations and concerns, in *China Under the Four Modernizations*, ed. U.S. Congress, Joint Economic Committee. Washington, DC: U.S. Government Printing Office.

Oshima, Harry T. 1987. *Economic Growth in Monsoon Asia: A Comparative Study*. Tokyo: University of Tokyo Press.

———. 1993. *Strategic Processes in Monsoon Asia's Economic Development*. Baltimore, MD: Johns Hopkins University Press.

Paarlberg, R.L. 1997. Feeding China: A confident view, *Food Policy* 22(3): 269–79.

Palmer, Monte. 1989. *Dilemmas of Political Development: An Introduction to the Politics of the Developing Areas*. Itasca, IL: F. E. Peacock Publishers.

Pandit, Kavita. 1990. Service labor allocation during development: Longitudinal perspectives on cross-cultural patterns, *Annals of the Association of American Geographers* 24: 29–41.

Pannell, Clifton W. 1981. Recent growth and change in China's urban system, in *Urban Development in Modern China*, eds. Laurence J.C. Ma and Edward W. Hanten, pp. 91–113. Boulder, CO: Westview Press.

———. 1984. Urbanization and economic development in Mainland China, Conference on Urban Growth and Economic Development in the Pacific Region, Taipei, Taiwan, January 9–11.

———. 1985. Recent Chinese agriculture, *Geographical Review* 75(2): 170–85.

———. 1986. Recent increase in Chinese urbanization, *Urban Geography* 7(4): 291–310.

———. 1987–88. Economic reforms and readjustment in the People's Republic of China and some geographic consequences, *Studies in Comparative International Development* 22(4): 54–73.

———. 1988. Regional shifts in China's industrial output, *Professional Geographer* 40(1): 19–32.

———. 1989. Employment structure and the Chinese urban economy, in *Urbanization in Asia: Spatial Dimensions and Policy Issues*, eds. Frank J. Costa, Ashok K. Dutt, Laurence J.C. Ma, and Allen G. Noble, pp. 385–408. Honolulu: University of Hawaii Press.

———. 1990. China's urban geography, *Progress in Human Geography* 14(2): 214–36.

———, and Elizabeth J. Leppman. 1997. Urbanization and regional change in contemporary China, paper presented at the Southeastern Conference of the Association for Asian Studies annual meeting, Savannah, Georgia, January 19.

Pannell, Clifton W., and Laurence J.C. Ma. 1983. *China: The Geography of Development and Modernization*. London: Edward Arnold.

Payne, Philip R. 1985. The nature of malnutrition, in *Nutrition and Development*, eds. Margaret Biswas and Per Pinstrup-Andersen, pp. 1–19. Oxford: Oxford University Press.

Perkins, Dwight H. 1969. *Agricultural Development in China, 1368–1968*. Chicago: Aldine.

———. 1990. The influence of economic reforms on China's urbanization, in *Chinese Urban Reform: What Model Now?*, eds. R. Yin-Wang Kwok, William L. Parish, Anthony Gar-On Yeh, and Xu Xueqiang, pp. 78–106. Armonk, NY: M. E. Sharpe.

———, ed. 1977. *Rural Small-Scale Industry in the People's Republic of China*. Berkeley and Los Angeles: University of California Press.

Piazza, Alan. 1986. *Food Consumption and Nutritional Status in the PRC.* Boulder, CO: Westview Press.

Pillsbury, Richard. 1998. *No Foreign Food: The American Diet in Time and Place.* Boulder, CO: Westview Press.

Pollock, Nancy J. 1975. The risks of dietary change: A Pacific atoll example, in *Gastronomy: The Anthropology of Food Habits*, ed. Margaret L. Arnott, pp. 121–30. The Hague: Mouton.

Popkin, Barry M. 1993. Nutritional patterns and transitions, *Population and Development Review* 19(1): 138–57.

Quan, Zhang Xing. 1991. Urbanisation in China, *Urban Studies* 28(1): 41–51.

Quandt, Sara A. 1987. Methods of determining dietary intake, in *Nutritional Anthropology*, ed. Francis E. Johnston, pp. 67–84. New York: Alan R. Liss.

Ran, Maoxing, and Brian J.L. Berry. 1989. Underurbanization policies assessed: China, 1949–1986, *Urban Geography* 10(2): 111–20.

Ranis, Gustav, and John C.H. Fei. 1964. *Development of the Labor Surplus Economy.* Homewood, IL: Richard Irwin.

Rappaport, R.A. 1971. Nature, culture, and ecological anthropology, in *Man, Culture and Society*, ed. Harry L. Shapiro, pp. 237–67. London: Oxford University Press.

Redfield, Robert. 1930. *Tepoztlán, A Mexican Village: A Study of Folk Life.* Chicago: University of Chicago Press.

———. 1941. *The Folk Culture of Yucatan.* Chicago: University of Chicago Press.

———. 1947. The folk society, *American Journal of Sociology* 52(4): 293–308.

———. 1953. *The Primitive World and Its Transformations.* Ithaca, NY: Cornell University Press.

———. 1956. *Peasant Society and Culture.* Chicago: University of Chicago Press.

———, and Milton B. Singer. 1954. The cultural role of cities, *Economic Development and Cultural Change* 3(1): 53–73.

Redfield, Robert, and Alfonso Villa R. 1934. *Chan Kom, a Maya Village.* Washington, DC: Carnegie Institution of Washington Publication No. 448.

Reid, Janice. 1986. "Land of milk and honey": The changing meaning of food to an Australian aboriginal community, in *Shared Wealth and Symbol: Food, Culture and Society in Oceania and Southeast Asia*, ed. Lenore Manderson, pp. 49–66. Cambridge: Cambridge University Press.

Reiss, Albert J., Jr. 1955. An analysis of urban phenomena, in *The Metropolis in Modern Life*, ed. Robert Moore Fisher, pp. 41–51. New York: Doubleday and Co.

Reissman, Leonard. 1964. *The Urban Process: Cities in Industrial Societies.* New York: Free Press of Glencoe.

Roberts, Leslie. 1988. Diet and health in China, *Science* 240(4848): 27.

Ross, Eric B. 1980. Introduction, in *Beyond the Myths of Culture: Essays in Cultural Materialism*, ed. Eric B. Ross, pp. xix–xxix. San Francisco: Academic Press.

Rozelle, Scott, Jikun Huang, and Linxiu Zhang. 1997. Poverty, population and environmental degradation in China, *Food Policy* 22(3): 229–51.

Rozelle, Scott, and Mark W. Rosegrant. 1997. China's past, present and future food economy: Can China continue to meet the challenges? *Food Policy* 22(3): 191–200.

Rozin, Paul. 1976. The selection of foods by rats, humans, and other animals, in *Advances in the Study of Behavior*, eds. Jay S. Rosenblatt, Robert A. Hinde, Evelyn Shaw, and Colin Beer, pp. 21–76. New York: Academic Press.

———. 1987. Psychobiological perspectives on food preferences and avoidances, in *Food and Evolution: Toward a Theory of Human Food Habits*, eds. Marvin Harris and Eric B. Ross, pp. 181–205. Philadelphia: Temple University Press.

_____. 1990. Social and moral aspects of food and eating, in *The Legacy of Solomon Asch: Essays in Cognition and Social Psychology*, ed. Irvin Rock. Hillsdale, NJ: Lawrence Erlbaum Assocs.

Sanjur, Diva. 1982. *Social and Cultural Perspectives in Nutrition*. Englewood Cliffs, NJ: Prentice-Hall, Inc.

Sauberlich, Howerde. 1990. Ascorbic acid, in *Present Knowledge in Nutrition*, 6th ed., ed. Myrtle L. Brown, 132–141. Washington, DC: International Life Sciences Institute Nutrition Foundation.

Sauer, Carl O. 1969. *Agricultural Origins and Dispersals: The Domestication of Animals and Foodstuffs*, 2nd ed. Cambridge, MA: M.I.T. Press.

Scandizzo, Pasquale L., and I. Tsakok. 1985. Food price policies and nutrition in developing countries, in *Nutrition and Development*, eds. Margaret Biswas and Per Pinstrup-Andersen, pp. 60–76. Oxford: Oxford University Press.

Schafer, Edward H. 1977. T'ang, in *Food in Chinese Culture: Anthropological and Historical Perspectives*, ed. K.C. Chang, pp. 85–140. New Haven, CT: Yale University Press.

Schlosser, Eric. 2001. *Fast Food Nation: The Dark Side of the All-American Meal*. Boston: Houghton Mifflin Company.

Schell, Orville. 1986. *To Get Rich Is Glorious: China in the 80s*, rev. and updated ed. New York: New American Library.

_____. 1989. *Discos and Democracy: China in the Throes of Reform*. New York: Anchor Books Doubleday.

Schinz, A. 1989. *Cities in China*. Berlin: Betruder Borntraeger.

Schutz, Howard G. 1988. Beyond preference: Appropriateness as a measure of contextual acceptance of food, in *Food Acceptability*, ed. David M. H. Thomson, pp. 115–34. London: Elsevier Applied Science.

Scupin, Raymond, and Christopher DeCorse. 1995. *Anthropology: A Global Perspective*, 2nd ed. Englewood Cliffs, NJ: Prentice Hall.

Shen, Jianfa. 2000. Modelling national or regional grain supply and food balance in China, *Environment and Planning A* 32: 539–57.

Shen, Tiefu, Jean-Pierre Habicht, and Ying Chang. 1996. Effect of economic reforms on child growth in urban and rural areas of China, *New England Journal of Medicine* 335(6): 400–406.

Shortridge, Barbara, and James R. Shortridge. 1989. Consumption of fresh produce in the metropolitan United States, *Geographical Review* 79: 79–98.

Simoons, Frederick J. 1980. The determinants of dairying and milk use in the Old World: Ecological, physiological, and cultural, in *Food, Ecology and Culture: Readings in the Anthropology of Dietary Practices*, ed. J.R.K. Robson, pp. 83–91. New York: Gordon and Breach Science Publishers.

_____. 1991. *Food in China: A Cultural and Historical Inquiry*. Boca Raton, FL: CRC Press.

_____. 1994. *Eat Not This Flesh*, 2nd ed. Madison: University of Wisconsin Press.

Sjoberg, Gideon. 1952. Folk and "feudal" societies, *American Journal of Sociology* 53(3): 231–39.

_____. 1960. *The Preindustrial City*. Glencoe, IL: Free Press.

Skinner, G. William. 1977. Regional urbanization in nineteenth-century China, in *The City in Late Imperial China*, ed. G. William Skinner, pp. 211–49. Stanford, CA: Stanford University Press.

Smil, Vaclav. 1985. China's food, *Scientific American* 253(6): 116–24.

_____. 2000. *Feeding the World: A Challenge for the Twenty-first Century.* Cambridge, MA: M.I.T. Press.

Smith, Christopher J. 1991. *China: People and Places in the Land of One Billion.* Boulder, CO: Westview Press.

_____. 1993. (Over) eating success: The health consequences of the restoration of capitalism in rural China, *Social Science and Medicine* 37(6): 761–70.

Snyder, Janet. 1992. China: Last frontier for saturated beer market, Reuters, September 24, reprinted in *China News Digest* (Global), September 27, n.p.

Soemardjan, Selo. 1985. Influence of culture on food and nutrition: The Indonesian case, in *Nutrition and Development*, eds. Margaret Biswas and Per Pinstrup-Andersen, pp. 163–81. Oxford: Oxford University Press.

Sokolov, Raymond. 1990. The China syndrome, *Natural History* (April): 114–18.

Sorokin, Pitirim, and Carle C. Zimmerman. 1929. *Principles of Rural–Urban Sociology.* New York: Henry Holt and Co.

Sorre, Maximillian. 1962. The geography of diet, in *Readings in Cultural Geography*, eds. Philip L. Wagner and Marvin W. Mikesell, pp. 445–56. Chicago: University of Chicago Press.

Spence, Jonathan. 1977. Ch'ing, in *Food in Chinese Culture: Anthropological and Historical Perspectives*, pp. 259–94. New Haven, CT: Yale University Press.

_____. 1999. Paradise lost, *Far Eastern Economic Review* 162(15): 40–6.

State Statistical Bureau (SSB). 1995. *China Statistical Yearbook 1995.* Beijing: China Statistical Publishing House.

Stavis, Benedict. 1991. Market reforms and changes in crop productivity: Insights from China, *Pacific Affairs* 64(3): 373–83.

Stewart, Charles T. 1958. The rural–urban dichotomy: Concepts and uses, *American Journal of Sociology* 64: 152–58.

Stoecker, Barbara. 1990. Chromium, in *Present Knowledge in Nutrition*, 6th ed., ed. Myrtle L. Brown, pp. 287–93. Washington, DC: International Life Sciences Institute Nutrition Foundation.

Stover, Dawn. 1996. The coming food crisis, *Popular Science* 429(2): 49–55.

Stover, Leon E. 1974. *The Cultural Ecology of Chinese Civilization.* New York: Pica Press.

_____, and Takeko Kawai Stover. 1976. *China: An Anthropological Perspective.* Pacific Palisades, CA: Goodyear Publishing Co.

Swaminathan, M.S. 1984. Rice, *Scientific American* 251: 81–93.

Swann, Nancy, trans. and ann. 1950. *Food and Money in Ancient China: The Earliest Economic History of China to A.D. 25: Han Shu 24.* Princeton, NJ: Princeton University Press.

Swedner, Harald. 1960. *Ecological Differentiation of Habits and Attitudes.* Lund: CWK Gleerup.

Sydney Morning Herald. 1991. Unemployed peasants flood Chinese cities, *Sydney Morning Herald,* June 14, reprinted in *China News Digest,* June 15, pp. 2–3.

Szepesi, Béla. 1990. Carbohydrates, in *Present Knowledge in Nutrition*, 6th ed., ed. Myrtle L. Brown, pp. 47–55. Washington, DC: International Life Sciences Institute Nutrition Foundation.

Taimni, K.K. 1994. Powerhouse in the making, *Ceres* 26(3): 27–32.

Tan, K.C. 1986. Revitalized small towns in China, *Geographical Review* 76: 138–48.

Taylor, Jeffrey R., and Judith Banister. 1991. Surplus rural labor in the People's Republic of China, in *The Uneven Landscape*, ed. Gregory Veeck, pp. 87–120. Geoscience and Man, Vol. 30. Baton Rouge: Department of Geography and Anthropology, Louisiana State University.

Taylor, Will. 1995. Selenium and viral diseases: Facts and hypotheses, posted to Internet Newsgroup sci.med.aids, August, updated October.

Terjung, W.H., J.T. Hayes, H-Y. Ji, P.E. Todhunter, and P.O. O'Rourke. 1985. Potential paddy rice yields for rainfed and irrigated agriculture in China and Korea, *Annals of the Association of American Geographers* 75(1): 83–101.

Thomas, Stephen C. 1990. Catching up, *China Business Review*, November-December, pp. 6–11.

Thomson, Carol A., and Ernesto Pollitt. 1977. Effects of severe protein-calorie malnutrition in human populations, in *Malnutrition, Behavior, and Social Organization*, ed. Lawrence S. Greene, pp. 19–37. New York: Academic Press.

Tiger, Lionel. 1992. *The Pursuit of Pleasure*. Boston: Little, Brown and Company.

Todaro, Michael P. 1989. *Economic Development in the Third World*, 4th ed. New York: Longman.

Tönnies, Ferdinand. 1887/1940. *Gemeinschaft und Gesellschaft*, trans. and ed. by Charles P. Loomis as *Fundamental Concepts in Sociology*. New York: American Book Company.

Torbert, Preston M. 1984. Windows on Liaoning Province, *China Business Review*, November-December, pp. 20–3.

Travers, Lee. 1986. Peasant non-agricultural production in the People's Republic of China, in *China's Economy Looks Toward the Year 2000*, Vol. I: *The Four Modernizations*, U.S. Congress, Joint Economic Committee, pp. 376–86. Washington, DC: U.S. Government Printing Office.

Trewartha, Glenn T. 1952. Chinese cities: Origins and functions, *Annals of the Association of American Geographers* 42(1): 69–93.

Tsang, Ka Bo. 1996. Chinese pig tales, *Archaeology* 49(2): 53–7.

Tyler, Patrick E. 1996. No rights means no incentive for China's farmers, *New York Times*, December 15, p. 10.

Unwin, Tim. 1989. Urban–rural interaction in developing countries: A theoretical perspective, in *The Geography of Urban–Rural Interaction in Developing Countries: Essays for Alan B. Mountjoy*, pp. 11–32. London: Routledge.

Veeck, Ann. 2000. The revitalization of the marketplace: Food markets in Nanjing, in *The Consumer Revolution in Urban China*, ed. Deborah S. Davis, pp. 107–23. Berkeley: University of California Press.

Vermeer, Donald E., and Dennis A. Frate. 1975. Geophagy in a Mississippi county, *Annals of the Association of American Geographers* 65: 414–24.

Vidal de la Blache, Paul. 1903. *Tableau de la géographie de la France*. Paris: Colin.

von Thünen, Johann Heinrich. 1966. *Von Thünen's Isolated State: An English Edition of Der isolierte Staat*, trans. Carla M. Wartenberg. Elmsford, NY: Pergamon Press.

Walker, Kenneth R. 1984. Chinese agriculture during the period of adjustment, *China Quarterly* No. 100: 783–812.

_____. 1988. Trends in crop production, 1978–86, *China Quarterly* No. 116: 592–633.

_____. 1989. 40 years on: Provincial contrasts in China's rural economic development, *China Quarterly*, No. 119: 448–80.

Wallerstein, Immanuel M. 1974. *The Modern World-System: Capitalist Agriculture and the Origins of the European World-Economy in the Sixteenth Century*. New York: Academic Press.

Wan, Guang H. 1996. Using panel data to estimate Engel functions: Food consumption in China, *Applied Economics Letters* 3: 621–24.

_____. 1998. Nonparametric measurement of preference changes: The case of food demand in rural China, *Applied Economics Letters* 5: 433–36.

Wang, Jan. 1990. Leaving behind the iron rice bowl, *Globe and Mail* (Toronto), February 2, reprinted in *China News Digest*, February 3, 1991, pp. 1–4.

Wang, Lingjun. 1990. My view on absorbing surplus rural labor, *Jingji Ribao* [*Economic Daily*], April 14, p. 2; reprinted in FBIS-CHI, May 10, pp. 29–31.

Wang, Tai, Jinjun Liu, and Yuqi Wang. 1989. Warning of the first lunar month — A look at the rural employment crisis in light of the labor outflow, *Nongmin Ribao* [*Farmers' Daily*], March 11, pp. 1, 8; reprinted in FBIS-CHI, March 24, pp. 95–7.

Wang, Yonghong. 1993. Fish population endangered by large harvests, *China Daily*, October 2.

Wang, Zhi, and Wen S. Chern. 1992. Effects of rationing on the consumption behavior of Chinese urban households during 1981–1987, *Journal of Comparative Economics* 16: 1–26.

Webb, F.J. 1994. Personal interview, Shenyang, Liaoning, November 9.

Webb, Shwu-Eng H. 1991. Regional economic growth in China since 1979: Emphasis on agricultural development, in *The Uneven Landscape*, ed. Gregory Veeck, pp. 53–85. Geoscience and Man, Vol. 30. Baton Rouge: Department of Geography and Anthropology, Louisiana State University.

Wen, Jia. 1989. Project to raise output of nonstaple food, *China Daily*, FBIS-CHI, January 11, p. 49.

Wen, Simei. 1990. Government policies and food sector performance: The Chinese experience, in *Increasing Access to Food: The Asian Experience*, eds. D. S. Tyagi and Vijay Shankar Vijas, pp. 145–184. New Delhi: Sage Publications.

Whitney, Eleanor Noss, Eva May N. Hamilton, and Sharon Rady Rolfes. 1990. *Understanding Nutrition*, 5th ed. St. Paul, MN: West Publishing.

Williams, William D. 1990. The Giffen effect: A note on economic purposes, *American Behaviorial Scientist* 34(1): 106–9.

Wilson, Christine S. 1977. Research methods in nutritional anthropology: Approaches and techniques, in *Nutrition and Anthropology in Action*, ed. Thomas K. Fitzgerald, pp. 62–68. Amsterdam: van Gorcum, Assen.

Wirth, Louis. 1938. Urbanism as a way of life, *The American Journal of Sociology* 44(1): 1–24.

Wittwer, Sylvan, Yu Youtai, Sun Han, and Wang Lianzheng. 1987. *Feeding a Billion: Frontiers of Chinese Agriculture*. East Lansing: Michigan State University Press.

Woodruff, C.W. 1975. Ascorbic Acid—Scurvy, *Progress in Food and Nutrition Science* 1: 493–506.

World Health Organization. 1987. *Selenium*. Environmental Health Criteria 58: A Report of the International Programme on Chemical Safety. Geneva: World Health Organization.

Wu, Weidan. 1994. Personal interview, Shenyang, Liaoning, September 19.

WuDunn, Sheryl. 1992. China removes some price controls on food, *New York Times*, November 29, 19.

_____. 1993. As China leaps ahead, the poor slip behind, *New York Times*, May 23, 3.

Xiang, Hu. 1992. Reform results in nationwide vegetable circulation, XINHUA, May 2, reported in FBIS-CHI–92, May 4, p. 31.

Xiao, Zheng. 1993. Grain yield falls as industry soars in Guangdong, *China Daily Business Weekly*, November 21–7.

Xie, Yichun, and Frank J. Costa. 1991. The impact of economic reforms on the urban economy of the People's Republic of China, *Professional Geographer* 43(3): 318–35.

Xin, Changxing. 1991. An analysis of the "labor tide," *Gongren Ribao* [*Workers' Daily*], May 3, p. 3, FBIS-CHI–91, May 28, pp. 43–4.

XINHUA. 1989. Change in diet could relieve food shortage, FBIS-CHI, April 20, pp. 49–50.

Yan, Rui-Zhen. 1990. Economic reforms in rural areas and access to food: The Chinese experience, in *Increasing Access to Food: The Asian Experience*, eds. D. S. Tyagi and Vijay Shankar Vijas, pp. 185–39. New Delhi: Sage Publications.

Yan, Yunxiang. 1997. McDonald's in Beijing: The localization of Americana, in *Golden Arches East: McDonald's in East Asia*, ed. James L. Watson, pp. 39–76. Stanford, CA: Stanford University Press.

Yang, Hong, and Xiubin Li. 2000. Cultivated land and food supply in China, *Land Use Policy* 17(2): 73–88.

Ye, Shunzan. 1989. Urban development trends in China, in *Urbanization in Asia: Spatial Dimensions and Policy Issues*, eds. Frank J. Costa, Ashok K. Dutt, Laurence J.C. Ma, and Allen G. Noble, pp. 75–92. Honolulu: University of Hawaii Press.

Yeates, Maurice. 1975. *Main Street: Windsor to Quebec City*. Toronto: Macmillan.

Young, Michael W. 1986. "The worst disease": The cultural definition of hunger in Kalauna, in *Shared Wealth and Symbol: Food, Culture and Society in Oceania and Southeast Asia*, ed. Lenore Manderson, pp. 111–26. Cambridge: Cambridge University Press.

Yü, Ying-shih. 1977. Han, in *Food in Chinese Culture: Anthropological and Historical Perspectives*, ed. K.C. Chang, pp. 53–83. New Haven, CT: Yale University Press.

Zelinsky, Wilbur. 1985. The roving palate: America's ethnic restaurant cuisines, *Geoforum* 16(1): 51–72.

Zhai, Fengying, Xuguang Guo, Parry M. Popkin, Linmao Ma, Quing Wang, Wentao Yu, Shuigao Jin, and Keyou Ge. 1996. Evaluation of the 24-hour individual recall method in China, *Food and Nutrition Bulletin* 17(2): 154–61.

Zhang, Cungen. 1995. China's meat supply and demand to the year 2000 and how to increase supply, *Nongye Jingji Wenti* [*Problems of Agricultural Economy*], May 23, reprinted and trans. as *Expert Views Current, Future Meat Production*, FBIS-CHI–95–140, July 21, pp. 52–8.

Zhang, Fan, and Zhangping Ma. 1988. Establish a consumption pattern which accords with the national conditions of our country, *Guangming Ribao* [*Bright Light News*], FBIS-CHI, March 1, pp. 20–2.

Zhang, Mengyi. 1990. A new mode of population shift and mobility in China, *Liaowang Overseas Edition*, No. 2, January. 8, pp. 16–17, FBIS, February. 9, 1990, pp. 18–20.

Zhang, Tianxin. 1993. Tradition binds village life, *China Daily*, December 28.

Zhao, Fei. 1988. *Jinri Yingyang yu Jiankang* [*Nutrition and Health for Today*]. Beijing: Jindun Chubanshe.

Zhao, Songqiao. 1986. *Physical Geography of China*. New York: John Wiley.

_____. 1991. Zhongguo nongye (zhongzhiye) de lishi: Fazhan he dili fenbu [Historical development and geographic distribution of agriculture (farming) in China], *Dili Yanjiu* [*Geographical Research*] 10(1): 1–11.

_____. 1993. The spread of agriculture in China, *Chinese Geographical Science* 3(3): 194–202.

_____. 1994. *Geography of China: Environment, Resources, Population, and Development.* New York: John Wiley.

Zheng, Zungu. 1990. A preliminary study of food problem in China and its countermeasures, paper presented at the International Geographical Union Regional Conference, Beijing, August.

Zhou, Yixing. 1991. The metropolitan interlocking region in China: A preliminary hypothesis, in *The Extended Metropolis: Settlement Transition in Asia,* eds. Norton Ginsburg, Bruce Koppel, and T. G. McGee, pp. 89–111. Honolulu: University of Hawaii Press.

Zweig, David. 1987. From village to city: Reforming urban-rural relations in China, *International Regional Science Review* 11(1): 43–58.

Appendix A
Nutrients and Their Role in Human Health

In addition to energy, food supplies a host of chemical substances that the body uses for building, repair, and various biochemical reactions necessary for life. Nutrients are divided into energy-producing and non-energy-producing. The former include carbohydrates, proteins, and fats; the latter include vitamins and minerals.

Energy-Producing Nutrients

Carbohydrates

Carbohydrates include sugars, starches, and fiber. All plant foods contain carbohydrates, as does milk. Carbohydrates, as a proportion of food intake, range from 50% to 70%, due mostly to economic and cultural factors (Szepesi, 1990: 47).

Chemically, sugars are simple carbohydrates; starches are complex carbohydrates. Sugars add flavor and appeal to foods and are generally harmful only when eaten in excess, especially in concentrated form. All energy-yielding foods eventually metabolize into simple sugars.

Starches, or complex carbohydrates, occur along with fiber in vegetables, fruits, grains, and legumes. The nutritional role of starches primarily is to supply a source energy to the body (National Research Council, 1989).

Fibers are present in many plants, primarily in the cell walls. Unless refining processes remove the fiber, it is consumed as part of plant foods. Water-soluble fiber lowers blood cholesterol and glucose (sugar) absorption, while water-insoluble fiber speeds up the transit time of food in the digestive tract and, thus, acts as a natural laxative (Life Sciences Research Office, 1987; National Research Council, 1989).

Proteins

While carbohydrates provide energy, proteins literally provide much of the building material for the human body. Chemically, proteins are composed of about 20 amino acids.

Of these, 11 are considered nonessential—not because they are unimportant, but because the body manufactures them. The nine essential amino acids, on the other hand, must come from food (National Research Council, 1989: 53). Once all nine essential amino acids are available in sufficient quantities, the body manufactures protein. All nine must be consumed at the same time to yield nutritional benefit— an all-or-nothing situation.

Proteins have many uses in the body. They are used to make enzymes; to maintain the balance of fluids and acids versus bases; to make pigments, antibodies, and hormones; to transport other proteins; and to build such body tissues as bones, teeth, muscles, brain cells, organs, and scar tissue (to promote healing) (National Research Council, 1989: 52). The most efficient source of protein in the diet is foods of animal origin because they contain all nine essential amino acids in the proportions that the body needs. This is an important reason for the value that most people and cultures place on such foods (Abrams, 1987; Harris, 1986; Lieberman, 1987; Simoons, 1994). A vegetarian diet that provides adequate protein is possible by combining various plant foods (primarily a grain and a legume) that contain different assortments of amino acids, but it requires more complicated calculation and planning.

Fats

Fats are actually a subset of lipids, which include triglycerides (fats and oils), phospholipids, and sterols. In spite of media attention to the evils of fat, lipids are important to nutrition (Alfin-Slater and Aftergood, 1968; National Research Council, 1989: 46-7). Their most important role is to provide energy for bodily functions. Fats provide nine Calories per gram, more than any other nutrient (National Research Council, 1989: 45). The body stores fat in its adipose cells (what we mean when we refer to body fat) to create a readily available source of energy (National Research Council, 1989: 45).

Fats are found in foods of animal origin and in legumes and grains. Because animal foods are an excellent source of fats (as well as protein), these foods have long been prized. In the long period of prehistoric human development, when people lived by hunting and gathering, they ate at irregular intervals, when food was available. Killing an animal meant an immediate feast of protein- and fat-rich meat; the only way to store food was within the body as fat, which could provide energy until the next meal. This adaptation to irregular eating has survived, into modern times, as a taste for foods that have a high fat content—to the point of over-consumption of fats among the world's prosperous (Tiger, 1992).

Body fat also insulates the internal organs against extremes of temperature, protects the kidneys from shock, and protects a woman's mammary glands from temperature extremes and shock. Fats also provide flavor and appeal, aid in digestion and absorption of certain other nutrients, and help maintain the structure and health of cells. They are carriers of the fat-soluble vitamins (National Research Council, 1989: 45).

Non-Energy-Producing Nutrients

Vitamins

Vitamins are organic substances available in foods, but they provide no energy. Instead, they work as co-enzymes (molecules that aid the work of enzymes), facilitating the work of enzymes in breaking down foods to release nutrients. There are two classes of vitamins: the water-soluble and the fat-soluble.

Water-soluble vitamins

Water-soluble vitamins are carried in the bloodstream, and excessive quantities easily are excreted through the kidneys. Consequently, they are needed in small amounts at regular and frequent intervals, and it is hard to overdose on them.

There are eight different B vitamins. Some serve as co-enzymes in metabolizing carbohydrates, fats, and proteins; others assist the assembly of compounds, such as protein. They also aid in cell multiplication, especially the short-lived cells, such as those of the gastrointestinal tract and red blood cells.

Thiamin (Vitamin B_1) plays a significant role in energy metabolism, especially in nerve cells. Deficiency of thiamin causes beriberi (from Chinese words meaning "I cannot"), first studied among East Asians when they began eating mostly highly polished rice and, thus, losing the thiamin present in rice hulls (Hilker and Sonogyi, 1982). Because of the importance of thiamin in the health of the nervous system, it is not surprising that symptoms of beriberi include weakness, paralysis, difficulty walking, and mental confusion (Brown, 1990; Horwitt, Liebert, Kreisler, and Wittman, 1948; Inouye and Katsura, 1965). Meat from pigs (pork and ham), vegetables, unrefined grains, and legumes are rich in thiamin (Brown, 1990).

Riboflavin (Vitamin B_2) is also important in energy metabolism and supports normal vision and skin health. Deficiency symptoms include cracks at the corner of the mouth, a magenta color to the tongue, hypersensitivity to light (photophobia), and skin rash (National Research Council, 1989: 132-3). Sources of riboflavin include meat, fish, and poultry; vegetables; and milk and milk products.

Niacin (Vitamin B_3) is involved in the metabolism of glucose (sugar), fat, and alcohol. Humans derive part of their needed niacin from an amino acid, tryptophan (National Research Council, 1989: 137). Deficiency of niacin plus exposure to sunlight causes pallagra, marked by diarrhea, inflamation of the mucous membranes, and skin rash. Formerly common in the southern United States among people whose nearly meat-free diet was mostly maize, it is still found in parts of Africa and Asia (National Research Council, 1989: 137), including parts of China (Jacob and Swendseid, 1990: 167). Meats are a significant source of this vitamin; the availability to the body of niacin in grains is enhanced by treating the grain with lime (National Research Council, 1989: 138-9).

Vitamin B_6 is important in the metabolism of amino acids and the construction of nonessential amino acids from the essential ones in food. The requirement for vitamin B_6 varies with the amount of protein: the more protein eaten, the more vitamin B_6 the diet must supply (National Research Council, 1989). Deficiency usually occurs together with deficiencies of other B vitamins; its symptoms include weakness, irritability, insomnia, anemia, and convulsions. Meats, eggs, unmilled rice, soybeans, oats, whole-wheat products, peanuts, and walnuts are the main dietary sources (National Research Council, 1989: 143).

Folate (or folic acid) aids in metabolizing amino acids and in the construction of DNA. Consequently, it is important in cell building, especially where rapid cell multiplication is taking place, as in the gastrointestinal tract and red blood cells, and in pregnancy (National Research Council, 1989). Deficiency leads of anemia, frequent infections, glossitis (smooth red tongue), diarrhea, depression, confusion, fainting, and fatigue (Whitney, Hamilton, and Rolfes, 1990). Leafy green vegetables, liver, legumes, and seeds are the main dietary sources.

Vitamin B_{12} maintains the sheath that surrounds and protects nerve fibers and promotes their normal growth. It also is vital to bone cell activity and metabolism. Bacteria, fungi, and algae synthesize their own Vitamin B_{12}, but yeasts, higher plants, and animals cannot. In human diets, it is mainly supplied by the products of animals. Animal bodies have accumulated it by bacterial synthesis (National Research Council, 1989: 159). Deficiency of this vitamin causes pernicious anemia and various neurological symptoms.

Biotin is a sulfur-containing vitamin that is found in many different foods and is synthesized in the lower gastrointestinal tract by microorganisms and by some fungi (National Research Council, 1989: 165-6). Deficiencies have been found only in artificially induced conditions (such as intravenous feeding) and produce nausea, vomiting, glossitis, pallor, mental depression, and skin rash (National Research Council, 1989: 166). No recommended daily allowance has been set for biotin; it is apparently needed in very small amounts.

Pantothenic acid is important because it is part of a co-enzyme that releases energy from carbohydrates and fatty acids and synthesizes certain hormones. Deficiency is rare, as it is found in many foods and is needed in small quantities. Induced deficiencies in animals produce retarded growth rates, infertility, abortion, abnormalities of the skin and hair, neuromuscular disorders, and gastrointestinal distress (National Research Council, 1989).

Vitamin C (L-ascorbic acid) may assist a specific enzyme in breaking down foods, but it also performs an important role as an antioxidant. In this role, it protects another substance from destruction by destroying itself. In the intestine, for example, it protects iron and aids in its absorption (Hallberg, Brune, and Rossander-Hulthén, 1987). It also helps form the fibrous, structural protein collagen, which serves as the matrix for the formation of bones and teeth, forms the "glue" of scars (Levenson, Manner and Seifter, 1971), keeps cells together, and assists in the metabolism of several amino acids, some of which become hormones that are important in the body's responses to stress, including fever. Orange juice is the best-known provider of Vitamin C, but it is also found in other fruits and vegetables, such as green peppers, collard greens, broccoli, potatoes, tomatoes, spinach, and others.

Vitamin C deficiency causes scurvy (Hornig, 1975; Sauberlich, 1990; Woodruff, 1975). Because of the importance of collagen in maintaining flexibility in the walls of blood vessels, one of the first signs of scurvy is hemorrhage, especially in the gums. Other symptoms include depression, frequent infections, muscle degeneration, hysteria, bone fragility, joint pain, rough skin, blotchy bruises, and failure of wounds to heal.

Fat-soluble Vitamins

Fat-soluble vitamins are found in the oils and fats of foods. They require bile for digestion, and they enter the lymphatic system before being used. They are stored in the liver and body fat (adipose cells), from which they can be called upon as needed. Hence, they need be consumed only in small quantities, infrequent consumption is adequate, and over consumption is a greater risk than it is with water-soluble vitamins (Whitney, Hamilton, and Rolfes, 1990: 238). Fat-soluble vitamins include A, D, E, and K.

Vitamin A plays a number of roles. Perhaps the best known is in maintaining night vision (Dowling, 1966). It also helps promote healthy skin and mucous membranes and aids in the growth of body cells. It helps maintain thyroid function, the stability of cell membranes, nerve-cell sheaths, and the manufacture of red blood cells (Olson, 1990). Liver, fish, dairy products, and vegetables are rich sources of Vitamin A (National Research Council, 1989: 81; Olson, 1990).

Because the body stores Vitamin A, deficiency symptoms appear only after the stores are consumed, which may take a period of years. Then bones cease to grow, tooth enamel decays, anemia sets in, vision (especially night vision) deteriorates, and the hair follicles become plugged with keratin, forming white lumps (hyperkeratosis). Immune reaction also suffers, and the brain and spinal cord may grow too fast for the stunted skin and spine, causing damage to the central nervous system (National Research Council, 1989: 80; Olson, 1990).

Vitamin D normally is synthesized by the body from sunlight. Skin color however, determines the amount of ultraviolet light absorbed and thus the amount of Vitamin D that is synthesized; dark-skinned people need more sunlight than light-skinned people. Clothing customs; confinement of the sick, the young, and the aged to the indoors; and other cultural factors can inhibit Vitamin D supplies. In countries where Vitamin D-fortified milk commonly is consumed, deficiencies are rare.

Vitamin D is vital in the creation and maintenance of bones, and the signs of Vitamin D deficiency are similar to signs of calcium deficiency. In children, the deficiency leads to rickets, characterized by bowed legs (Loomis, 1970). In adults who do not consume dairy products or get enough sun, it promotes bone loss (osteoporosis) and fractures. Women are especially at risk who undergo repeated pregnancy, are nursing almost constantly, and get little sunshine (National Research Council, 1989: 93).

Vitamin E plays a number of roles, including protecting other substances (such as Vitamin A and polyunsaturated fatty acids) from oxidation. It seems to have a protective function for blood cells as they pass through the lungs, especially in a polluted environment (Whitney, Hamilton, and Rolfes, 1990: 257-8), and experiments in animals suggest that a diet deficient in Vitamin E increases vulnerability to heart disease (Beck, Kolbeck, Rohr, et al., 1994b). Vitamin E is found in many foods, especially vegetable and seed oils and products made from them: margarine, salad dressings, and shortenings. It also is found in fruits and green leafy vegetables. Deficiencies are rare except in premature infants and other individuals who, for a variety of reasons, do not absorb fat normally (National Research Council, 1989).

Vitamin K is vital in the production of proteins involved in blood clotting, as well as those in plasma, bone, and kidney. Bacteria in the digestive tract manufacture some Vitamin K; foods such as liver, green leafy and cabbage-type vegetables, and milk are other supplies. Deficiency shows up in the failure of blood to clot (National Research Council, 1989).

Minerals

Minerals are single-atom elements; 16 of them have been determined to be essential nutrients. They are divided into two groups, based on the amount present in a human body: the major minerals, and the trace minerals.

Major Minerals

Major minerals include calcium, phosphorus, sodium, potassium, sulfur, chloride, and magnesium. All strongly influence the body's fluid balance and blood pressure, as well as performing other functions.

Calcium is the most abundant mineral in the human body; 99 percent of it is in the bones, where it gives the bones rigidity, with the remaining in blood and body fluids (Arnaud and Sanchez, 1990; National Research Council, 1989: 174). Vitamin D, normally obtained from sunlight but also available in fortified milk, aids in calcium absorption, but the body's regulator is calcium-binding protein (National Research Council, 1989: 177-8). When the body needs more calcium, as during pregnancy, lactation, and childhood growth, the body produces more of this protein, and more of the calcium in foods actually is absorbed. Excess protein in the diet reduces the amount of calcium absorbed because it increases the amount that is excreted. Consequently, recommended daily allowances of calcium are lower in countries where diets typically contain less protein (National Research Council 1989: 179). Dairy products provide a rich source of calcium.

Deficient calcium (or Vitamin D) causes rickets: stunted growth and deformed bones in children (Loomis, 1970; National Research Council, 1989: 92). Among older persons, especially women, lack of calcium can lead to osteoporosis, or bone loss (Arnaud and Sanchez, 1990). Bones may become brittle and fail to heal when broken, and vertebrae in the backbone "collapse," leading to a stooped posture (National Research Council, 1989: 176-8).

Phosphorus, as calcium, is an essential element of bone tissue; the ratio of phosphorus to calcium is approximately 1 to 2 (National Research Council, 1989). It is present in many foods, especially protein-rich foods and grains. Consequently, a deficiency of phosphorus is rare.

Sodium chloride (salt) has been regarded as a valuable substance since ancient times (Bloch, 1963; Kurlansky, 2002). It was an important item in trade; even the English word "salary" is derived from the word for "salt." It is the prime regulator of extracellular fluid volume and the body's acid-base balance (National Research Council, 1989). In addition to familiar table salt, many foods supply sodium. Except in certain medical conditions or prolonged, heavy sweating, the body can maintain an adequate supply of sodium.

Potassium is an electrolyte that, along with sodium, maintains a normal fluid balance in the cells, especially the nerve cells. It also facilitates various reactions in the body, including making of protein; it supports cell integrity and assists in the transmission of nerve impulses and the contraction of muscles, including the heart. Consequently, a deficiency in potassium, though rare, can interfere with heart action. It also causes general muscle weakness, even paralysis, and confusion (National Research Council, 1989: 255).

Chloride, along with sodium and potassium, regulates the body's extracellular fluid volume. It is a major component of stomach acid, which is important in the chemical breakdown of food during digestion. It occurs widely in foods along with sodium, and deficiencies do not occur naturally in the diet (Whitney, Hamilton, and Rolfes, 1990).

Sulfur alone is not a separate nutrient; it occurs as part of protein and of certain vitamins. Therefore, there are no recommended allowances for sulfur, and there is no deficiency of the mineral apart from deficiencies of substances of which it is a part (Whitney, Hamilton, and Rolfes, 1990: 302).

Magnesium is stored in bones, but it is important in muscles, where it plays a role in contraction and relaxation. It also is important in the transmission of nerve impulses and the maintenance of teeth. Deficiency inhibits muscle relaxation and causes weakness, convulsions, and hallucinations. The deficiency must be extreme for symptoms to show; American diets have contained declining amounts of magnesium since the early twentieth century without widespread symptoms appearing (National Research Council 1989). Legumes, seeds, nuts, and vegetables are sources of dietary magnesium.

Trace Minerals

Trace amounts of at least nine minerals are known to be essential to good health: iron, zinc, iodide, copper, manganese, fluoride, chromium, selenium, and molybdenum. There is increasing evidence of the importance of minute amounts of nickel, silicon, tin, vanadium, cobalt (present in Vitamin B_{12}), and boron. Silver, mercury, lead, barium, cadmium, and even arsenic also may prove to be vital in minute quantities (Whitney, Hamilton, and Rolfes, 1990). **Iron** is vital to the process by which cells generate energy. It also is found in many enzymes and is required for making new cells, amino acids, hormones, and neurotransmitters. It forms part of hemoglobin (the protein in red blood cells that carries oxygen) and myoglobin (the protein in muscle cells that holds protein) (National Research Council, 1989: 195).

Iron deficiency is a major nutritional problem world-wide, especially among young children, adolescents, and women of child-bearing age who lose blood each month from menstruation (National Research Council, 1989: 197). Although grains and legumes contain substantial amounts of iron, the iron in these foods is absorbed poorly if they are the primary diet (Dallman, 1990:

244; DeMaeyer, Adiels-Tegman, and Rayston, 1985). Severe deficiency can lead to anemia, when there is insufficient iron to form hemoglobin (National Research Council 1989: 196). An anemic person may be noticeably pale, suffer headaches, and feel fatigued, but even before anemia sets in, the deficiency affects behavior. The capacity for physical work is impaired, and iron-deficient children become restless, apathetic, and irritable (Dallman, 1990; Lozoff and Brittenham, 1986). Tolerance for cold declines (Dallman, 1990).

Zinc is a factor in most major metabolic processes (National Research Council, 1989: 205-6). It seems to be especially important in the translation of the genetic code into actual cell development; zinc deficiency appears in sluggish cell growth and repair. Wounds heal slowly, growth is retarded, appetite decreases, and the immune system becomes less efficient (Cousins and Hempe, 1990; National Research Council, 1989). The best sources of zinc are protein-rich foods, especially meat and milk, as well as vegetables and legumes.

Iodine, in the form of iodide, is vital in tiny amounts for proper thyroid action. Deficiency causes goiter, marked by swelling of the thyroid gland (Gillie, 1971). A deficiency during pregnancy causes a complex of birth defects, including severe mental retardation and physical abnormalities, called cretinism. Iodide is abundant in seafood, other meats, and plants grown in iodine-rich soils (principally in areas that were once submerged under the sea). Lacking one of these sources, iodized table salt makes up any deficiency (National Research Council, 1989).

Copper plays a role in the absorption and use of iron in hemoglobin and in the protective sheath of nerve cells. Its main sources are organ meats, seafood, nuts, seeds, and even drinking water, especially if it flows through copper pipes. Deficiencies, rare in humans, cause anemia and bone changes (National Research Council, 1989; O'Dell, 1990).

Manganese is apparently vital to the action of many enzymes in dozens of metabolic processes. Deficiencies, which are almost unknown in people who eat normal diets, cause problems with bones, reproduction, the nervous system, and the metabolism of fat (Keen and Zidenberg-Cherr, 1990; National Research Council, 1989). Whole grains and cereal products are the best dietary sources; tea is also high in manganese (National Research Council, 1989).

Fluoride has as its main role the strengthening of tooth enamel, thus, preventing dental caries (cavities). The main natural source is drinking water; fluoride is now added to drinking water in scores of communities in the United States and Canada. It also is added to toothpaste, and it can be applied topically by a dentist, as is usually done in the United States and Canada (National Research Council, 1989; Ophaug, 1990).

Chromium acts with insulin to regulate blood sugar levels and metabolism. A deficiency, which is unlikely under normal circumstances, produces symptoms similar to diabetes (high blood sugar). Many foods, especially meats, unrefined foods, fats, and vegetable oils, contain chromium; eating mostly refined foods reduces the amount of the mineral available to the body (National Research Council, 1989; Stoecker, 1990).

Selenium functions as part of an enzyme, which acts with Vitamin E as an antioxidant, protecting polyunsaturated fats from destruction. The best sources of selenium are seafoods, liver, kidney, and other meats. The amount in grain varies with the selenium content of the soil in which it was grown (WHO, 1987). The mineral is of particular interest because the greatest ranges in selenium consumption occur in different parts of China (Levander, 1987: 228).

Deficiency of selenium causes heart disease, most noticeably in children — so-called Keshan disease, named after the county in Heilongjiang Province, China, where it was first studied — apparently by increasing the power of a specific kind of virus (Beck, Kolbeck, Rohr et al., 1994a; Beck, Kolbeck, Shi et al., 1994; Chen et al., 1980; *China Daily*, December 26, 1995; Gauntt and Tracy, 1995; Gu, 1983; Keshan Disease Research Group, 1979a, 1979b; Lockitch et al., 1990). Laboratory experiments with mice indicate that sufficient selenium, in fact, can counter the effects of deficient Vitamin E (Levander, Ager, and Beck, 1995). Selenium deficiency also may increase the risk of developing AIDS from the HIV virus (Taylor, 1995).

Excessive selenium (selenosis) causes lesions of the skin, nervous system, and possibly teeth, as well as loss of hair and nails. It was reported in Hunan Province in the 1960s and seems to have been related to consumption of vegetables of exceptional selenium content during the famine of those years (Yang, Wang, Zhou, and Sun, 1993).

Other minerals needed in minuscule amounts include molybdenum, nickel, silicon, tin, vanadium, cobalt, boron, silver, mercury, lead, barium, cadmium—and even the famous poison, arsenic (Nielsen, 1990).

Appendix B
Forms Used in Field Study

Liaoning Province Urban Household Food Survey Questionnaire

Date: _____, 19__   Household Number: _____

Address: _____

Household data:

Name   Gender   Age   Birthplace   Occupation   Income

Do you have a vegetable garden? If so, how big is it (in square meters)? What do you grow?

What proportion of your food do you produce yourself?

Food-related chores:
In your household, who decides daily menus?

Who decides what to grow in the vegetable garden?

Who does the grocery shopping?

    Cooking?

Dishwashing?

Does anyone in your household have a health condition that limits the diet? If so, who is it? What is the limitation?

Is anyone in your household pregnant? Nursing? What effect does this have on diet?

Influences on Diet:

What are your family's favorite foods? Why?

What are the ways you find out about new foods? (Mark as many as apply.)

_____ Relatives and friends: Who?

_____ Health care workers: Who?

_____ Radio, television, press: Which?

_____ School (for example, children's school lessons)

Do you try any of these ideas? Why or why not?

Do you eat any particular foods because you think they will improve your health or appearance? Which ones?

Regular foods: What did you eat yesterday for

Breakfast:

Lunch:

Dinner:

Snacks:

What did you eat for the last major holiday?

辽宁省城市户口家庭食物状况调查表

日期: 一九___年___月___日   编号: _____号

	地 址						
家 庭 资 料	姓 名	性别	年龄	出 生 地 点	职 业	收 入	
	家里是否有菜园? 如有, 菜园有多少平米? 种些什么?						
	你估计自产蔬菜占多大比重?						
家 务 分 担	你们家谁决定每天吃什么?						
	谁决定菜园里种什么?						
	谁购买食物		谁做饭		谁洗碗		
	你们家是否有谁因健康状况而影响食物选择? 如有, 是谁? 什么问题?						
	你们家是否有怀孕的妇女? 是否有吃奶的婴儿? 他们的饮食如何?						

Figure B.1a

影 响 因 素	你们最喜欢的食物有哪些? 为什么?
	你们的食物知识从哪里来? (请在所选项画√) _____亲友、同事, 是谁_____ _____医疗保健人员, 是谁_____ _____广播、电视、报纸是什么_____ _____学校 (如: 在学校上的课) _____
	你试着吃与新的食物知识有关的食物吗? 为什么?
	你吃哪些食物是为了保健和美容? 其效果如何?
食 谱	你昨天吃了些什么? 早餐: 午餐: 晚餐: 其它:
	上个节日吃些什么?

Figure B.1b

Liaoning Province Rural Household Food Survey Questionnaire

Date: _____, 19__   Household number: _____

Address: _____

Household data:

Name   Gender   Age   Birthplace   Occupation   Income

Does your household have a vegetable garden? Orchard? Grainfield? If so, how big is each (in *mu*)? What do you grow?

Food sources:
What proportion of your food (grain, vegetables, fruit, poultry, etc.) do you produce yourselves?

Food-related chores:

Who decides what to eat each day?

Who decides what to grow in the vegetable garden?

Who does the
    Grocery shopping?
    Cooking?
    Dishwashing?

Does anyone in your household have a health condition that limits diet? If so, who? What is the limitation?

Is anyone in your household pregnant? Nursing? What is the effect on her diet?

Influences on food choices:

What are your family's favorite foods? Why?

From what sources do you obtain information about new foods? (Mark as many as apply.)

_____ Relatives and friends: Who?

_____ Health-care workers: Who?

_____ Radio, television, press: Which?

_____ School (for example, children's school lessons)

Do you try these ideas? Why or why not?

Regular foods: What did you eat yesterday for
    Breakfast:

    Lunch:

    Dinner:

    Snacks:

What did you eat for the last major holiday?

辽宁省农村户口家庭食物状况调查表

日期: 一九＿＿年＿＿月＿＿日　　　　　　编号:＿＿＿＿＿号

家庭资料	地　址					
	姓　　　名	性别	年龄	出　生　地　点	职　　业	收　入
	家里是否有菜园、果园、粮田？如有，分别有多少亩？具体各种些什么？					

食物来源	你估计自产各种食物(粮食、蔬菜、水果、家禽等)占多大比重？

家务分担	你们家谁决定每天吃什么？				
	谁决定菜园里种什么？				
	谁购买食物		谁做饭		谁洗碗
	你们家是否有谁因健康状况而影响食物选择？如有，是谁？什么问题？				
	你们家是否有怀孕的妇女？是否有吃奶的婴儿？他们的饮食如何？				

Figure B.2a

影	你们最喜欢的食物有哪些? 为什么?
响	你们的食物知识从哪里来? (请在所选项画√) ____亲友、同事，是谁_____ ____医疗保健人员, 是谁_____ ____广播、电视、报纸是什么_____ ____学校 (如: 在学校上的课)_____
因	你试着吃与新的食物知识有关的食物吗? 为什么?
素	你吃哪些食物是为了保健和美容? 其效果如何?
食	你昨天吃了些什么? 早餐: 午餐: 晚餐: 其它:
谱	上个节日吃些什么?

Figure B.2b

一九_____年_____月_____日

1、早饭   吃饭人数：_____

食 物 名 称	内 容 成 份

2、午饭   吃饭人数：_____

食 物 名 称	内 容 成 份

3、晚饭   吃饭人数：_____

食 物 名 称	内 容 成 份

4、其他   吃饭人数：_____

食 物 名 称	内 容 成 份

Figure B.3

Food Diary Page

Date_____

1.　Breakfast　　　　　　　　　　　Number served_____

Food
Ingredients

2.　Lunch　　　　　　　　　　　　Number served _____

Food　　　　　　　Ingredients

3.　Dinner　　　　　　　　　　　Number served _____

Food　　　　　　　Ingredients

4. Snacks　　　　　　　　　　　Number served _____

Food　　　　　　　Ingredients

Appendix C
Glossary of Chinese Characters

baijiu 白酒
baozi 包子
bao jiaozi 包饺子
cai 菜
chou doufu 臭豆腐
chun juan 春卷
cong 葱
da dou 大豆
da mai 大麦
di gua 地瓜
Dongbei 东北
doufu 豆腐
dou nai 豆奶
fanqie 番茄
fan 饭
fei nongye 非农业
gan doufu 干豆腐
gaoliang 高粱
gua 瓜
hong cha 红茶
hu luobo 胡萝卜
huasheng 花生
huang gua 黄瓜
hundun 馄饨
jiaozi 饺子
jin 斤
jiucai 韭菜
li tu, bu li xiang 离土，不离乡

mantou 馒头
Manzu 满族
nongye 农业
nu 奴
Qian Shan 千山
qin cai 芹菜
rou 肉
shi 食
suan 蒜
suan cai 酸菜
suan tai 蒜薹
tu dou 土豆
xi gua 西瓜
xi hong shi 西红柿
xian bing 馅饼
xiang 乡
xiao mai 小麦
xiao mi 小米
xiao mi zhou 小米粥
yang cong 洋葱
yin 饮
yinshi 饮食
youcai 油菜
zhen 镇
zhenxiang 镇乡
zhenxianghua 镇乡化
Zhong Yuan 中原
zhushi 主食

Index